Handmade: A collection of beautiful things to make
Includes index
ISBN 1-56426-252-9
Library of Congress Cataloging-in-Process
Printed in Hong Kong

F E D C B
4 3 2 1 0 9

Cole Publishing Group, Inc. is not responsible for unsolicited
manuscripts, photographs, or illustrations.

Cole Publishing Group, Inc.
13750 Arnold Drive
P.O. 2199
Glen Ellen, CA 95442-2199 USA
Voice   (707) 939-9400
Fax   (707) 939-9496
www.coleshomelibrary.com

Cole's Home Library Craftbooks
Project Editor: Carolyn Watanabe Barbulesco
Project Coordination: Zazen Design, Santa Rosa, CA
Special Graphics: Costill Graphics, Santa Rosa, CA

Distributed to the book trade by:
ACCESS Publishers Network, Grawn, MI 49637

Cole books are available for
quantity purchase for sales promotions,
presentations, fund-raising,
or educational use.
For further information on Cole books,
contact the publisher.

HANDMADE

A COLLECTION OF
BEAUTIFUL THINGS TO MAKE

CONTENTS

NEEDLEWORK

PATCHWORK AND APPLIQUÉ

TOYS

KNITTING AND CROCHET

PAINTING AND STENCILING

PAPER AND DÉCOUPAGE

GENERAL CRAFT

NEEDLEWORK

NASTURTIUM CROSS STITCH

They were the flowers you could pick with impunity as a child because they grew in such profusion that nothing seemed to exhaust their colorful generosity. Their strange flat leaves held a magical drop of dew that slithered like quicksilver and fairies reputedly drank. They are, of course, nasturtiums, **Tropaeolum majus**, those humble, hardy, cheerful little plants that we often take for granted in a garden, because they ask so little.

For cross stitch enthusiasts, this exquisite bouquet of nasturtiums will be a joy to stitch. An original design has been reworked on Dublin linen, and, in the translation from painting to embroidery, the beautiful detail and subtle shading of the original have been carefully maintained.

Project based on a painting by Mignon Parker and stitched by Alison Snepp
Photography by Andrew Elton
Styling by Lisa Hilton

MEASUREMENTS

Embroidered image measures approximately $9^{1}/_{4}$" x 9".

MATERIALS

- 20" square off-white evenweave linen, 25 threads/inch
- One skein DMC Six-strand Cotton Embroidery Floss in each of the following colors: very light fern green 524, dark drab brown 611, light old gold 676, dark orange spice 720, medium orange spice 721, light olive green 734, medium tangerine 741, off-white 746, light peach flesh 754, golden olive 832, very dark garnet 902, very light sportsman flesh 951, light yellow-beige 3047, dark green-grey 3051, medium green-grey 3052, or equivalent
- Size 24 or 26 tapestry needle
- Sewing thread in a medium color

METHOD

Before commencing, refer to the instructions for cross stitch in the **Embroidery Stitch Guide** on page 58.

Mark center point of linen.

The embroidery chart is printed below. Using a red pen, connect center arrows across chart both vertically and horizontally to mark center lines. Start embroidery at center point.

Using two strands of embroidery floss over two threads of linen, work cross stitch, following the chart. When cross stitch is complete, work backstitch as shown, using one strand of floss.

When embroidery is complete, remove tacking and press work on wrong side on a well-padded surface, to prevent stitches becoming flattened.

Mount and frame as desired.

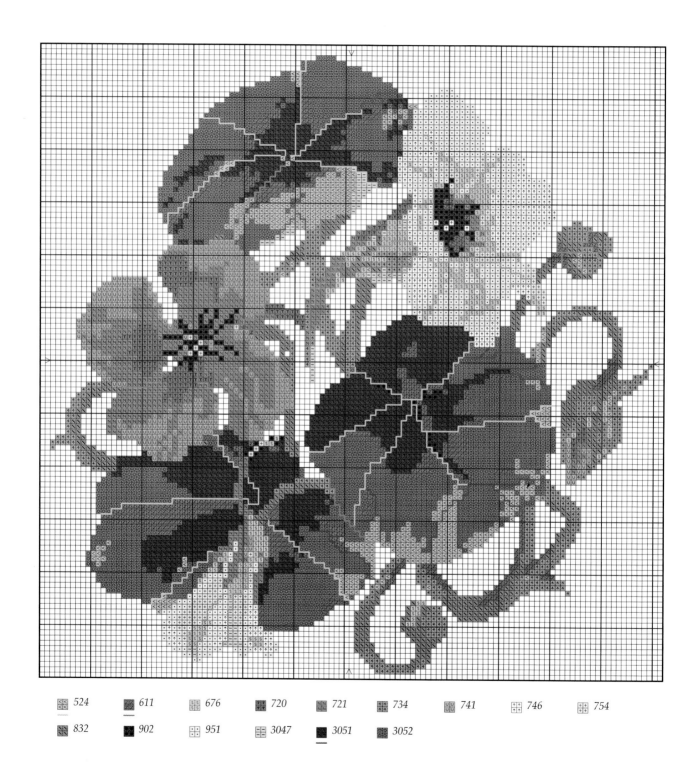

524	611	676	720	721	734	741	746	754
832	902	951	3047	3051	3052			

STAMPED EMBROIDERED PICTURES

I f needlework is your passion, consider the possibilities of combining stamping with embroidery. A stamp can be used like an embroidery transfer and completely covered with tiny stitches, or sections can be left visible and tinted with acrylic paint to complement your needlework. This project uses three stamps with a floral theme, worked in straight stitch, lazy daisy stitch, French knots, stem stitch, buttonhole stitch and bullion stitch roses with six-strand cotton floss and embroidery ribbon. Fused-on scraps of patchwork fabric are blanket stitched around their edges, and buttons have been added for a decorative finish. The pictures are backed with batting and quilted around each design border with a simple running stitch. The results, displayed in simple wooden frames, speak for themselves.

Embroidered pictures designed and worked by Lynda Maker

WORKED
IN WOOL

These wool-embroidered items amply prove that making things for tiny people is one of the purest pleasures. The beautiful embroidery on the blanket and matching pincushion is exquisitely detailed but quite simple to work — the design incorporates only a few different stitches and the flowers can be placed at random. Bearing all the qualities of future family heirlooms, these nursery treasures will be a delight to stitch and a joy to give.

This project uses the following stitches:

- satin stitch • stem stitch • lazy daisy stitch
- straight stitch • fly stitch • French knot

See **Embroidery Stitch Guide** on page 58.

Project designed and stitched by Lynda Maker
Photography by Andre Martin
Styling by Kathy Tripp

Wool-embroidered Blanket

This blanket, although intricate-looking, is not difficult. Once the ribbon design is in place, the flowers can be placed randomly — just keep filling up the spaces. There's no need to stick to the pattern rigidly. A combination of different yarn weights and thicknesses gives a textured look, making the blanket lovely to look at and feel. You may have wool yarns that you'd like to incorporate; feel free to use your imagination and include as many colors as you desire. This will make your blanket unique. Remember, the combination of different shades only adds more depth to the piece.

MEASUREMENTS

The blanket is approximately 43$\frac{1}{2}$" x 32", to fit a bassinet, but the method can be adapted to any sized blanket.

MATERIALS

- 43$\frac{1}{2}$" x 32" wool blanket fabric, or size to fit bassinet
- Tracing paper
- Dark sewing thread
- One skein embroidery wool in each of the following brands and colors (or substitute your own): **Paterna:** deep gold A701, light gold A711, cream A756, light grey-blue A514, buttermilk A704, yellow A727, dusty rose A923, green A652, light green A653; **DMC Medici:** mushroom pink 8120A, burgundy 8123, yellow 8026, deep brown-green 8309, green 8405, lilac 8331, rust 8176; **Appletons:** light grape 603, grape 604, moss green 292
- Two skeins Paterna Embroidery Wool, smoke blue A504
- DMC light gold thread (Art 282), or similar
- Crewel embroidery needle
- 48" x 36" cotton fabric, for backing
- Three skeins DMC Cotton Pearl No. 5, color 332

METHOD

Preparation Fold blanket fabric in half crosswise and lengthwise to find center. The embroidery design is printed opposite. Enlarge it 165 percent on a photocopier. Trace circle from design onto tracing paper, and cut out, leaving a $\frac{3}{8}$-inch border all around. Place on back of blanket fabric, positioning center of circle directly in center of fabric, or slightly below center, depending on preference.

Pin circle in place and baste around outline with dark sewing thread. Alternatively, trace circle onto fabric with a light pencil, remove pattern and baste around outline.

Trace bow and ribbon pieces from the design onto tracing paper. Cut out and place in position on back of fabric, over basted circle, in reverse. (Because you are working on the back, you must work in mirror image.) A quick tracing of circle, bow and ribbon, taken from the design and flipped over, provides a guide to positioning your pieces.

Trace lightly around pattern pieces and baste over tracings in dark thread, to mark pattern outline thoroughly.

Turn blanket to right side and you'll have a perfect outline of circle, ribbon and bow.

Positioning the ribbon pattern is probably the most difficult part of the whole procedure. Spend a little time getting it right, as it sets the framework for the whole piece. No other flowers are marked on the blanket, allowing you complete freedom to fill the spaces using the design as a guide.

Embroidery Start your embroidery by practicing a few stitches on a scrap of fabric first, following the **Wool Embroidery Guide** on page 17 and the **Embroidery Stitch Guide** on page 58.

The ribbon and bow should be embroidered first, as many of the flowers overlap them. They are worked in slanted satin stitch, using smoke blue. The ribbon is outlined in stem stitch, using gold thread.

To start the flowers, embroider three or four large daisies in a section. Daisies are made up of a number of lazy daisy stitches filled with straight stitches of a different color. Try using Paterna yarns in different combinations, such as buttermilk filled with straight stitches of cream, and light gold with straight stitches of yellow. Slightly smaller daisies have been embroidered in clusters, using deep gold filled with light gold. Other small daisies have been stitched in cream lazy daisy stitch, but not filled with straight stitch.

All centers of daisies are French knots. To fill the larger daisies, use four or five knots; for the smaller daisies, use one, two or three. Choose a center to match the flower, such as deep brown-green to add a dark center to the stronger daisies, light gold for the lighter large daisies, and yellow (Paterna A727) for the smaller cream daisies.

Add leaves of lazy daisy stitch around flowers. Green (Paterna A652) is good for darker daisies, and light green (Paterna A653) for cream daisies.

Embroider lavender using lazy daisy stitches in a fishbone pattern, referring to design for approximate positioning. Curve the stitches as you sew, to make

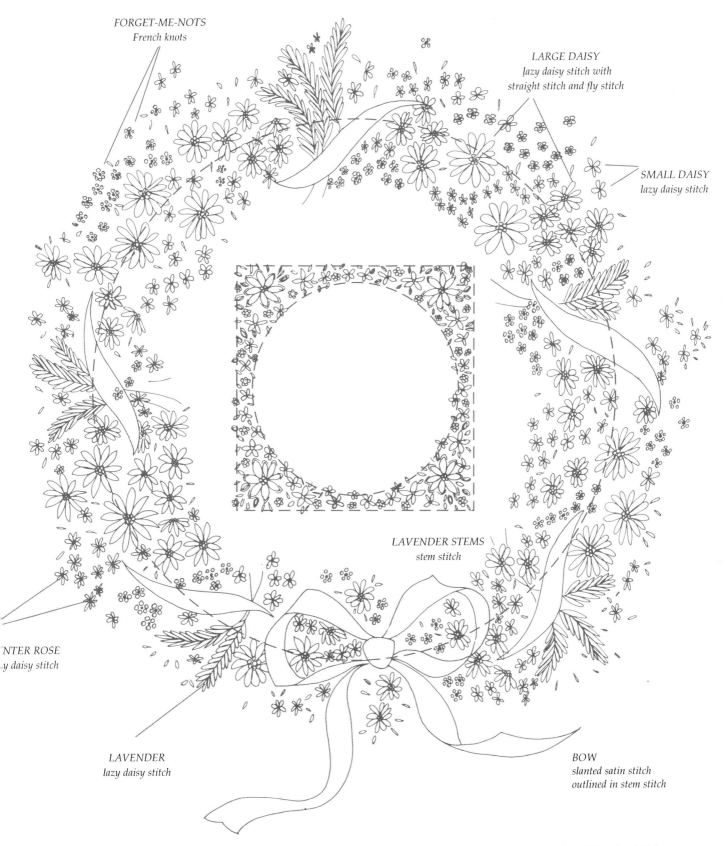

FORGET-ME-NOTS
French knots

LARGE DAISY
lazy daisy stitch with
straight stitch and fly stitch

SMALL DAISY
lazy daisy stitch

LAVENDER STEMS
stem stitch

NTER ROSE
y daisy stitch

LAVENDER
lazy daisy stitch

BOW
slanted satin stitch
outlined in stem stitch

lavender look more natural. Use two different threads at once, such as light grape and grape, to give greater depth of color. Stems are worked in stem stitch, using moss green. Add random straight stitches of moss green along the lavender flower for interest.

Now you can fill the remaining area to your heart's delight! Add flurries of forget-me-nots in smoke blue and light grey-blue, working five blue French knots with a center French knot in yellow (DMC Medici 8026). Add small lazy daisy stitches randomly in green (DMC Medici 8405). Add clusters of winter roses, working three lazy daisy stitches from the same point downwards, using mushroom pink. Two leaves are added in lazy daisy stitch, from the same starting point but pointing upwards, in green (DMC Medici 8405). Extra leaves should also be added randomly.

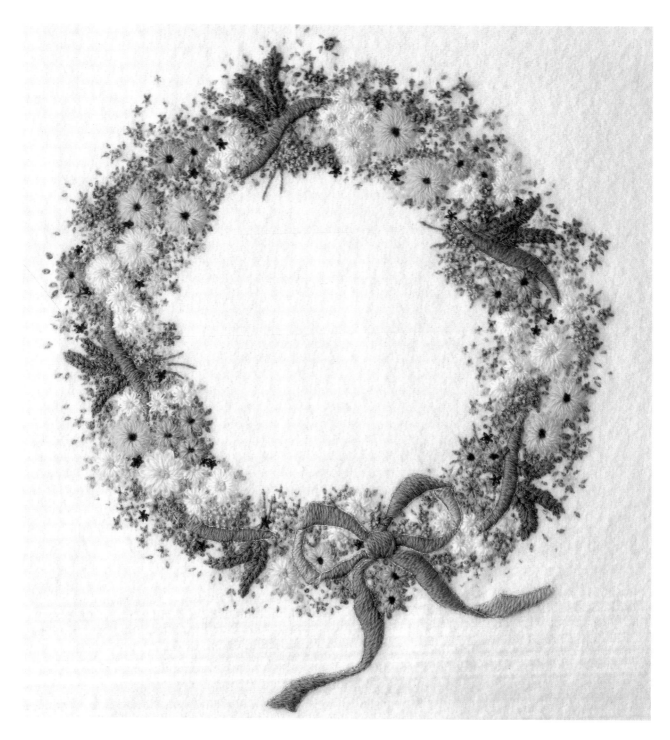

Fill any remaining spaces with little flowers, worked with five lazy daisy stitches in colors of your choice, such as lilac, dusty rose or yellow. Tiny five-pointed flowers, worked in burgundy, also add depth and interest. Other five-pointed flowers of deep gold can be filled with straight stitches of rust.

Some flowers should overlap the ribbon, to give a more natural look, as though the ribbon were weaving through the flowers. Use the circle as a guide and keep approximately equidistant either side of the basted line.

When you are happy with the effect, repeat your work in different sections, but do not try to repeat it exactly. Work slightly different combinations of flowers; for example, instead of four daisies, you may decide to work only three, along with more small cream daisies. Add flurries of forget-me-nots in different areas.

Stop every now and then to look at your work. You will see what it needs.

When you are happy with the final piece, fill any spaces with flowers to balance the circle. Add French knots randomly throughout the design in DMC gold thread and DMC Cotton Pearl, to add luster.

Pull out basting thread.

Wool Embroidery Guide

Small daisy
Lazy daisy

Large daisy
Work a straight stitch in the center of each lazy daisy petal, and a group of French knots at center. Fly stitch can be added to points of random flowers, for extra color.

Forget-me-not
Work five blue French knots, with a yellow knot at center.

Lavender
Work lazy daisy flowers and stem stitch stems. Add random green straight stitches for leaves.

Winter rose
Work three pink lazy daisy stitches from the same hole, fanning downwards, and two green smaller lazy daisy stitches from the same hole, pointing upwards.

Ribbon and bow
Work in slanted satin stitch and outline with gold stem stitch.

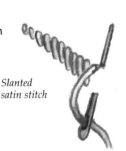

Slanted satin stitch

To assemble blanket Place backing fabric, right side down, on floor and center blanket, right side up, on top. Fold under $3/8$ inch on edges of backing fabric, then fold again to form a 2-inch binding, and pin in place. Slipstitch folded edges of binding to blanket, sewing right through both layers to catch backing fabric, and mitering corners for neatness.

Finish your blanket with a twisted cord, stitched to the front of the blanket, along inner edge of binding. Alternatively, you could use piping, purchased or homemade, and secure it when stitching the binding in place.

To make a twisted cord: Take six strands of Cotton Pearl and two strands of gold thread, each $2^3/4$ yards. Knot each end, and either ask someone to hold one end, or fix it to a door, window or chair. Stretch threads and twist until you feel a resistance, then, without loosening tension on threads, find the middle point and allow cords to twist back on one another from this middle point, forming a thick cord. Make two of this length for two longer sides of blanket, and repeat process, starting with two lengths of $6^1/2$-foot threads for shorter sides.

To neaten ends when sewing cord to blanket, tuck them into corners or make small loops at each corner.

METHOD

Preparation Fold one blanket fabric square in half crosswise and lengthwise to find center point. The embroidery design is printed on page 15. Enlarge the design 165 percent on the photocopier. Trace circle and square from design onto tracing paper. Cut out square, center on back of fabric, and baste outline in dark thread, as for blanket. Repeat for the circle. Do not trace any flowers onto blanket fabric; design should be used as a guide only.

Embroidery On front of fabric, work large daisies first, using deep gold lazy daisy stitch, filling in with straight stitches of light gold. Work centers using four French knots of deep brown-green. A fly stitch of rust can also be worked at point of each petal. Add buds, using lazy daisy stitch in deep gold. Add leaves in green.

Work smaller five-pointed daisies in deep gold lazy daisy stitch; fill with rust straight stitches.

Forget-me-nots are worked in French knots, using smoke blue with yellow centers.

Add more five-pointed flowers in yellow, lilac and mushroom pink, scattering green leaves randomly throughout. Stay approximately within the pattern lines to achieve the shaped effect.

Gold beads or French knots made with gold thread can be added randomly. French knots of Cotton Pearl are also added for luster.

Using the alphabet opposite, trace desired initial onto thin tracing paper. Pin to right side of fabric and baste through paper along marked lines.

Remove paper and fill initial using satin stitch in smoke blue.

Pincushion

MEASUREMENTS

Finished pincushion is approximately 5$\frac{1}{2}$" square.

MATERIALS

- Two 6$\frac{1}{4}$" squares wool blanket fabric
- Tracing paper
- One skein embroidery wool in each of the following brands and colors (or substitute your own): **Paterna:** smoke blue A504, deep gold A70l, light gold A711; **DMC Medici:** deep brown-green 8309, mushroom pink 8120A, burgundy 8123, yellow 8026, green 8405, lilac 8331, rust 8176, or equivalent.
- Crewel embroidery needle
- DMC light gold thread (Art 282), or similar
- DMC Cotton Pearl No. 5, color 332
- A few tiny gold seed beads (optional)
- Bran or fiberfill, to stuff

A few random flowers may be stitched in the center of the remaining fabric square as a pretty detail for the back of the pincushion.

To assemble pincushion Place fabric squares right sides together. Allowing a $^3/_8$-inch seam, machine-stitch along edges, leaving a small opening. Clip corners and turn right side out. Stuff with bran or fiberfill. Slipstitch opening closed.

To finish, make a twisted cord, as for blanket, allowing two and a half times desired finished length.

Slipstitch cord to edge of pincushion, attaching a tassel at a corner, if desired, and allowing some excess cord at one corner to form a loop.

To make tassel: Wind Cotton Pearl and gold thread (approximately 50 times per tassel) around small rectangle of cardboard (width of cardboard equals approximate length of tassel). Slip a length of thread under wound threads to secure tassel at top. Cut threads at bottom to release tassel from cardboard and wind approximately 12 inches of gold thread around tassel near top, to form neck.

A B C D E F G
H I J K L M
N O P Q R S T
U V W X Y Z

PRETTY AS A PICTURE

T*hese tiny pictures make a charming set. Each miniature features a different ribbon-embroidered flower in a hand-drawn vase, but you don't need any drawing skills — simply trace the outline onto calico, before completing the needlework.*

This project uses the following stitches:

- *lazy daisy stitch* • *straight stitch*
- *French knot*

*See **Embroidery Stitch Guide** on page 58.*

MEASUREMENTS

Each finished framed picture measures $4^3/_4$″ square; glass size is $2^3/_8$″ square.

MATERIALS

For frame:
- $4^3/_4$″ unfinished wooden frame
- Fine sandpaper
- Artist's acrylic gouache, such as Jo Sonja's: Burnt Umber, Yellow Oxide, Raw Umber
- Clear glazing medium, such as Jo Sonja's
- Satin acrylic finishing varnish, such as Liquitex
- Paintbrushes
- Old toothbrush

Mini pictures designed and stitched by Alison Snepp
Photography by Andre Martin
Styling by Lisa Hilton

- Beeswax
- Three small brass hooks
- Two small eye hooks, for hanging

For picture:
- $4^3/_4$″ square calico (per picture)
- Fine blue pen
- $1/_8$-inch-wide silk ribbons in the following colors:
  Roses: dark green, rose pink, salmon pink;
  Jonquils: medium green, yellow, terracotta, white;
  Dahlias: dark red, magenta, bright pink, pale pink, dark green, yellow-green, yellow, or equivalent
- Size 6 crewel embroidery needle

METHOD

Frame Sand frame lightly to remove any roughness and wipe clean. Mix a stain of one part Burnt Umber and one part Yellow Oxide, plus enough clear glazing medium to make the mixture the consistency of cream. Apply mixture in direction of wood grain, using a damp soft cloth (not a dry one). If necessary, wipe off excess stain with a clean part of the damp cloth. For a deeper color, apply a second or third coat, allowing to dry between coats.

When stain is thoroughly dry, apply a thin coat of varnish and allow to dry.

Using old toothbrush (or old flat brush), spatter frame lightly with Raw Umber — any unsightly blobs can be removed with tip of a damp cloth. Allow to dry.

Apply a little Burnt Umber around outside and inside edges of frame, to enhance aged effect; allow to dry.

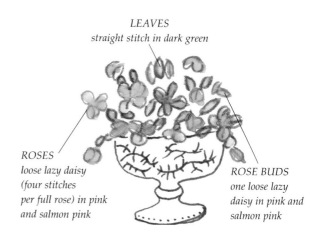

LEAVES
straight stitch in dark green

ROSES
loose lazy daisy
(four stitches
per full rose) in pink
and salmon pink

ROSE BUDS
one loose lazy
daisy in pink and
salmon pink

Apply one or two coats of varnish. When dry, apply a coat of beeswax, and buff.

Screw brass hooks to lower edge of frame, and eye hooks to back of frame, for hanging.

Embroidery Using fine blue pen, trace your chosen design for the vase, printed below, onto calico square. Allow ink to dry before pressing calico with a dry iron.

Use only short lengths of ribbon for the embroidery and work the stitches in the colors indicated in the diagrams below. Work the leaves first, and then the flowers. When the embroidery is complete, lace or glue to backing board and secure in frame.

JONQUILS
Work lower sections first, with a small horizontal straight stitch in yellow; add top section next, with a small vertical straight stitch in terracotta; finally, add random French knots, some in white and some in yellow

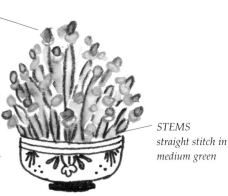

STEMS
straight stitch in medium green

DAHLIA
French knots on stems in magenta

BUDS
French knots in pale pink

LEAVES
straight stitch in light and dark green

DAHLIA
straight stitch in bright pink

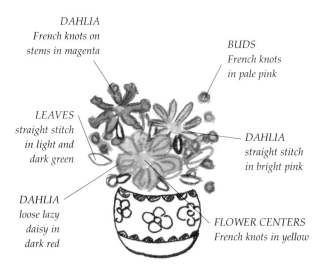

DAHLIA
loose lazy daisy in dark red

FLOWER CENTERS
French knots in yellow

NATURE NOTES SAMPLER

The vivid spring colors of the Australian bush are celebrated in this lovely cross-stitched sampler. The purple flowers of boronia (Boronia ledifolia) adorn the side borders, while a boronia bouquet forms a resting place for a pair of superb fairy wrens. Galahs strut about under a panel of golden wattle (Acacia longifolia), and a bright blue fairy wren is guarded by the golden candle cones of a heath banksia (Banksia ericifolia). Borders of yellow egg-and-bacon pea flowers (Papilionaceae) and a couple of nodding black-eyed Susans (Tetratheca ericifolia) complete the design. The finished sampler will be a permanent reminder of spring as well as a tribute to the beauty of Australia's native flora.

Sampler designed and stitched by Marianne Porteners
Photography by Andre Martin

MEASUREMENTS

Finished embroidery measures approximately 5" wide x 11" high, excluding frame.

MATERIALS

- 14" x 20" white 14-count Aida cloth
- One skein DMC Six-strand Cotton Embroidery Floss in each of the following colors: very dark ash grey 3799, light steel grey 318, pearl grey 415, light brown-grey 3023, dark beige-grey 642, very dark beige-grey 640, medium drab brown 612, very dark topaz 780, light copper 922, copper 920, medium Christmas red 304, dark lemon 444, bright yellow 972, light yellow-beige 3047, medium yellow-green 3347, dark yellow-green 3346, royal blue 797, medium electric blue 996, medium blue-violet 340, light cranberry 604, very light plum 3608, light plum 3607
- Size 24 tapestry needle
- Sewing thread in medium color

METHOD

Before commencing, refer to the instructions for cross stitch in the **Embroidery Stitch Guide** on page 58.

Following the graph on page 24, embroider motifs in cross stitch. Each symbol represents one cross stitch, embroidered with two strands of embroidery floss in the indicated color, over one fabric square. Work the lines of the outer frame in backstitch, and the details in straight stitch or backstitch, as indicated on the graph.

Commence embroidery with the outer frame, approximately $4^1/_2$ inches in from the edges at lower righthand corner. For the first stitch, leave a short end of embroidery thread hanging free at the back of the work, to be laced under embroidery when work has progressed.

Work personal initials from the alphabet graph on page 25, using light brown-grey, and graphed "M P" initials for position.

To finish, press work on the wrong side on well-padded surface, then mount and frame as desired.

	304		920
	318		922
	340		972
	415		996
	444		3023
	604		3047
	612		3346
〉 galah beaks			
	640		3347
	642		3607
	780		3608
◁ female wren beak			
	797		3799
		7 male wren beaks	
		birds' eyes	

Handmade tags are quick to make and add a special finishing touch to gifts. Choose single motifs from the sampler and work on scraps of 14- or 18-count Aida. Cut into squares, fray one square of cloth for a narrow fringe, then glue lightly to colored cardboard tag shapes. Punch a hole in each tag and finish with a ribbon tie.

Small but perfect scented sachets — embroider the boronia motif from the sampler as a repeating pattern on a small amount of white 18-count Aida cloth. Stitch the cloth into a small bag, approximately $2^1/2$" x $1^1/2$", fill with lavender and tie with ribbon at the top.

Here's another dainty gift that would make a great craft sale item. Paint small wooden or cardboard boxes white, then cover lid with a scrap of Aida on which you've worked motifs from the larger sampler. Glue lace or ribbon around the lid edge to disguise raw Aida edges, and decorate with seed pods or a tiny bow. Inside the lid could also be padded to make the box into a pin or needle box.

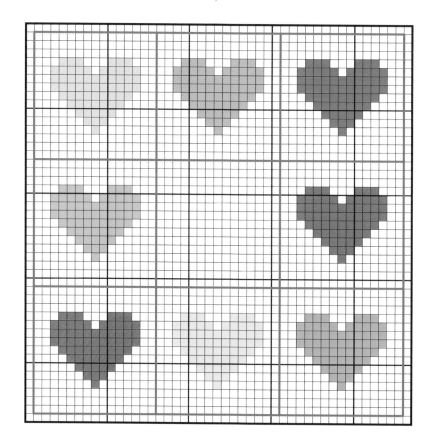

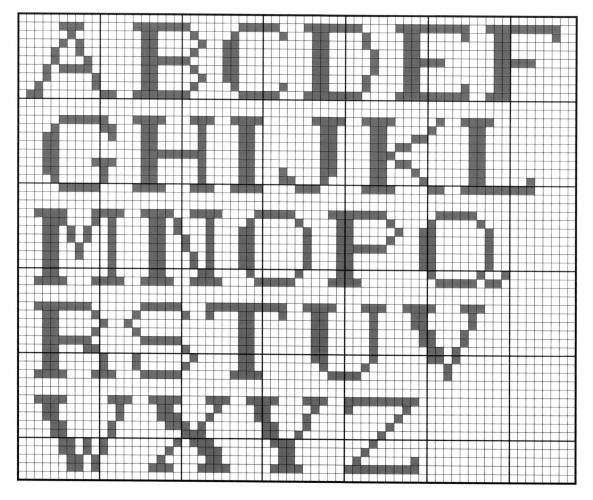

CROSS MY HEART

Featuring a repeating heart motif, this simple cross-stitched sampler can be worked in a jiffy. It would make a marvelous gift for a newborn when you haven't made industrious use of the nine months' notice! There are no precise instructions for the sampler — using the graphs opposite and following the instructions for cross stitch in the **Embroidery**

Stitch Guide on page 58, simply work on the fabric of your choice, using colors that please you. As a guide, our embroidery is approximately $2^3/4$" square, and is worked on Belfast linen (32 threads/inch).

Sampler designed by Caroline Lobsey and worked by Caroline Halliday
Photography by Andre Martin

VARIATIONS ON A THEME

Combining the jewel-bright colors of variegated pearl threads and delightfully easy canvas stitches, these cases are a treat to stitch and make superb use of the multi-colored thread. They have been sized for glasses, but they could also provide an elegant cover for small cellular phones, and could easily be adapted to fit a larger one.

This project uses the following canvas stitches:

- Milanese stitch • reverse cushion stitch
- leaf stitch • cross-cornered cushion stitch

See **Diagrams 1–4** on pages 30 and 31.

Cases designed and stitched by Alison Snepp
Photography by Valerie Martin

MEASUREMENTS

Finished case measures approximately $3^1/2''$ wide x $6^3/4''$ long.

MATERIALS

- $17^3/4''$ x 6" 18-count interlock tapestry canvas (per case)
- Watercolor thread: Forest Fire (5 skeins), **or** Aurora (5 skeins), **or** Caribbean (5 skeins), **or** Lilac (5 skeins, plus 2 skeins each DMC Cotton Pearl No. 5, colors 223 and 224) (see **Note**, below)
- Size 22 tapestry needle
- Size 5 crewel embroidery needle
- Embroidery scissors
- 1"-wide masking tape
- $17^3/4''$ x 6" lining fabric, to match Watercolor thread
- Sewing thread, to match lining

Note: *Watercolor Thread is made by The Caron Collection, 67 Poland Street, Bridgeport CT 06605, ph (203) 333 0325.*

METHOD

Preparation Cover the edges of the canvas with masking tape to stop them fraying and to prevent the embroidery threads becoming snagged.

The embroidery on each case is started $1^1/8''$ inches in and down from the top lefthand corner of the canvas.

Milanese stitch in Forest Fire To outline area to be worked, use sewing thread and, beginning $1^1/_8$ inches in from edge and top of canvas, baste a rectangle measuring 64 threads across and 232 threads down.

Milanese stitch is also known as arrowhead stitch. Following **Diagram 1** and using one strand of thread, start with the point of an arrowhead in the top lefthand corner of the case and work diagonal rows of embroidery down the case to the righthand side. To stitch the second row, you can turn the work upside down and work back down towards the right again, or start a new row, below the first. Whichever method you choose, work the next diagonal row with the arrowhead pointing downward (opposite to the first), but note that your starting arrowhead will not be complete, because of the side edge. At the edges, partial stitches will have to be worked to finish the embroidery crisply in a straight line. These should be worked in the same direction as a full stitch would have been worked.

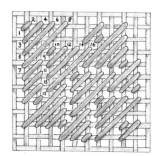

DIAGRAM 1 — Milanese stitch
Red thread shows direction of first row

Reverse cushion stitch in Aurora To outline area to be worked, use sewing thread and, beginning $1^1/_8$ inches in from edge and top of canvas, baste a rectangle measuring 64 threads across and 232 threads down.

Using one strand of thread and following **Diagram 2**, begin embroidery $1^1/_8$ inches in from the top lefthand corner and work 16 squares diagonally down the canvas, across the width of the case. To stitch the next

row, you can turn the work upside down, or start a new row beneath the first, leaving one empty square in between. Continue working the square-shaped cushion stitches until there are 58 squares down the length of the canvas. Every second square should be stitched, with all the diagonal stitches worked in the same direction. Next, start working into the blank rows of squares between the stitched cushions, working the diagonal stitches for these rows in the opposite direction to the first.

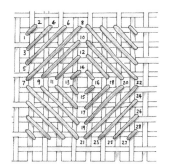

DIAGRAM 2 — Reverse cushion stitch
Darker thread shows direction of first row

Leaf stitch in Caribbean To outline area to be worked, use sewing thread and, beginning $1^1/_8$ inches in from edge and top of canvas, baste a rectangle measuring 66 threads across and 232 threads down.

Using one strand of thread and following **Diagram 3**, work one row of 11 complete leaf stitches across the top of the glasses case. The second row will have one half leaf stitch at each end and ten complete stitches nestled in between the bottom of the complete stitches in the row above. Continue to fill the basted area of the case with leaf stitches worked in this manner.

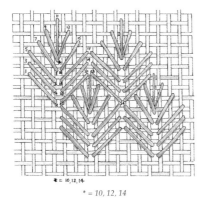

＊ = 10, 12, 14

＊ = 10, 12, 14

DIAGRAM 3 — Leaf stitch
Green thread shows direction of first row

Cross-cornered cushion stitch in Lilac and Cotton Pearl

To outline the area to be worked, use sewing thread and, beginning $1^1/8$ inches in from edge and top of canvas, baste a rectangle measuring 64 threads across and 232 threads down.

Beginning at the top lefthand corner of marked area and using one strand of Cotton Pearl No. 5, color 223, work reverse cushion stitch, as shown in **Diagram 2**, working all the squares in one diagonal direction with this color. Work all the "cushions" on the opposite diagonal with one strand of Cotton Pearl No. 5, color 224.

Using one strand of Lilac thread and following **Diagram 4**, half cover each Pearl thread square with diagonal stitches as shown. Work back and forth across the rows of cushion stitches to create a pretty see-through effect.

DIAGRAM 4 — Cross-cornered cushion stitch
Pink thread shows reverse cushion stitch,
worked before overlaying with second color

Finishing

Blocking: Spray wrong side of embroidered canvas with cold water to dampen. Use rustproof nails or pins to fasten edge of canvas to a wooden board, with right side of embroidery facing the board so that it is tight and straight. Allow canvas to dry thoroughly. Remove embroidery from board.

Lining: Trim excess canvas from around the embroidery leaving a 12-thread border of unstitched canvas on each side. Turn back the unstitched canvas to the wrong side of the embroidery, mitering the corners as you go. Stitch the unstitched canvas to the back of the embroidery with sewing thread.

Turn in the edges of the lining fabric to fit the back of the embroidery and hand-stitch it around the edges to line the back of the embroidery.

Fold embroidery in half to form glasses case — note that the fold forms bottom of case. Slipstitch long sides of canvaswork together, leaving top edges open.

Cord: Cut six lengths of thread, each 7 feet long. Place the six lengths of thread together and tie them in a knot at one end. Close the knot in a tightly fitting drawer. Hold the other end of the threads and twist them together, following the twist of the threads, until they are tightly twisted.

With a finger at the halfway point, bring the end held to the ends in the drawer and allow the threads to twist around each other smoothly, forming a cord.

Using sewing thread, slipstitch the cord to the glasses case, starting at the folded end of the cord. Push the folded end inside the glasses case at one corner of the embroidery and stitch it to the edge of the glasses case in the following sequence of sides: across the top of one side, down one long side, across the bottom, up the other long side and then across the top of the other side.

Tie a tight knot in the end of the cord to fit, and push knot inside the glasses case before finishing stitching. Finish the four corners with small simple tassels.

SITTING PRETTY

These beautiful ribbon-embroidered pillows bloom all year round, giving a wonderful display of the softest pastel colors. As a variation on the more usual silk ribbon, the flowers have been worked in a combination of cotton and linen ribbons. If cotton or linen ribbon is unavailable, substitute synthetics, which come in a variety of textures, weights and widths.

This project uses the following stitches:

- whipped backstitch • lazy daisy stitch
- pistil stitch • ribbon stitch • loop stitch
- French knots • straight stitch

See **Embroidery Stitch Guide** on page 58.

Pillows designed and worked by Lynda Maker
Photography by Andre Martin
Styling by Vicki Liley

Basket of Flowers Pillow

MEASUREMENTS

Finished pillow measures approximately 20" square, including ruffle. Embroidered panel measures $15^1/_2$" square.

MATERIALS

- 20" square cream-colored cotton damask
- Fabric for backing and ruffle
- Mokuba Cotton Ribbon (No. 1513) in the following amounts and colors: $3^1/_3$ yards x No. 10, $5^1/_2$ yards x No. 31, $5^1/_2$ yards x No. 29, $5^1/_2$ yards x No. 16, $3^1/_3$ yards x No. 42, $2^3/_4$ yards x No. 15, $2^1/_4$ yards x No. 23, or equivalent (see **Note**, below)
- Mokuba Acrylic/Linen Ribbon (No. 1501) in the following amounts and colors: $3^1/_3$ yards x No. 15, $5^1/_2$ yards x No. 2, $5^1/_2$ yards x No. 17, $4^1/_3$ yards x No. 31, $3^1/_3$ yards x No. 27, $1^2/_3$ yards x No. 12, $3^1/_3$ yards x No. 23, or equivalent
- One skein DMC Flower Thread in each of the following colors: 2727, 2745, 2833, 2831
- Sewing thread to match Cotton Ribbon Nos. 29 and 31
- Assorted buttons in complementary colors, including seven x $^3/_8$" buttons with four holes, for basket
- Air erasable marking pen
- Sizes 18 and 22 candlewicking needles
- Small, sharp tapestry needle
- Small sewing needle
- 14" embroidery hoop
- 16" pillow form

Note: *Mokuba ribbon can be mail ordered from Designer Trim, 134 Bridge Road, Richmond, Vic 3121, Australia.*

METHOD

Cut a 16½-inch square of cotton damask, centering damask pattern, if necessary. Mark center of square.

Basket Outlines for basket and flower embroidery are printed on page 36. Enlarge each of them 180 percent on a photocopier. Using erasable marking pen, trace the outline of both the basket and the handle onto damask, matching center cross on outline to center mark on fabric. (The pattern appears to be slightly low on the fabric, but this is to allow space for ribbons at the top.) Place fabric in embroidery hoop and cut a 20-inch length of Cotton Ribbon No. 10. Thread into Size 18 candlewicking needle and knot the end (refer to **Embroidery Stitch Guide** on page 58 for how to thread embroidery ribbon).

Using **Diagram 1** as a guide and starting at the center bottom of the basket, make large straight stitches, keeping the ribbon flat as you draw it through the fabric.

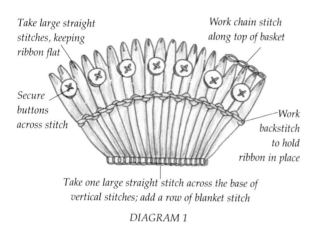

Take large straight stitches, keeping ribbon flat

Work chain stitch along top of basket

Secure buttons across stitch

Work backstitch to hold ribbon in place

Take one large straight stitch across the base of vertical stitches; add a row of blanket stitch

DIAGRAM 1

To avoid wasting ribbon, bring the needle out at the top of the next stitch and work the next straight stitch down (**Diagram 2**). The stitches need to fan out to fill the shape of the basket. To achieve this effect, the spaces between the stitches at the top of the basket are ⁵⁄₁₆ inch apart, while those at the base are only ⅛ inch apart. Working from the middle, stitch one side completely before returning to middle to complete the other side — this will maintain the symmetry.

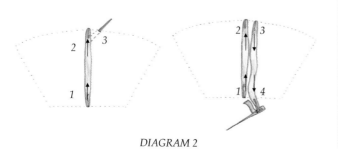

DIAGRAM 2

Now run a single, long, horizontal straight stitch across base of other stitches.

Thread a Size 22 candlewicking needle with a length of Acrylic/Linen Ribbon No. 15, and work a row of blanket stitch over this straight stitch, taking needle through the fabric between the vertical straight stitches.

Again using Acrylic/Linen Ribbon No. 15, work a row of chain stitch along the top of the basket. Now work a row of backstitch across the vertical straight stitches, approximately halfway up the basket, as shown in **Diagram 1**. Change to a tapestry needle and, using the same thread, weave in and out of the backstitches to achieve a pretty effect. Position ⅜ inch buttons across the basket, as shown on the outline on page 36, and secure each in place with a cross stitch of Acrylic/Linen Ribbon No. 31.

Thread Size 18 candlewicking needle with Cotton Ribbon No. 10 and, using **Diagram 3** as a guide, run a line of backstitch along the length of the traced handle. Use a whipstitch into each stitch to add bulk, using your finger or another needle to keep the thread flat. Whip twice into each stitch. Using Acrylic/Linen Ribbon No. 15 and Size 22 candlewicking needle, work a row of blanket stitch along the length of the handle.

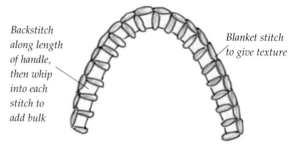

Backstitch along length of handle, then whip into each stitch to add bulk

Blanket stitch to give texture

DIAGRAM 3

Flowers Trace approximate areas for flowers onto fabric, but there is no need to be too exact.

Daisies: Trace circles onto fabric using erasable marking pen. Using Size 22 candlewicking needle and Acrylic/Linen Ribbon No. 2, work a circle of lazy daisy stitches. Fill each stitch with a straight stitch of the same color. Using a strand of yellow Flower Thread (2727 or 2745), work flower centers in French knots. Leaves are worked in lazy daisy, using Acrylic/Linen Ribbon No. 17.

Gathered roses: The gathered roses are worked in Cotton Ribbon Nos. 31 and 29. Cut a 14- to 16-inch length of Cotton Ribbon (shorter for smaller flowers), and knot one end. Take a piece of matching sewing thread, secure at the knotted end and make small running stitches along the length of the ribbon. Thread the ribbon through the Size 18 candlewicking needle and bring up through fabric at center of flower. Thread

loop flowers

purple sage

pink sprays

daisies

forget-me-nots

straight-stitch flowers

gathered roses

BASKET OF FLOWERS

Forget-me-nots: Using Acrylic/Linen Ribbon No. 23 and Size 22 candlewicking needle, work French knots in a tight circle. Use Flower Thread (2727) to work French knot centers. Work leaves in straight stitch using Acrylic/Linen No. 17.

Purple sage: Make a long straight-stitch stem, using Acrylic/Linen Ribbon No. 17. Make tiny straight stitches side by side on either side of stem at intervals, to top of stem. Using Acrylic/Linen No. 27, fill these two-stitch "cups" with lazy daisy stitches or straight stitch. Using Cotton Ribbon No. 42, make large loose ribbon stitches at base of each stem.

a small sharp needle with matching sewing thread. Gently gather the ribbon a little at a time, pulling on the sewing thread. Secure gathered edge to fabric with tiny stitches in matching sewing thread. Work two or three circles of gathers, then pass the ribbon to the back of the fabric and secure. Cut a length of Cotton Ribbon, the same color as the gathered center, and work straight stitches around the gathers.

Roses worked in No. 29 have been left very full; those worked in No. 31 have centers worked in pistil stitch, using Flower Thread 2833 and 2831.

Leaves are worked in Cotton Ribbon Nos. 16 and 42, using ribbon stitch.

Loop flowers: Using Size 18 candlewicking needle, thread Cotton Ribbon No. 15 and bring up through fabric. Make six loop stitches in a circle. Thread tapestry needle with Flower Thread (2831) and work a pistil stitch into the center of each loop petal to secure. Leaves are worked in straight stitch, using Cotton Ribbon No. 16.

Straight-stitch flowers: These simple flowers are worked using Cotton Ribbon No. 23 and Size 18 candlewicking needle, stitching five or six straight stitches in a circle. Centers are worked in Flower Thread (2745), using a French knot. A few leaves can be worked in straight stitch, using Cotton Ribbon No. 16.

Pink sprays: Draw a center line for these, using erasable marking pen. Make a straight-stitch stem, using Acrylic/Linen Ribbon No. 17, halfway along marker line. Using Acrylic/Linen No. 31, work up each side of the remainder of the marker line in lazy daisy. Work 8–10 stitches, depending on the spray, finishing with a middle stitch. Work a straight stitch inside each lazy daisy, using Acrylic/Linen No. 12. Use Acrylic/Linen No. 17 to add lazy daisy leaves along the stem.

Fill any extra spaces on the fabric with leaves, French knots, extra flowers and assorted odd buttons.

Bows: Cut 1 yard each of Cotton Ribbon Nos. 31 and 29. Thread into a needle together and stitch from the top of the handle through the fabric and up again below handle. Pull half the length of ribbon through to give 20 inches of each ribbon on either side of handle. Tie a knot around the handle. Take both ends together and secure about 1 inch above the handle with a small stitch of matching sewing thread. Tie a real bow and secure with tiny stitches of matching thread. Arrange ribbon tails in attractive loops and secure with tiny stitches. Turn under raw ends on ribbons to neaten and secure.

When embroidery is finished, pillow can be made up into any style you desire. We added a 2-inch (finished size) ruffle, using fabric one and a half times the outside measurement of pillow front, and finished the seam with a twisted cord of matching threads.

Basket of flowers outline
enlarge 180%

Basket
and
handle
outline
enlarge
180%

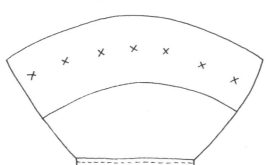

Bouquet Pillow

MEASUREMENTS

Finished pillow measures approximately 20″ square, including ruffle. Embroidered panel measures $15^{1}/_{2}$″ square.

MATERIALS

- 20″ square fabric (we used a pale green furnishing check)
- Extra fabric for backing and frill
- Mokuba Cotton Ribbon (No. 1513) in the following amounts and colors: $1^{1}/_{4}$ yards x No. 15, $2^{3}/_{4}$ yards x No. 29, $2^{1}/_{5}$ yards No. 31, $1^{1}/_{4}$ yards x No. 42, $1^{1}/_{4}$ yards x No. 16, $^{5}/_{8}$ yard x No. 23
- Mokuba Acrylic/Linen Ribbon (No. 1501) in the following amounts and colors: $3^{3}/_{8}$ yards x No. 17, $1^{2}/_{3}$ yards x No. 2, $1^{2}/_{3}$ yards x No. 23, $2^{3}/_{4}$ yards x No. 31, $1^{1}/_{4}$ yards x No. 12
- One skein DMC Flower Thread in each of the following colors: 2727, 2745, 2833, 2831
- Sewing thread to match Cotton Nos. 29 and 31
- Assorted buttons in complementary colors

- Erasable marking pen
- Sizes 18 and 22 candlewicking needles
- Small sharp tapestry needle
- Small sewing needle
- 14" embroidery hoop
- 16" pillow form

METHOD

Cut a 16 $\frac{1}{2}$-inch square of fabric, and mark center of the square. Enlarge the bouquet outline, printed below, 125 percent on a photocopier, and roughly trace the position of the flowers. Referring to the photograph, at right, and the techniques in Basket of Flowers, work the bouquet, adding buttons as required. Using Acrylic/Linen No. 17, work stems in large straight stitches.

BOUQUET OF FLOWERS

Bow: Cut a 20-inch length each of Cotton Nos. 29 and 31 and thread into needle. Insert needle on one side of stems, take it beneath fabric, then re-emerge on other side of stems, leaving half the thread on each side of stem bunch. Tie a bow across front of stems, and secure bow and tails in place with tiny stitches in matching sewing thread, curling the tails into attractive loops as you work. Make up pillow as desired.

Bouquet of flowers outline enlarge 125%

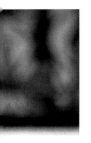

CONVERTED TO THREAD

Wheel Flower Tapestry Pillow

This lovely tapestry is based on Preston's *Wheel Flower* (c. 1929), a hand-colored woodcut of *Stenocarpus snuatus*.

MEASUREMENTS

Finished tapestry measures approximately $14^1/_4$" square.

MATERIALS

For tapestry:

- 20" square mono canvas, 12 holes/inch
- Anchor Tapisserie Wool in the following colors and amounts: charcoal grey 9798 (7 skeins), medium olive green 9178 (2 skeins), spruce green 9078 (1 skein), dark spruce green 9080 (3 skeins), grey-green 9066 (2 skeins), grass green 9168 (2 skeins), camel brown 9424 (12 skeins), flame red 8200 (3 skeins), or equivalent
- Size 18 tapestry needle
- Tapestry frame (optional)

For pillow cover:

- Blotting paper, tapestry size
- Board slightly larger than canvas
- Spray container of water
- Hammer and rustproof nails or pins
- Piece of backing fabric, slightly larger than finished cover size (we used velvet)
- Zipper, 3" shorter than width of cover, to match backing fabric
- Matching sewing thread
- Cord trim, enough for outer edge of pillow cover, plus 4 inches extra
- Adhesive tape
- Pillow form $1^1/_2$" larger than finished cover size

*B*etween the wars Margaret Preston was arguably Australia's foremost woman painter, and her decorative and vividly colored images remain as popular today as they were in the 1920s and 1930s. Her distinctive style, with its often vivid colors and sculptural lines, seems peculiarly fitted to the Australian flora that she loved to depict. The strong, slightly stylized lines of her woodcuts also make them very suitable for translation into tapestry and cross stitch, as you can see from the beautiful designs featured here.

Wheel Flower tapestry colored by Coats Patons Crafts, graphed by David Marsh of Crafted Software, and stitched by Kerry Stibbe
Photography by Andre Martin
Styling by Kathy Tripp

METHOD

Tapestry Mark center point on canvas, and attach canvas to frame, if using. Following graph and key on these pages, work tapestry in tent (continental) stitch (see **Embroidery Stitch Guide** on page 58). Each square on the graph equals one tent stitch. When you have completed the design, work 10 rows of tent stitch around all four edges in 9424.

To assemble pillow cover When tapestry is finished, it will have become slightly distorted in shape, and will need to be squared again, or "blocked". Rule correctly squared dimensions of finished canvas onto blotting paper and lay this on a wooden board. Lightly spray the back of the canvas with water to dampen and leave for a few minutes to soften. Gently pull the canvas square, fixing it in place on the ruled blotting paper, using nails or pins

and a hammer (**Pic 1**). Don't pull the canvas too tightly or the edges will distort. When tapestry is dry — this may take two or three days — remove it from the board. Cut away excess canvas, leaving $^1/_2$ inch of unsewn canvas around all four edges.

From backing fabric, cut a piece the same size as trimmed canvas, but adding 2 inches to width measurement to accommodate zipper seam. Fold fabric in half crosswise and cut along crease, for zipper opening. Neaten raw edges of backing pieces.

With right sides facing and allowing 1-inch seams, stitch zipper seam 2 inches in from each end (**Pic 2**). Adapt this measurement if zipper is more or less than 3 inches shorter than width of cover so that zipper will be inserted in center of seam. Press seam open, pressing zipper seam allowance to wrong side at same time. If using velvet, use a pressing cloth. Baste zipper in place, with pressed opening edges meeting at center of zipper teeth. Using a zipper foot, stitch zipper in place. Leave zipper open so that you can turn cover right side out.

With right sides together, pin pillow cover back to tapestry. Working from the canvas side, machine-stitch around outer edges of tapestry (**Pic 3**), leaving a 1-inch opening along the bottom edge. Machine-stitch close to last row of hand stitches to prevent the canvas from showing on the right side. Work a second row of stitching over the first.

Trim seams at corners and turn cover to the right side, pushing out the corners carefully.

Using double thread, hand-stitch cord to pillow cover edge from bottom opening, leaving a 2-inch "tail" of cord as you begin. Wrap ends of cord with adhesive tape to prevent them from fraying. Working from the canvas side, pick up a little canvas then a small amount of cord with each stitch (**Pic 4**).

To finish the cord ends neatly, lay one end of cord over the other and slightly unroll the top piece so that twists of this cord can be pushed into twists of the cord below. Using double thread, sew a few stitches through the two layers of cord to hold them in place securely. Untwist the ends of the cord, tape together and push down into opening. Slipstitch gap closed. Insert pillow form into cover.

8200   9066   9078   9080   9168   9178   9424   9798

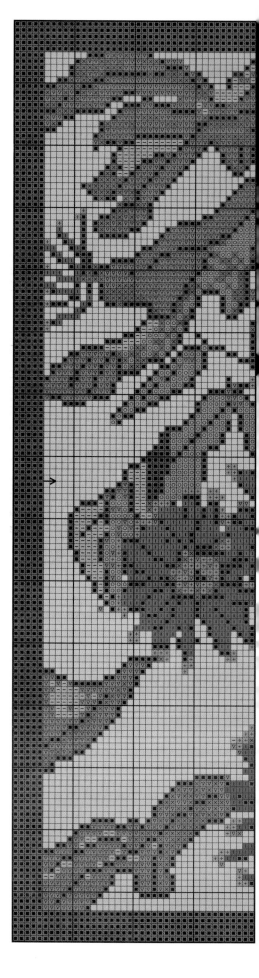

Framed Cross-stitch Pictures

These handsome cross-stitched pictures have been graphed and colored with careful reference to the original woodcuts, Cinerarias (1927) and Dahlia and Sunflower (1933).

This project uses the following stitches:

• *cross stitch* • *half cross stitch*

• *backstitch* • *French knot*

*See **Embroidery Stitch Guide** on page 58.*

MEASUREMENTS

Each finished design measures approximately 6" square.

MATERIALS

For each design:

• 12" square cream 14-count Aida
• Size 24 tapestry needle
• Embroidery hoop (optional)

Cinerarias:

• DMC Six-strand Cotton Embroidery Floss in the following amounts and colors: one skein each of maroon 221, light brownish pink 224, mauve-pink 316, dark green 319, light green 320, mid green 367, light tan 738, light mauve-pink 778, deep blue 792, light blue 793, deep tan 976, mid tan 977, purple 3041, light purple 3042, brownish pink 3722; two skeins black 310, or equivalent

Dahlia and Sunflower:

• One skein DMC Six-strand Cotton Embroidery Floss in each of the following colors: black 310, faded red 349, gold 726, light gold 744, pink 760, light pink 761, dark red 817, dark orange 920, mid orange 921, light orange 922, deep gold 972, écru, or equivalent

METHOD

Graphs for the cross stitch are printed on pages 44 and 45. Using the colors indicated on the key accompanying each graph, work the design in cross stitch, using two strands of embroidery floss over one Aida square.

When a square contains two symbols and you are in doubt, black is the dominant color. The square will either be divided by black backstitch or contain a black $^3/_4$ stitch and a $^1/_4$ stitch in contrasting color.

When cross stitch is complete, work backstitch using one strand of thread. All French knots are stitched over the top of a black cross stitch, except for full stop after 'M' on Dahlias. Add French knots in the color indicated on the key, using one strand of embroidery floss, and encircling the needle twice.

Press finished embroidery on the wrong side on a well-padded surface and frame as desired.

Photography by Joe Filshie
Styling by Georgina Dolling

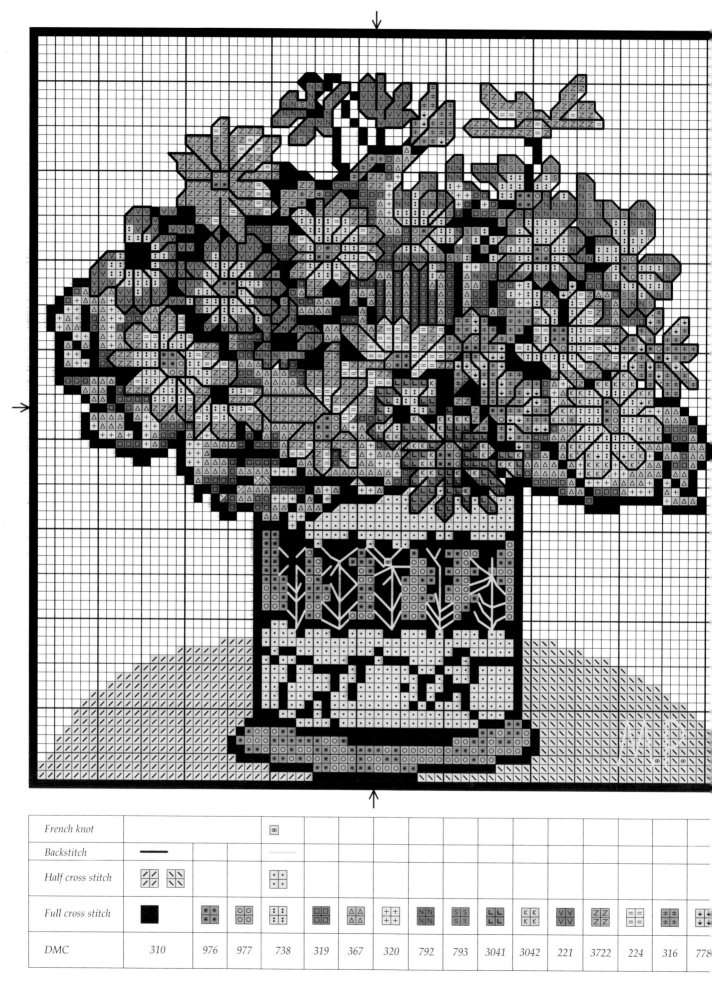

French knot						⊕												
Backstitch	—																	
Half cross stitch	◹ ◺					⋮⋮												
Full cross stitch	■		✶✶	○○	⋮⋮	□□	△△	++	NN	SS	LL	KK	VV	ZZ	==	‡‡	‡✦
DMC	310		976	977	738	319	367	320	792	793	3041	3042	221	3722	224	316	778

French knot	·	✗			S				‖		■
Backstitch	—										
Half cross stitch	⁄⁄	⁂				▦	▦					
Full cross stitch	■	QQ QQ	✳✳	◉◉	▢▢	▦	✚✚	◉◉	=‖=	ZZ ZZ	VV VV	WW WW
DMC	310	écru	920	921	922	817	349	760	761	972	726	744

WARM THOUGHTS

Add the cheerful little faces of these exquisite pansies to your teatime ritual and brighten up the coldest morning. The pure wool tea cozy features embroidered blooms in a wonderfully subtle array of soft colors and is lined with a matching pansy fabric. This is not a difficult project, but it will take a little patience and practice with long and short stitch if you haven't done it before.

This project uses the following stitches:

• long and short stitch • straight stitch • fly stitch • stem stitch • satin stitch

*See **Embroidery Stitch Guide** on page 58.*

MEASUREMENTS

Finished tea cozy measures approximately 16" x 10", but you can adapt the pattern to suit your own teapot.

*Tea cozy designed and worked by Gabrielle Henderson
Photography by Andre Martin
Styling by Vicki Liley*

MATERIALS

• 20" x 16" pure wool blanket fabric
• $2/3$ yard x 45" lining fabric
• 20" x 16" batting
• Thin tracing paper (such as tissue paper or waxed paper)
• Water erasable marking pen, fine tip
• Size 22 tapestry needle or Size 22 candlewicking needle
• One skein Appletons 2-ply Wool in each of the following colors: light purple 893, mid purple 894, dark purple 895, light blue 741, mid blue 743, dark blue 744, mauve 885, dark yellow 553, mid yellow 996, light yellow 872, cream 991, black 993, green 352, or equivalent
• Matching sewing thread

PATTERN PIECE AND EMBROIDERY OUTLINE

Tea Cozy pattern and embroidery outline are both printed on page 49. On a photocopier, enlarge pattern 112 percent and embroidery outline 117 percent, and trace.

CUTTING

Note: *Do not add seam allowance to pattern pieces, as edges are bound.*

From blanketing, cut two Tea Cozies to length indicated on pattern piece for wool and batting.

From lining fabric, cut two Tea Cozies to length indicated on pattern piece, for lining. Cut also one bias strip, 2" x 34", for binding (or join pieces to achieve this length).

From batting, cut two Tea Cozies to the same length as blanketing.

METHOD

Embroidery Run a line of basting along lower edge of both blanketing Tea Cozies, $1^{1}/_{2}$ inches from raw edge (to indicate line to which lining comes on finished cozy).

Center your traced design above the basted line, on the right side of one of the wool fabric pieces, and pin in place. Using erasable marking pen, pierce the paper and put a dot onto the fabric in the center of each flower and at intervals around the edge of the petals. Remove the paper and join the dots, using the drawing as a guide. It's a good idea to draw and embroider one flower at a time, adding all leaves and buds last.

Using the individual pansy diagrams for color placement and the embroidery outline for stitch placement, embroider design on blanketing. The flowers and leaves are not meant to be botanically correct and it is not necessary to follow the diagrams exactly to get a pleasing result. If you have not done long and short stitch before, it is a good idea to practice on a scrap of fabric until you are happy with the tension of your stitching.

All leaves, stems and bases of buds are worked in green 352. All buds are worked in satin stitch. Bud A is worked in mid yellow 996 and dark yellow 553; Bud B is worked in mauve 885; Bud C is worked in dark purple 895. All leaves are worked in fly stitch, starting each with a straight stitch first to give a nice point.

To assemble Tea Cozy Pin or baste batting to wrong side of both blanketing pieces.

With right sides together, pin lining to blanketing so that lower edge of lining aligns with the basted line on blanketing. Stitch lining to blanketing, allowing $^{3}/_{8}$-inch seam. Do this for both front and back of cozy. Turn lining around to wrong side of front and back so that wrong side of lining faces batting and raw curved edges are even.

Place front and back together, with linings facing each other, and baste outer edge together through all thicknesses.

Leaving a small amount for hem allowance at lower edge, pin and stitch bias strip to edge of Tea Cozy, right sides together, embroidery face up. Trim seam and neaten all layers; fold in remaining raw edge of bias and slipstitch to back of cozy over seam, turning and neatening raw ends of binding at both lower edges.

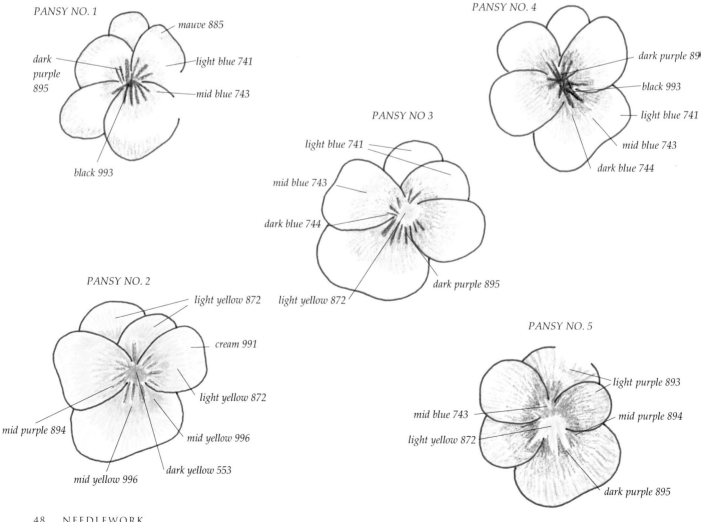

PANSY NO. 1
— mauve 885
dark purple 895
light blue 741
mid blue 743
black 993

PANSY NO. 2
light yellow 872
cream 991
light yellow 872
mid purple 894
mid yellow 996
dark yellow 553
mid yellow 996

PANSY NO 3
light blue 741
mid blue 743
dark blue 744
light yellow 872
dark purple 895

PANSY NO. 4
dark purple 895
black 993
light blue 741
mid blue 743
dark blue 744

PANSY NO. 5
light purple 893
mid purple 894
mid blue 743
light yellow 872
dark purple 895

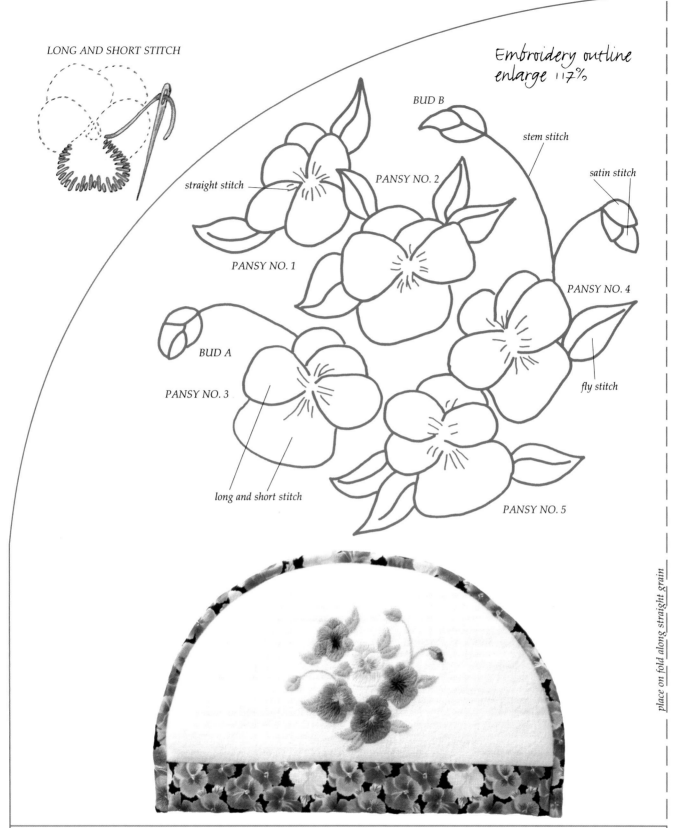

LONG AND SHORT STITCH

Embroidery outline enlarge 117%

BUD B

straight stitch

PANSY NO. 2

stem stitch

satin stitch

PANSY NO. 1

BUD A

PANSY NO. 4

PANSY NO. 3

fly stitch

long and short stitch

PANSY NO. 5

place on fold along straight grain

cutting line for wool and batting

Half Tea Cozy pattern enlarge 112%

cutting line for lining

THE PERPETUAL GARDEN

Two perennial garden favorites — shy sweet violets and fragrant silvery lavender — bloom all year round in these delicate silk ribbon embroideries. Each piece is, in fact, a mix of appliqué, and silk ribbon and thread embroidery — tiny silk violets nestle among appliquéd leaves in a simple vase, and sprays of Italian lavender, worked in a combination of silk ribbon and stranded cotton, seem so real that you could almost pick them. Neither piece is very difficult to stitch and either would brighten a wintry corner with the promise of spring to come.

These projects use the following stitches:

- straight stitch • stem stitch • ribbon stitch
- satin stitch • lazy daisy stitch
- pistil stitch

See **Embroidery Stitch Guide** on page 58.

Silk ribbon embroideries designed and worked by Heather McCallum

Photography by Jaime Plaza

Violet appliqué outlines

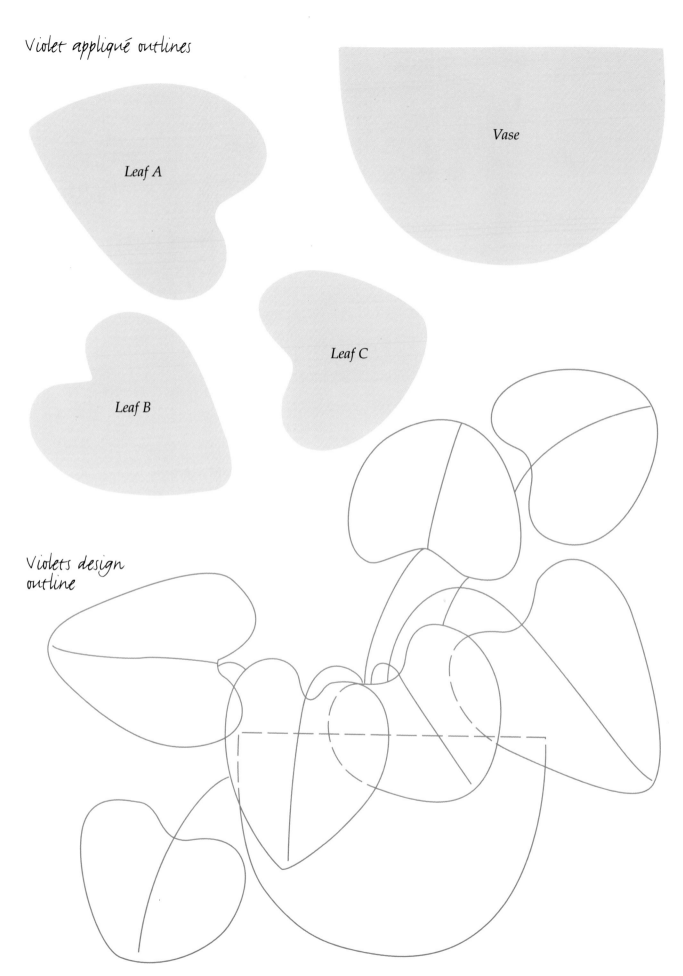

Leaf A

Vase

Leaf B

Leaf C

Violets design outline

If you wish, the Violets design can be made into a cushion by bordering it with a toning background fabric.

Violets

MEASUREMENTS

Design area is $6^3/4$" wide x $6^1/4$ high.

MATERIALS

- 14" square background fabric (see **Note**, below)
- $4^3/4$" square brown cotton fabric, for Vase
- 8" square green cotton fabric, for Leaves
- Matching sewing thread
- One skein DMC Six-strand Cotton Embroidery Floss in each of the following colors: green 520, gold 782, mauve 3743, or equivalent
- $6^1/2$ yards x $^1/4$"-wide purple silk ribbon
- Size 5–8 straw, or milliner's, needle
- Size 18 candlewicking needle
- Fabric scissors
- Paper scissors
- 10" square freezer paper (see **Note**, below)
- 8" embroidery hoop

Note: *Any firm even-weave fabric will do. We used cotton Osnaburg for the cushion and tea-dyed calico for the picture. Belfast linen would* also be suitable. Freezer paper is available at supermarkets. It has the advantage of sticking temporarily to fabric when ironed, but if it is unavailable, ordinary photocopy paper does a good job — simply use pins to hold it in position and proceed as for freezer paper.

APPLIQUÉ OUTLINES

Appliqué outlines are printed on page 52. Onto freezer paper, trace one Vase, one Leaf A, two Leaf Bs, and four Leaf Cs. Cut out to make templates.

CUTTING

Iron Vase template onto wrong side of brown fabric and cut out, adding a $^1/4$-inch seam allowance. The freezer paper will temporarily stick to fabric when ironed, making it easier to manage. Repeat with Leaf templates on green fabric.

METHOD

Appliqué Finger press seam allowance to the wrong side of each appliqué piece, and baste into place, stitching through paper.

Using design outline on page 52, pin Vase in position on background fabric and, with matching sewing thread, appliqué using a small slipstitch. Leave top of Vase unstitched. Remove basting and freezer paper.

Pin Leaves into position one at a time, working from the underneath Leaves to the top, using the design outline on page 52 and photograph below. Start slipstitching on a straight edge so that when you remove the paper it is easier to maintain the shape of the leaf.

Embroidery When all Leaves have been appliquéd into position, work a vein down the center of each, using three strands of green 520 in stem stitch with a straw, or milliner's, needle.

Continue the stem stitch to form stems on the violet leaves. When stitching is complete, place work in embroidery hoop and work violets in ribbon stitch,

using silk ribbon in the candlewicking needle. Some of the violets should overlap and single stitches can be used to fill in spaces. The aim is to have a heavily worked area in the center of the design, softening towards the edges.

Work buds and half-open violets randomly through the design, using the photograph below as a guide.

Work centers of violets with one strand of mauve 3743. Stitch small straight stitches radiating out from the center, then, with three strands of gold 782, work one straight stitch for the throat. Using two strands of green 520 and straight stitch, add a calyx and stem to the violets that look as if they should have them.

The combination of appliqué, silk ribbon and thread embroidery creates texture and gives a realistic feel to the Violets design.

Italian Lavender

MEASUREMENTS

Design area is 6$\frac{1}{4}$" wide x 8" high.

MATERIALS

- 16" x 20" background fabric, such as calico or Belfast linen
- Anchor Stranded Embroidery Cotton in the following colors and amounts: grey-green 8581 (1 skein), mauve 871 (1 skein), purple 873 (1 skein), black 403 (1 skein) and green 860 (2 skeins), or equivalent
- 2$\frac{1}{4}$ yards x $\frac{3}{16}$"-wide purple silk ribbon
- Small and large candlewicking needles
- Straw, or milliner's, needle
- Water erasable marking pen
- Small embroidery hoop

METHOD

Transfer the embroidery outline, printed on page 56, to the background fabric using erasable marking pen and light box or sunny window. Place the fabric into an embroidery hoop.

Work base of flower head in satin stitch, using three strands of mauve 871 and three strands of grey-green 8581 threaded into the same needle (**Diagram 1**). Thread large candlewicking needle with six strands of purple 873 and three strands of mauve 871. Work one lazy daisy (detached chain) stitch into each of the four sections of satin stitch up the center of the flower head and work small straight stitches up both sides, one at either end of each satin stitch section (**Diagram 2**).

Thread one strand of black 403 and one strand of purple 873 into the straw, or milliner's, needle and work a pistil stitch (or straight stitch finished with a two-twist French knot) coming from each straight stitch on both sides. A row of pistils is also worked up the center, one from each lazy daisy (**Diagram 3**). These pistil stitches represent the small flowerets on the Italian lavender and can be varied for each head, some with all stitches included, some with a couple missing.

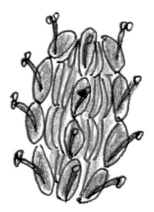

DIAGRAM 3

Work stems from base of flower head down to the first or second set of leaves with two strands of purple 873 and four strands of green 860 in the same needle, in stem stitch. Work stems from the first or second set of leaves to the bottom with six strands of green 860 in stem stitch. Work leaves in straight stitch with six strands of grey-green 8581, working random leaves with a mix of three strands of grey-green 8581 and three strands of green 860.

Work buds with three strands each of grey-green 8581 and mauve 871, with three straight stitches of varying length (**Diagram 4**). Add leaves on either side of bud with three strands of green 860 (**Diagram 5**).

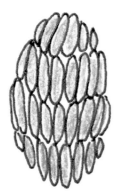

DIAGRAM 1

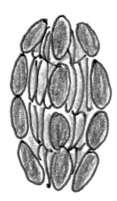

DIAGRAM 2

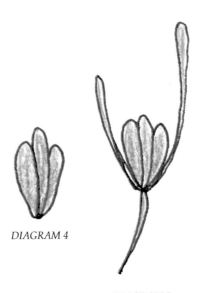

DIAGRAM 4

DIAGRAM 5

Before beginning silk embroidery, remove erasable marking pen by dipping embroidery into cold water. Roll in a towel to remove excess water and press on the wrong side on a padded ironing board. Stitch the ribbon flower tops after pressing. Do not press the silk ribbon, as pressing will spoil the lovely loose texture of the stitches.

Thread purple ribbon into a large candlewicking needle; work long, loose straight stitches, some twisted, some straight, for flower tops (**Diagram 6**).

DIAGRAM 6

Italian lavender embroidery outline

Embroidery Stitch Guide

Ribbon stitch

Bring needle up at A and flatten ribbon as it emerges from fabric. Extend ribbon just beyond length of stitch and insert needle through top surface of ribbon at B. Pull ribbon gently through fabric as the sides of ribbon curl inward to form a point. Leave the curls showing by not pulling tightly.

Loop stitch

Bring needle up through fabric and lay ribbon flat as if you were going to make a ribbon stitch, but pierce the ribbon again, almost where it came up. Pull through, keeping ribbon flat around an extra needle. Come up for the next loop and make the next stitch while still keeping the extra needle in place. (This holds the first stitch in place.) When the second loop is formed, you can remove the extra needle from the first loop. Hold this needle in the second loop while you make the third.

Bullion stitch

Bring needle up at A and insert it at B, about $1/8$ inch from A, bringing tip out again at A. Keeping thread to right of needle, wind thread clockwise around needle 3–7 times. Maintain tension on twists with finger or thumb, and push needle through fabric, pulling thread gently through twists. Holding twists in place with a finger, insert needle again at B to anchor the stitch.

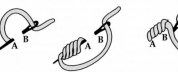

Cross stitch

Zigzag or bind by machine or whipstitch by hand around cut edges of fabric to prevent fraying (but never use sticky tape or masking tape). To find center of fabric, fold it in half lengthwise and crosswise and baste along the length of these center lines with a single sewing thread. If desired, insert fabric into embroidery hoop.

Work cross stitch from left to right in sequence shown, then work back from right to left to complete stitches, taking care that top stitch of every cross is worked in same direction. To work $3/4$, $1/2$ and $1/4$ cross stitch, refer to diagram, at right.

$3/4$ $1/2$ $1/4$

Whipped backstitch (ribbon)

Work backstitch as required. Bring ribbon back up at A. Wrap the backstitch by slipping needle once or twice under the backstitch. Continue in this manner to end.

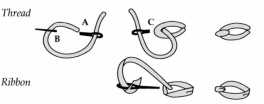

Lazy daisy or detached chain stitch

Bring needle out at A and reinsert it at A, leaving thread (or ribbon) in a loop under the needle. Exit at B, pulling thread through. Insert needle at C over thread loop.

Thread

Ribbon

French knot

Bring needle out at A and wrap thread counter-clockwise twice (or more) around needle. While holding thread taut, reinsert needle at B (close to A). Hold knot firm with thumb while pulling thread through fabric.

When using ribbon, work knots more loosely than with thread.

Thread

Ribbon

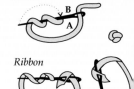

How to thread embroidery ribbon

Thread one end of ribbon into needle and pull through eye of needle for approximately 2 inches. Pierce threaded end of ribbon with needle, about $3/8$ inch from end, and pull long length of ribbon until ribbon "locks" at the eye of needle. This stops needle from unthreading. To begin stitching, draw ribbon through fabric, leaving a small tail behind your work. As you make your first stitch, pierce the tail with the needle to secure the ribbon. When finishing the stitch, work a small backstitch at back of fabric.

Blanket stitch

Bring needle out at A, then insert at B and bring it out again at C, making sure that thread is under point of needle before pulling needle through. Point C now becomes Point A of next stitch.

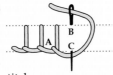

Stem stitch

Work stitch from left to right if righthanded. Bring needle up through fabric at A, go back down at B, making a straight stitch diagonally along traced embroidery line. Take needle back through to C (the midpoint of the previous stitch), keeping thread below needle, and proceed in this manner for desired length.

Palestrina knot stitch

Pick up a small piece of fabric with the stitch. Pass the needle under the stitch just made — not through the fabric. Pass the needle under the same part of the stitch made in Diagram 1 (not through the fabric), beneath Diagram 2's stitch, keeping the thread under the needle. Pull through gently. Repeat the steps.

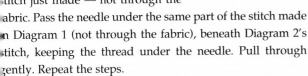

Long and short stitch

Work first row as series of alternating long and short satin stitches. Work remaining rows as same-length satin stitches, fitting them into gaps left by preceding rows.

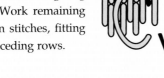

Feather stitch

Work from top to bottom. Bring needle up on center line, at A, then take it down at B and bring out again at C, on center line, looping thread under needle. Pull needle through. Insert needle at D, below and to the left of C, bring out at E, on center line. Pull needle through with thread under needle, and so on.

Fly stitch

Bring needle up at A and insert again at B. Emerge at C, bringing the needle tip over the thread. Draw thread through fabric and insert needle again at D, making CD any length desired.

Buttonhole stitch

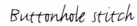

Herringbone stitch

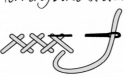

Tent (continental) stitch

row 1

row 2

ready to turn

row 2 (canvas turned)

satin stitch

straight stitch

Ladder stitch

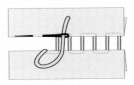

Backstitch

Pistil stitch

Bring needle up at A and wrap thread twice around shaft of needle. Swing point of needle clockwise and insert into fabric at B, some distance from A. Pull gently on working thread as you insert needle; hold twists with thumb and forefinger of your non-stitching hand as you pull needle through to back of fabric to complete stitch.

PATCHWORK AND APPLIQUE

PAINTED FINISH

Bring spring indoors with this pretty stenciled quilt. Baskets and garlands of fresh-faced pansies adorn a plain calico background, highlighted with simple bands of a small country print. The effect is quite charming and, once you've cut your stencils, it's all clear sailing from start to finish.

Stencils and quilt designed by Pam Jones
Quilt stitched by Chris Moss
Photography by Andre Martin
Styling by Louise Owens

MEASUREMENTS

Finished quilt measures approximately 69" square.

MATERIALS

- 4 yards x 45" seeded homespun or calico
- 2 yards x 45" checked fabric, for sashing and outer border
- 4 yards x 45" fabric (we used calico), for backing
- 4$^1/_2$ yards x 36" quilt batting
- $^2/_3$ yard x 45" dark print, for binding
- Matching sewing thread
- Two sheets Mylar film
- Fine black waterproof pen
- Craft blade or Xacto knife, and cutting board
- Masking tape
- Artist-quality flow formula acrylics, such as Jo Sonja's: Dioxazine Purple, Raw Sienna, Red Oxide, Antique White and Antique Green, or equivalent
- Artist-quality fabric fixative
- Palette knife or craft stick
- Plate or palette for mixing paint
- Five stencil brushes (one for each color)
- Paper towels

METHOD

Stenciling Pre-wash and dry all fabrics, except batting. The three stencil designs are on pages 66 and 67. Enlarge each design 122 percent on a photocopier. Place Mylar over each design and trace with waterproof pen (**Pic 1**). (If using good-quality Mylar, the designs can be photocopied directly onto Mylar.) Mark a cross on Mylar in the center of each design.

Cut the stencil. For greatest control, turn the stencil as you work so that you are pulling the blade towards you (**Pic 2**).

From homespun, cut or tear nine squares, each 13 inches, two border strips, each 6 inches x approximately 4 feet, and two border strips, each 6 inches x approximately 5 feet (these will be trimmed to fit when joining to quilt top). All measurements **include** 1/4-inch seam allowance.

Fold each square block in quarters and crease at center. Tape one block to work surface, matching center cross of stencil with crease-marked center of block.

Mix paints with Fabric Fixative, following manufacturer's instructions, and prepare palette with the following colors and color mixes:

Leaves and stems: Mix Antique Green with Antique White for basecoat. Use Diox Purple for shading leaves.

Purple pansies: Mix Raw Sienna with Antique White for light yellow base of lower petal. Use Raw Sienna for shading of lower petal. Mix Diox Purple with Raw Sienna and Antique White for basecoat of outer petals. Use Diox Purple mixed with Raw Sienna for shading of outer petals.

Dusky pink pansies: Mix Red Oxide with Diox Purple and Antique White for base of lower petal. Mix Red Oxide with Antique White for basecoat of outer petals. Use a mix of Red Oxide and Diox Purple for shading of outer petals.

To stencil, work with a fairly dry brush, dabbing brush on paper towels before working on fabric. Work from the edge of the stencil towards center, using a swirling motion. You can apply an even coating or, for greater shading, leave areas lighter in the middle. Begin stenciling leaves (and stems) first (**Pic 3**), then inner petals, applying the basecoat to each. Then work the basecoat of the outer petals of each flower.

Apply the deeper shading to each area, working in the same order as for the basecoat. Finish by adding purple shading to leaves (**Pic 4**).

Work four blocks of stencil 1 and five of stencil 2, and four border strips, centering stencil on border strip and working toward ends. Heat-set stenciling by ironing on wrong side with iron on hottest setting possible.

To assemble quilt top

Refer to the **Diagram** below when piecing quilt top.

From checked fabric, cut six sashing strips, each 13" x 2¹/₂". Using two of these strips, with right sides together and allowing ¹/₄-inch seams, join three blocks into a horizontal strip, placing a wreath block between two baskets. Join the next three blocks horizontally, placing a basket block between two wreaths (**Pic 5**). Join the last three blocks as for the first three.

From check fabric, cut four 2¹/₂-inch-wide sashing strips the length of these horizontal sections (approximately 43 inches). With right sides together and allowing ¹/₄-inch seams, stitch two sashing strips between horizontal block sections to join all together. Use remaining two strips for top and bottom of the blocks.

From check fabric, cut another two 2¹/₂-inch-wide sashing strips to fit sides (approximately 4 feet). With right sides together and allowing ¹/₄-inch seams, stitch these strips in place.

Borders

Measure width of quilt through center of quilt top. Taking care that stenciled pansy design is well placed, trim stenciled border strips to this measurement, and stitch to top and bottom of quilt, allowing ¹/₄-inch seams. Repeat for sides, measuring length of quilt through center of quilt top and trimming side border strips to fit.

Measure width of quilt again, and, from check fabric, cut 6-inch-wide outer border strips to fit this measurement. Stitch to top and bottom of quilt. Repeat for side outer borders, measuring length of quilt before cutting strips.

Quilting

From batting, cut two 2¹/₄-yard lengths and butt long edges together. Herringbone stitch (see **Embroidery Stitch Guide** on page 58) edges flat together. Cut two 2-yard lengths of calico. Cut one in half lengthwise and stitch halves to either side of remaining 2-yard length. Press seams open. Place batting on wrong side of quilt top and trim excess, leaving about 2 inches all around. Place backing on quilt top, wrong sides together, sandwiching batting between layers. Baste horizontally and vertically, keeping basting lines 3¹/₂ inches apart. Hand- or machine-quilt as desired. Trim edges even.

Binding

From binding fabric, cut enough 3-inch-wide strips across fabric width to cover two sides of quilt (when joined). Join where necessary and press seams open. Press binding strips in half lengthwise, wrong sides together. With right sides together and raw edges even, stitch binding to quilt sides, allowing ³/₈-inch seams. Trim binding ends even with quilt edge. Turn folded edge of binding to back of quilt and slipstitch in place over seam.

Cut more 3-inch-wide binding strips to fit across top and bottom of quilt (joining where necessary), and stitch to quilt, as for sides, but do not trim ends. Before slipstitching folded edges in place, turn in raw ends and slipstitch corners neatly together.

PIECING GUIDE

stencil 1
enlarge 122%

Border stencil
enlarge 122%

stencil 2
enlarge 122%

APPLIQUÉD ROOSTER AND PIG PICTURES

Simple animal shapes are appliquéd to calico and bound with a patchwork border in these eye-catching pictures. The same border could be stitched to a tablecloth to match.

MEASUREMENTS

Each finished appliquéd panel measures 10" x 12⁵/₈", excluding patchwork border and wooden frame.

MATERIALS

- 1¹/₄ yards x 45" calico, sufficient for background and backing of two pictures
- ¹/₃ yard each of seven or more different fabrics, in checks, plaids and stripes
- Scraps of yellow fabric, for Beak, Feet and Sun
- Threads to match appliqué fabrics
- Yellow, black and buff six-strand cotton embroidery floss
- ²/₃ yard x 43¹/₂" thin polyester or needle-punched cotton batting
- Black quilting thread

Rooster and Pig designed and stitched by Vivien Prince
Photography by Andrew Elton
Styling by Lisa Hilton

- Unfinished wooden frames, without glass, inner area approximately 12" x 14"
- Thick cardboard, for mounting (if not provided with frame)
- Strong fine string or six-strand cotton embroidery floss, for lacing
- Darning needle
- Artist-quality flow formula acrylics, such as Jo Sonja's: Antique Green and Spruce, or equivalent
- Stiff-bristled brush, such as a pastry brush
- Lint-free rag
- Fine sandpaper
- Thin cardboard, for backing picture
- Masking tape

APPLIQUÉ OUTLINES

All appliqué outlines are printed on pages 70, 71 and 73. Trace Rooster Body, Comb, Beak, Wattle, Foot, Tailfeather 1, Tailfeather 2, Tailfeather 3, Tailfeather 4, Sun, Pig, Patch 1 and Patch 2.

CUTTING

Pin pattern pieces to right side of chosen fabrics and cut out, allowing an extra ¹/₄ inch on all sides for hem. We cut Beak, Foot and Sun from yellow fabric, and Comb and Wattle from a red print. Remaining pieces can be cut from fabric scraps as desired.

From calico or background fabric, cut two rectangles, each 8³/₈" x 13¹/₂" (one for each picture).

METHOD

Appliqué To help turn under edges on appliqué pieces when sewing, clip into corners and curves and trim points. Note that in the narrow spaces around Pig's ears and feet you will be able to cut a slit in the fabric only between the two pattern lines.

Fold background rectangles in half, then half again, to find center, and finger-crease center folds. Match the center point of background fabric with the cross on Rooster or Pig Body and pin appliqué piece in place, right sides uppermost.

Rooster: Put Comb in place, tucking well under head, and stitch to background fabric, following **Appliqué Hints** on page 102. Change thread color and stitch head over raw edge of Comb, extending hem approximately $3/8$ inch beyond ends of Comb, then leave remaining thread in work. Position and stitch Beak in place with yellow thread, then continue stitching Rooster Body over raw edge of Beak and down towards leg. (Lefthanders may have left their excess thread towards the back of the Rooster's head, in which case, stitch from that point towards the leg and use a new length of thread to stitch head in place over Beak.) Finally, pin and stitch Foot in place, then finish stitching Body.

The Tailfeathers are applied from the lowest (1) to the topmost. The top edges of 1, 2 and 3 are left unhemmed, as they slip beneath the next feather, but the top feather (4) is hemmed on all sides.

Stitch the Wattle in place below the Beak. Next, stitch the yellow Sun in place in front of the Rooster. Use a pencil to mark the position of the eye and wing, then embroider these details in place with backstitch, using six strands of black embroidery floss.

Pig: Stitch Pig to background, then stitch Patches to Pig. Embroider eye and curly tail in backstitch, with six strands of black embroidery floss.

Borders The width of the border depends on the inside (glass) measurement of your picture frame. Measure your appliquéd picture to find the difference between it and your frame aperture (you may have to trim the calico background to make an equal border on all four sides). Calculate the required finished width of borders, making sure that they will fit behind the frame recess. Add at least $1^{1}/_{4}$ inches to this width measurement and that gives the required width for borders. (The bare measurement for our picture was $1^{1}/_{2}$ inches plus $1^{1}/_{4}$ inches = $2^{3}/_{4}$ inches.) Cut an assortment of check and plaid rectangles, each $2^{3}/_{4}$ inches (or your own measurement) x $4^{3}/_{4}$ inches.

With right sides together, join rectangles end to end with a $1/4$-inch seam. Make the border strips as either one long strip or four separate pieces, each slightly

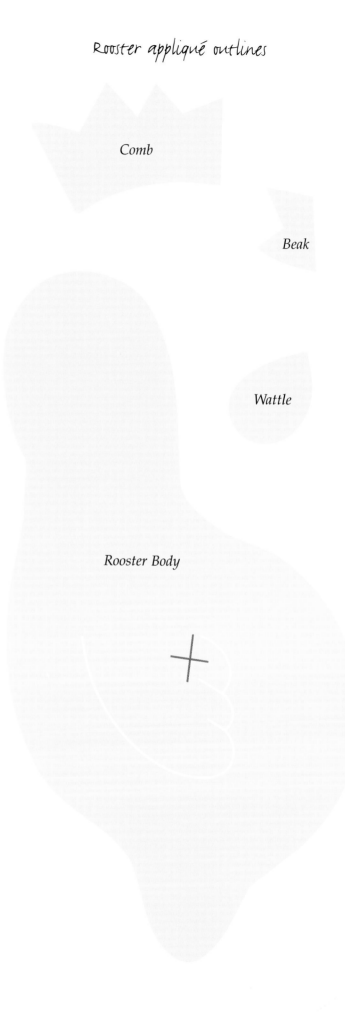

Rooster appliqué outlines

Comb

Beak

Wattle

Rooster Body

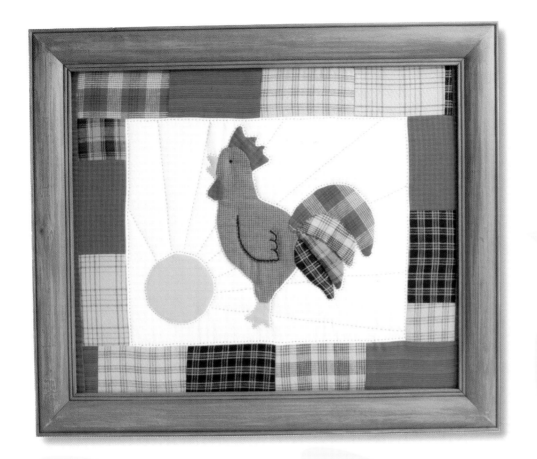

Foot

Tailfeather 4

Tailfeather 2

Tailfeather 1

Sun

Tailfeather 3

longer than the sides of the picture. Press border seams to one side, then, with right sides together, join borders to each opposite side of picture. Press seams towards outside edges, then join remaining border strips to top and bottom, stitching across side borders and calico.

Quilting Cut another piece of calico and a piece of batting, each $1^{1}/_{4}$ inches larger all round than bordered appliqué. Place backing, right side down, on a flat surface, top with batting, then place appliqué on top, right side up. Safety-pin or baste layers together, grid-fashion.

Using black quilting thread and a small running stitch or quilting stitch, outline Pig, Pig's Patches, Rooster, Rooster's wing, between Tailfeathers at upper edges of pieces 1, 2 and 3, and around Sun. Run a line of quilting stitches around the edge of the calico background, about $^{1}/_{8}$ inch inside border. Lightly pencil lines radiating from the Sun, and, using yellow embroidery floss, quilt along these lines, continuing the sunrays on the other side of the Rooster as well.

For background interest on the pig picture, draw three horizontal wavy lines across background and quilt with buff-colored embroidery floss. For a bit of variety, the lowest quilted line incorporates a cross-stitch "flower" at irregular intervals in the quilting line.

Mounting for frame Stitch through all layers close to outside edge of border, and trim excess batting and backing so that edges are even. Cut $2^{3}/_{8}$-inch-wide strips of calico or checked fabric and stitch to edges of border in the same way that border was attached to background. Make a narrow hem on all sides.

If backing cardboard is not provided with your frame, cut a backing piece from thick cardboard that fits into the frame recess.

Place work, face down, on a clean surface, center backing cardboard on it, then pull sides and ends of picture to back of card, using bulldog clips to hold in place. Thread a darning needle with 24–32 inches of fine strong string or embroidery floss and lace across back of card, starting at the center of one side and lacing across to the other side, tying a knot firmly without cutting string. Continue in this manner, knotting in extra lengths of string or floss as required and finishing off firmly. Miter-fold corners and ends, pin to hold in place, then lace across back of picture in the opposite direction.

Frame Sand frames to smooth and provide texture if frame is already lacquered.

Squeeze some Antique Green onto a clean tile or old plate, wet brush and mix in water just until paint has a creamy consistency. Smooth paint onto frame, working in direction of grain. Allow to dry for a few minutes, then wipe back gently along the grain with a dry rag. Apply a second coat and wipe back in the same way. Allow to dry for at least two hours or longer, then repeat the procedure with Spruce Green, this time using the paint sparingly on an almost-dry brush and just dragging it over the surface lightly to achieve the desired effect and wiping back slightly with the rag.

If desired, when frame is dry, it can be rubbed back a little again with sandpaper to expose wood in places.

Fit work into frame and cover with paper or thin card, cut $^{3}/_{4}$ inch larger than recess. Secure with masking tape.

Pig appliqué outlines

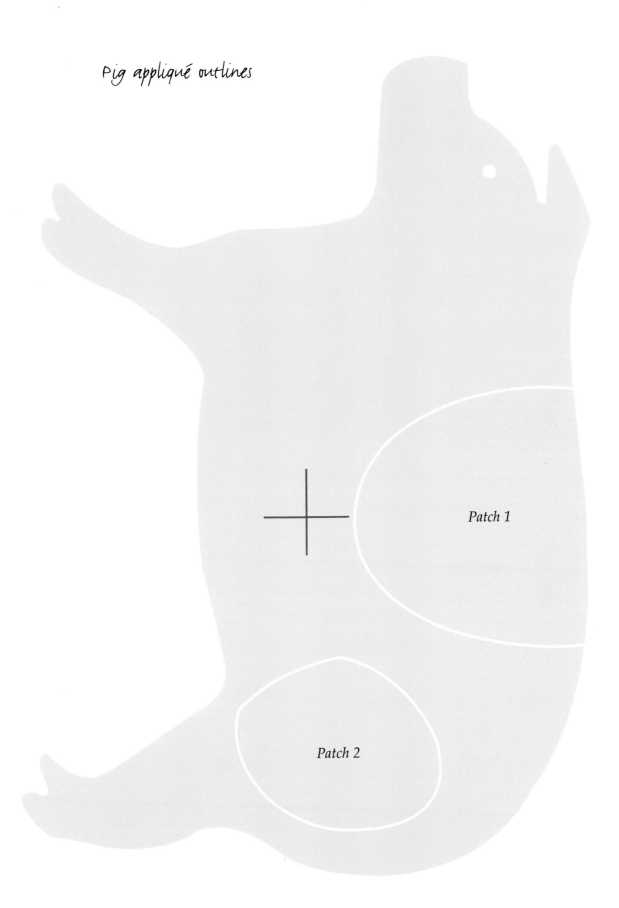

Patch 1

Patch 2

TAKE HEART

Hearts are a perennial favorite in country decorating and this miniature appliquéd quilt shows why they retain their popularity. For quick results, appliqué by machine — instructions are provided for both hand- and machine-stitching.

MEASUREMENTS

Finished quilt measures 18^1/$_2$″ square.

MATERIALS

- Nine rectangles, each 4^1/$_2$″ x 9^1/$_8$″, different but coordinating patchwork prints
- ^{1}/$_4$ yard x 45″ plain fabric, for inner border
- ^{1}/$_4$ yard x 45″ coordinating print, for outer border
- ^{1}/$_4$ yard x 45″ coordinating fabric, for binding
- 22″ square fabric, for backing
- 22″ square pure cotton batting
- Double-sided fusible webbing (if using machine appliqué)
- Matching thread
- Fine sewing needle (if using hand appliqué)

APPLIQUÉ OUTLINE

The Heart outline is printed on this page. Trace it onto stiff cardboard and cut out for template.

Quilt designed and stitched by Annette Blake
Photography by Catherine Muscat

CUTTING

Cut each 4^1/$_2$″ x 9^1/$_8$″ rectangle in half crosswise, forming nine pairs of 4^1/$_2$-inch squares. One set of squares will be used for backgrounds; the other will be used for appliqué.

If using hand appliqué, trace outline of Heart onto nine different squares, then add ^{1}/$_4$-inch seam allowance before cutting.

If using machine appliqué, trace outline of Heart onto double-sided fusible webbing nine times and cut out (without adding seam allowance). Iron webbing hearts onto wrong side of nine patchwork squares, then cut out.

METHOD

Appliqué Before proceeding, refer to **Appliqué Hints** on page 102.

If appliquéing by hand, fold under seam allowance around edge of heart and baste to hold. Center basted heart on contrasting background square and stitch invisibly in place around folded edge, using a fine needle and matching thread. Repeat process for all nine squares and hearts.

If appliquéing by machine, peel paper backing from fusible webbing and center heart on contrasting background square. Press with iron to secure in place. Machine appliqué around raw edge, using a fancy stitch or close zigzag. It helps to have a piece of waxed paper behind your fabrics to stabilize them while stitching. Repeat process for all nine squares and hearts.

To assemble quilt top With right sides facing and allowing ^{1}/$_4$-inch seams, stitch appliqué squares together in rows of three, then stitch the rows together, giving a quilt top of nine squares. Press.

Borders Measure length of quilt top through center and cut inner border fabric into two 1^3/$_8$-inch strips to fit this measurement. With right sides together and allowing ^{1}/$_4$-inch seams, stitch a border strip to opposite sides of block. Press. Measure width of quilt top through center and cut inner border fabric into two 1^3/$_8$-inch strips to fit this measurement. Stitch a border strip to top and bottom of block, press.

Repeat process to cut and join outer border strips, cutting strips 2^3/$_8$ inches wide.

Quilting

Press backing fabric and place on table, right side down. Top with batting, then quilt top, right side up. Pin and baste layers together, starting at center and working towards edges.

Quilt by hand or machine, around the squares, border lines and/or motifs, as desired. When quilting is complete, trim edges even with each other and baste around quilt by hand or machine, $1/8$ inch from the edge.

Binding

Cut binding fabric into four $2^3/4$-inch strips, each somewhat longer than desired finished length.

Press first strip in half lengthwise, wrong sides together, and mark the center point with a pin. Place another pin at the center point on one edge of quilt. With right sides together and raw edges even, pin binding to quilt, matching center points and allowing binding to extend beyond edges of quilt at each end.

With binding strip on top, stitch through all thicknesses, from end to end, allowing a $1/4$-inch seam and easing in any fullness by pulling binding taut while stitching. Trim excess binding from each end. Fold binding around to back of quilt and slipstitch folded edge to backing.

Repeat this procedure for the opposite side of the quilt.

Next, attach binding strips to remaining two sides of quilt, using the same technique, but do not cut off excess binding at ends, as this will be used to finish corners.

Press binding over seam and neatly fold under excess on ends. Holding the fold in place, fold binding around to back of quilt and hand-stitch folded edge in place to backing, as before, stitching corner edges neatly together, as well.

Repeat these steps for each corner.

WARM AND FUZZY

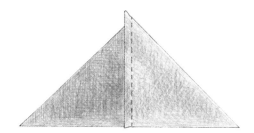

The is the sort of quilt that makes winter seem like the best of times, when the cat wants to stay inside and cuddle up, when the garden can take care of itself while you do cross stitch in front of the fire. Made up from a collection of snuggly cotton flannels in a simple nine-patch design, it's the sort of quilt that you'll want to wrap yourself in, not hang on a wall.

MEASUREMENTS
Finished quilt measures approximately 46" x 59".

MATERIALS

- Mixture of light colored flannels: $1^1/_4$ yards x 45" in total (see **Note**, below)
- Mixture of medium and dark colored flannels: $2^3/_4$ yards x 45" in total
- $^1/_4$ yard x 45" each of two plain flannels, for inner border
- 51" x 63" batting
- 51" x 63" backing fabric (joined where necessary if fabric is 45" wide)
- Assorted small buttons (optional)
- $^2/_3$ yard x 45", for binding

Note: *We used two lights, 12 mediums and five darks, but this can be varied as you prefer.*

Quilt designed and stitched by Jane Morgan
Photography by Louise Lister
Styling by Vicki Liley

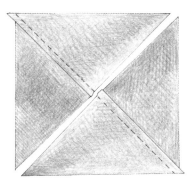

METHOD

Hourglass blocks From a mixture of light, medium and dark flannels, cut 24 squares, each $7^3/_4$ inches. Cut each square diagonally twice (four triangles), giving 96 triangles in all. Sort triangles into 48 matched pairs, keeping light, medium and dark in separate piles.

With right sides together, and combining pairs from different piles, stitch two triangles together along right-angle edge, allowing a $^1/_4$-inch seam (**Diagram 1**).

DIAGRAM 1

To save time and thread, stitch the next pair together right behind the first pair. This is called chain piecing. Do not cut the connecting thread, as it will act as a pin for the next seam. When all pairs are joined, snip joining threads and press seams of each matching pair in alternate directions (**Diagram 2**).

DIAGRAM 2

With right sides together, join pairs of triangles so that matching triangles are opposite each other, forming an "hourglass" shape (**Diagram 3**). You should have 24 hourglass blocks.

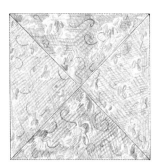

DIAGRAM 3

Nine-patch square-within-a-square blocks

From a mixture of light, medium and dark flannels, cut 2-inch strips across width of the fabric. You will need 12 strips altogether. Cut each strip crosswise into thirds, then, allowing $1/4$-inch seams, stitch strips together in groups of three, reversing the order of strips for each color combination (**Diagram 4**). Press seams to one side — towards the center on one group of three and towards the edges on the other.

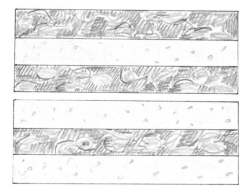

DIAGRAM 4

Using a rotary cutter and ruler, cut stitched strips across into 2-inch segments. Arrange these segments in groups of three into a nine-patch block, as shown in **Diagram 5**, and stitch, allowing $1/4$-inch seams. From each set of two full-width strips, you will be able to make four nine-patch blocks. Repeat this process to make 24 blocks altogether.

DIAGRAM 5

From a mixture of light, medium and dark fabrics, cut 48 squares, each 4 inches, making sure there are even numbers of each color. Cut each square in half diagonally, giving 96 triangles in all. Sort triangles into sets of four (all one color).

Allowing $1/4$-inch seams, stitch long side of each of the triangles in a set to the sides of a nine-patch block. Press seams towards the triangles.

To assemble quilt top

Alternating hourglass blocks and nine-patch blocks, lay out blocks in eight rows of six, and rearrange until satisfied with shading pattern. Stitch blocks together in sequence, one row at a time, allowing $1/4$-inch seams.

Next, stitch rows together, one after another, aligning seams.

Borders

Inner border: From each of two plain border fabrics, cut 2-inch strips across width of fabric. Join random lengths to form pieced border strips that are long enough to cover quilt edges.

Measure the length of your quilt through center of quilt top, and trim two border strips to this measurement. With right sides together and allowing $1/4$-inch seams, stitch a border strip to each side of quilt top. Have border strip uppermost when stitching so that you can ease quilt top into size of border strip if measurements are a little different. Open out, and press seam allowances towards border strip.

Measure width of quilt through center of quilt top, trim remaining strips to this measurement, and join to top and bottom of quilt.

Outer border: From a variety of quilt top fabrics, cut 4-inch strips of random length and join to form pieced lengths, long enough to form outer border strips.

Measure the length of your quilt through center of quilt top, and trim two border strips to this measurement. With right sides together and border strip uppermost, and allowing $1/4$-inch seams, stitch a border strip to each side of quilt.

Now measure width of quilt through center of quilt top, trim remaining strips to this measurement, then join to top and bottom of quilt to finish.

Quilting

Sandwich the batting between quilt top and backing, and baste or safety-pin layers together for quilting.

Our quilt has been quilted "in the ditch" by machine and finished off with an assortment of buttons at corners of blocks, and in random centers. Alternatively, the quilt could be tied, or hand-quilted. To make ties, push needle threaded with embroidery floss straight down through all layers, across $1/8$ inch, then straight back up again. Pull firmly and tie ends securely in a square knot, then trim ends.

Binding Cut and join required number of $2^1/_2$-inch fabric strips into a continuous length (measure edges of quilt for approximate length), then press in half, wrong sides together. Trim batting and backing even with edges of quilt top. With right sides together, pin binding to quilt edges, with all raw edges even. Allowing a $^1/_4$-inch seam, stitch binding to quilt. Stop stitching $^1/_4$ inch from the first corner and fold a miter into the corner, following **Diagram 6**. Repeat with three remaining corners. Turn folded edge of binding to back of quilt and slipstitch in place over seam, stitching folds or miters at the same time.

Label and sign your quilt.

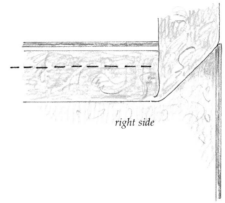

right side

DIAGRAM 6b

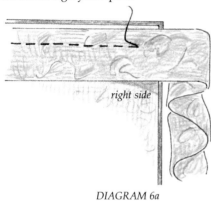

right side

DIAGRAM 6a

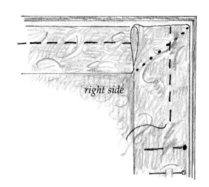

right side

DIAGRAM 6c

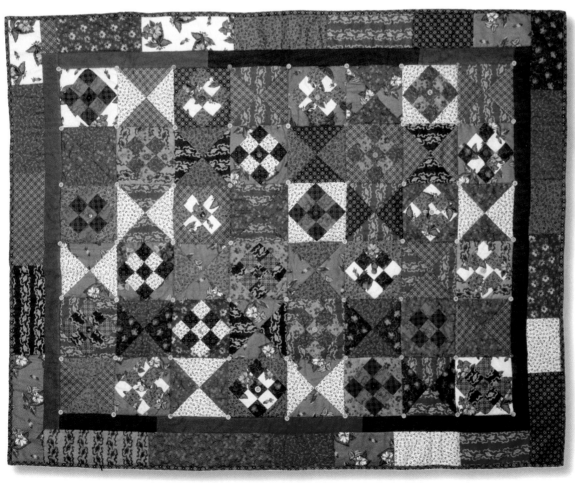

NAÏVE QUILT

A home among the eucalypts is the central image on this delightful appliqué quilt. With emus, kangaroos and even a whimsical angel keeping watch over proceedings, the quilt captures the essence of naïve style — unsophisticated, endearingly childlike and amusingly simple. And the good news is that it doesn't have to be exact; in fact, a tad less than perfect only adds to the charm.

MEASUREMENTS

Finished quilt measures approximately 34" x 39".

MATERIALS

- Scraps of various fabrics (see **Note**)
- 20" x 24" double-sided fusible webbing, for appliqué
- Black sewing thread
- Black fabric pen or black embroidery floss, for details
- Assortment of $2^1/_2$" fabric strips, for inner border — you will need a total length of approximately $3^1/_3$ yards
- Assortment of $3^1/_2$" fabric strips, for outer border — you will need a total length of approximately 4 yards
- $1^1/_2$ yards x 45" fabric, for backing
- Masking tape
- $1^1/_4$ yards x 47" thin quilt batting
- Assortment of $2^1/_2$-inch fabric strips, for binding — you will need a total length of approximately $4^1/_4$ yards
- Dowel rod and cord, for hanging (optional)

Note: *As this is a scrap quilt, precise amounts for the quilt top are not given. Using the **Diagram** on page 82, calculate the number and amounts of different fabrics needed for the background blocks, then gather enough scraps for the appliqué. Measurements on **Diagram** refer to finished size of block, so be sure to allow extra for seams.*

APPLIQUÉ OUTLINES

All appliqué outlines are printed on pages 84 to 89. Place fusible webbing, paper side up, over each picture and, using a pencil, trace around each shape, leaving about $1/_2$ inch between them. Some shapes are made up of several overlapping pieces, each of which needs to be cut separately. The shape is then reassembled on the background fabric. Some shapes are used more than once — use the photograph on page 85 as a guide to check this.

Quilt designed by Mary O'Roberts and stitched by Bev Peacock
Photography by Catherine Muscat

Block Diagram

15cm (6")
Emu
BLOCK 8
20cm (7⁷/₈") — $20cm\ (7^7/_8")$

Kangaroo
BLOCK 9
$20cm\ (7^7/_8")$
15cm (6")

22cm (8³/₄") — $22cm\ (8^3/_4")$
Stars
BLOCK 5
$11.5cm\ (4^1/_2")$

21.5cm (8¹/₂") — $21.5cm\ (8^1/_2")$
Angel
BLOCK 6
$11.5cm\ (4^1/_2")$

12.5cm (5")
Stars
BLOCK 7
$11.5cm\ (4^1/_2")$

10cm (4")
Windmill
BLOCK 4
$28.5cm\ (11^1/_4")$

41cm (16¹/₄") — $41cm\ (16^1/_4")$
Outhouse, House, Tree
BLOCK 1
$23.5cm\ (9^1/_4")$
leave unstitched until last

5cm (2")
Flying Geese
BLOCK 2
$23.5cm\ (9^1/_4")$

5cm (2") **20cm (8")**
Rabbit BLOCK 3

10cm (4")
Tree
BLOCK 12
$19.5cm\ (7^3/_4")$

6cm (2¹/₂") — $6cm\ (2^1/_2")$
17.5cm (7")
Stars
BLOCK 10

17.5cm (7")
Hen
BLOCK 11
$13.5cm\ (5^1/_4")$

17.5cm (7")
Rooster
BLOCK 13
$19.5cm\ (7^3/_4")$

11cm (4¹/₄") — $11cm\ (4^1/_4")$
Lamp
BLOCK 16
$24.5cm\ (9^3/_4")$

15cm (6")
Cup & Saucer
BLOCK 14
$10.5cm\ (4^1/_4")$

15cm (6")
Horseshoe
BLOCK 15
$14cm\ (5^1/_2")$

METHOD

Appliqué Cut out each shape roughly, leaving approximately $^1/_4$ inch on all sides (**Pic 1**).

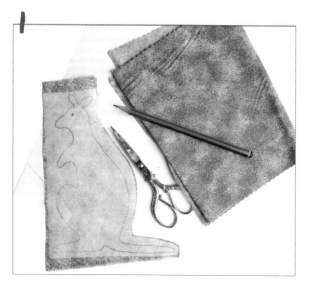

Place each traced shape, pencil side up, on the wrong side of chosen fabric and press with a hot iron, being careful that all edges are securely fused. Cut out each shape on the traced line.

Remove and discard paper backing, then place or assemble picture in position, right side up, on right side of background fabric. The shading on the appliqué outlines indicates where pieces overlap; for example, the tops of the emu's legs are tucked slightly under the emu's body. Press shapes in place with a hot iron.

Prepare all of the blocks in this manner, referring to the photograph on page 85 for placement.

To make the "Flying Geese" strip (Block 2 in the **Diagram** above), take the background fabric strip and mark a crease down the center as a placement guide. Fuse the first triangle in place with its top point centered on the crease, $^1/_4$ inch down from top edge of strip. You will also have $^1/_4$-inch seam allowance on each side of the lower points.

Place next triangle directly below the first, with its top point just touching the center of the base of first triangle. Repeat with remaining four triangles.

When all shapes have been fused in place, you can then begin to stitch them, as follows.

Using black sewing thread on the bobbin and spool, set your machine to a blind-hemming stitch, which looks like this:

On a scrap of fabric, stitch an inch or two and note how far apart the stitches are, and how deeply the zigzag stitch bites. If necessary, reduce the stitch width to about $1/8$ inch and stitch another inch or two. Next adjust the stitch length to slightly less than $1/8$ inch and stitch another inch or two. Alter as necessary until you obtain a stitch that looks similar to this:

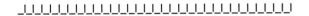

When you are satisfied, fuse a scrap to practice on and stitch with the straight stitches running alongside the outer edge of the fused shape, but on the background fabric only, and the long crosswise stitch biting onto the fused shape about $1/8$ inch, like this:

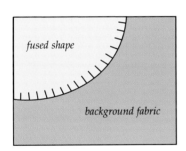

fused shape

background fabric

If your machine only has zigzag, just proceed as above, stitching samples until you have a zigzag that is not too big or too close (about $1/8$ inch should be right). To appliqué, try to keep one zigzag point on the background, close to the edge of the fused shape, and one point on the fused shape itself.

Whichever method you choose, when you have achieved a satisfactory stitch, make a note of the settings to save time when you want to use the stitch again.

For righthanders, place the block under the machine foot with the picture shape to the left of the needle, then stitch in a clockwise direction around edge (**Pic 2**). Lefthanders should reverse this.

Once all the shapes are stitched in place, you can draw or embroider any remaining detail, such as the legs on fowls, eyes, faces and angel hair.

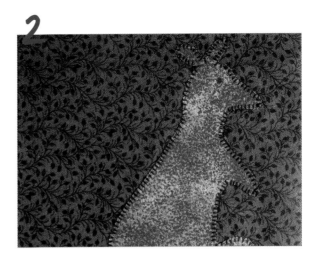

To assemble quilt top Referring to **Diagram** on page 82, and with right sides together and allowing $1/4$-inch seams, assemble units as follows:

Join Blocks 1, 2 and 3, leaving 2 inches unstitched at righthand upper edge of Block 3, until all others are added. Join on Block 4, and this section becomes the base.

Join Blocks 5, 6 and 7, then stitch this strip to top edge of base.

Join Blocks 8 and 9, then stitch this section to lefthand side of base.

Join Blocks 10 and 11, then add Blocks 12 and 13 to either side. This makes a second unit, which is then stitched to lower lefthand edge of base.

Join Blocks 14 and 15, then Block 16, and stitch this section to lower righthand corner, along edge of second unit.

Finally, complete the unstitched section of upper edge of Block 3, continuing seam along to join the rest of the lower section to the bottom of the base unit.

Borders **Inner border:** Measure length of quilt top through center (about $24^1/2$ inches). Join the assorted $2^1/2$-inch strips, pressing seams open as you stitch, to form two side border strips that measure length of quilt top. With right sides facing, stitch a border strip to each side of quilt top. Have border strip uppermost when stitching so that you can ease quilt top into size of border strip if measurements are different. Open out, and press seam allowances towards border strip. Repeat process to make top and bottom border strips from remaining $2^1/2$-inch strips, measuring width of quilt (about 34 inches) through center of quilt top after side border strips have been attached.

Outer border: Measure length of quilt top through center (about 28 inches). Join assorted $3^1/2$-inch strips, as before, to form two side border strips. Stitch a strip to each side of quilt top, then repeat to make and join top and bottom border strips (each about 40 inches long), measuring width of quilt after side border strips have been attached.

Quilting Press backing fabric and secure it to a hard surface with masking tape. Smooth batting on next, then quilt top, right side up. Safety-pin all layers together through each block and baste around outside edges.

Quilt can now be quilted by hand or machine. Keep quilting simple, such as stitching around all pictures, then echo quilting by hand, about $1/2$ inch from first quilting line (**Pic 3**).

For a primitive look, you may prefer to tie the quilt. Using embroidery floss, or yarn, sew through all layers, just at each block corner. To make ties, push threaded needle straight down at the corner, across just a scant $1/8$ inch, then straight back up again. Pull firmly and tie ends securely in a square knot, then trim ends back to $3/4$ inch.

Binding
Trim edges of quilt evenly, cutting away excess batting and backing.

With right sides together, join the binding strips to form two side bindings, each approximately 36 inches long, and top and bottom bindings, each approximately 42 inches long. Press all seams open.

Press binding strips in half lengthwise, wrong sides together. With right sides together and all raw edges even, pin and stitch first side binding to edge of quilt. Fold binding over to quilt back and whipstitch folded binding edge in place over seam. Repeat for other side. Trim raw edges even.

Apply top and bottom bindings in same way but fold in raw short ends to neaten and whipstitch those as well.

Remove basting, then sign and date your work on the back.

Hanging
From leftover backing fabric, make a fabric tube, or sleeve, as long as top edge of quilt and 2 inches wide. Hand-stitch this to upper quilt back. Push dowel rod through sleeve, tie cord at each end and hang.

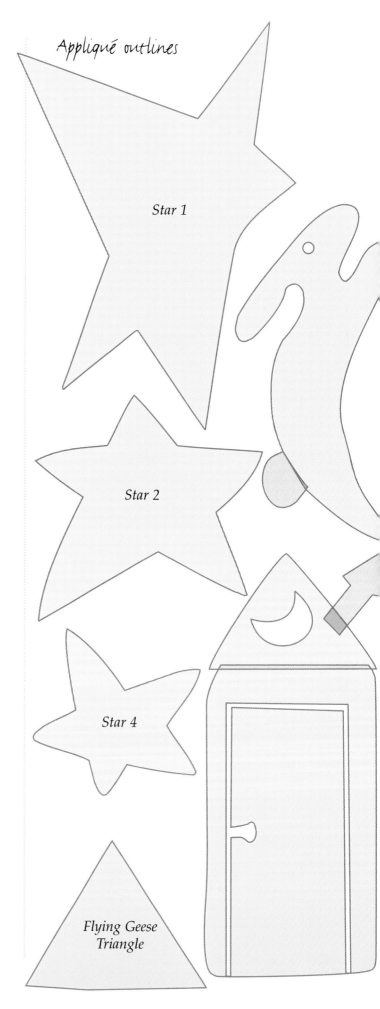

Appliqué outlines

Star 1

Star 2

Star 4

Flying Geese Triangle

Star 3

Star 5

Star 6

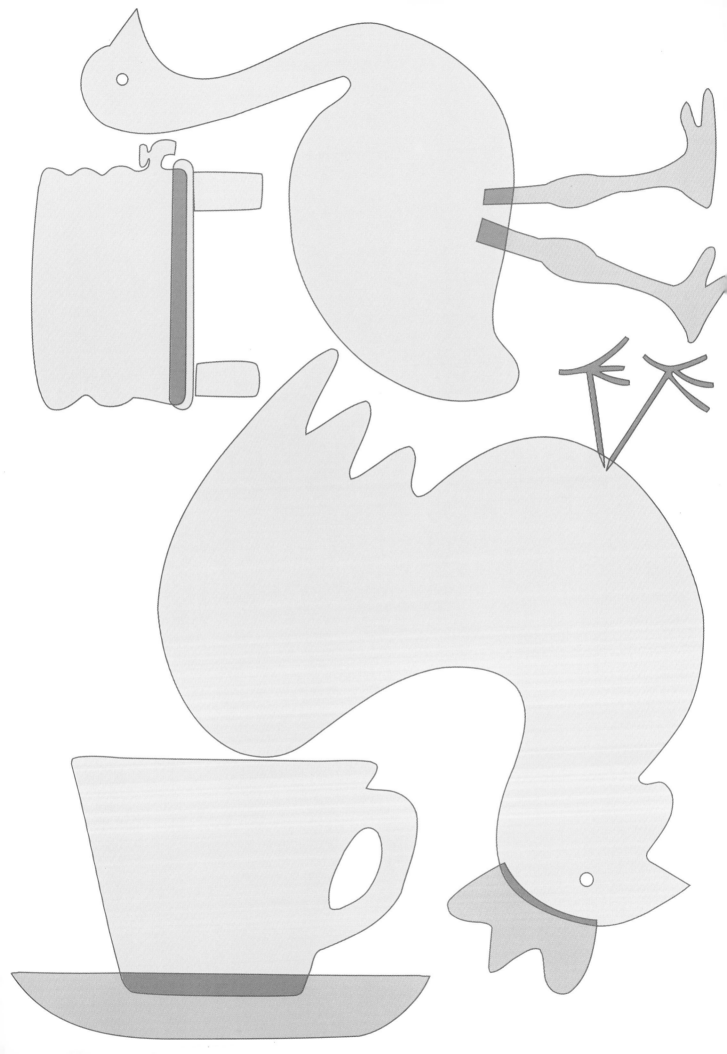

PATCHWORK TABLECLOTH

The time-honored Mediterranean color combination of blue and white adds a simple country freshness to any decorating scheme, but looks particularly at home with terracotta or old wood. This pretty tablecloth is quickly machine-pieced from a variety of inexpensive blue and white printed cottons, then hand-embellished with feather stitch. With added backing it would also make a lovely throw.

MEASUREMENTS
Finished cloth measures 79" x 64 1/2".

MATERIALS

- 2/3 yard x 45" each of six different indigo prints
- 2 1/2 yards x 45" fabric, for border
- Matching sewing thread
- 10 skeins DMC Cotton Pearl No. 3, white or écru, or equivalent
- Embroidery needle
- Thick cardboard or template plastic
- Rotary cutter
- Cutting mat

METHOD

From cardboard or plastic, cut an 8-inch-square template.

From indigo prints, cut a total of 80 squares, using template and a rotary cutter on a cutting mat. We cut 12 squares of each print, then another eight from the border print.

Lay squares out on the floor and rearrange until you are satisfied with the design. Pin and stitch squares together in 10 rows of eight squares, allowing 3/8-inch seams. Press all seams open. With right sides facing, stitch rows together and press seams open.

Using Cotton Pearl, work feather stitch (see **Embroidery Stitch Guide** on page 58) along all seam lines.

Before cutting border strips, check the length and width of your patchwork cloth, measuring through the center of the cloth, and adjust measurements of border fabric if necessary. Our cloth measured 72" x 58".

From border fabric, cut two strips, each 8" x 80", and two strips, each 8" x 65 3/8". Fold each strip in half lengthwise, wrong sides together, and press. Open flat again. Press under 3/8 inch on each long edge.

With right sides together, pin one long and one short strip together and stitch ends in a point, as shown in the **Diagram** below. Trim angled ends to 3/8 inch from stitching. Repeat for remaining strips so that strips form a "frame". Turn right side out, fold on lengthwise fold lines and press again.

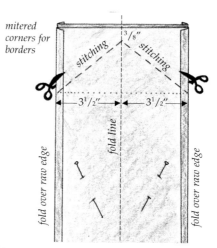

mitered corners for borders
3/8"
stitching   stitching
3 1/2"   3 1/2"
fold line
fold over raw edge
fold over raw edge

Slide raw edges of tablecloth between layers of frame, baste and topstitch close to pressed edge. Work feather stitch over stitching line.

COLOR YOUR WORLD

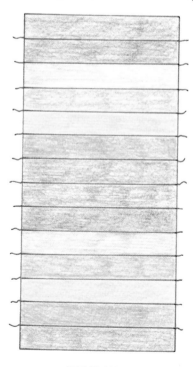

U*se the gorgeous colors of the rainbow to brighten a child's bedroom with this eye-catching quilt. Constructed from inexpensive poplin and calico, the quilt is pieced using a clever quick method that will have it finished in no time. You can also stitch a wonderful rainbow patchwork pillow to match from remaining scraps of fabric.*

MEASUREMENTS

Finished quilt measures approximately 48" x 68", but technique can be adapted to produce a quilt of any size.

MATERIALS

- $^2/_3$ yard x 45" polyester or cotton poplin in each of the following colors: red, orange, yellow, green, blue and violet
- 5 yards x 45" indigo polyester or cotton poplin
- $1^1/_2$ yards x 59" quilt batting
- Sewing thread

Quilt designed and made by Maria Ragan
Photography by Andre Martin
Styling by Vicki Liley

METHOD

Quilt top Cut 20 inches from indigo fabric, and place remaining $4^1/_3$ yards aside for borders and backing.

From each of the rainbow colors (including indigo), cut two strips, each 6" x $41^1/_2$" (14 strips in all). With right sides together and allowing $^3/_8$-inch seams, join the strips together in rainbow sequence: red, orange, yellow, green, blue, indigo, violet, red, orange and so on (**Diagram 1**). Press all seams open.

DIAGRAM 1

With right sides together, stitch the edges of this rainbow fabric together, joining red to violet, thus creating a tube of vertically striped fabric.

Now cut across the tube at right angles to the vertical stripes, measuring and cutting seven 6-inch-wide patchwork circles (**Diagram 2**).

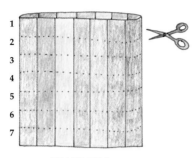

DIAGRAM 2

Using a seam ripper, rip one seam on each circle, ripping the seam between red and orange on the first circle, the seam between orange and yellow on the second circle, the seam between yellow and green on the third circle and so on, until all seven circles are flat strips again (**Diagram 3**).

Next, rip a two-square segment at the end of each strip (indicated by broken line on **Diagram 3**).

Take these two-square segments and stitch together in the correct sequence (as shown by the letters) to form Row 8 (**Diagram 4**). Segment A (yellow/orange) will be left over. These strips are now in the correct order for the complete quilt top.

With right sides together and allowing $^3/_8$-inch seams, stitch the strips together in order, making sure that crosswise seams match neatly. Press all seams in the same direction.

Border Measure the length of your quilt top through its center. From indigo fabric, cut two 4-inch-wide border strips to this measurement. With right sides together and allowing $^3/_8$-inch seams, stitch a border strip to each side of quilt. Now measure width of patchwork top through center, and cut two 4-inch-wide border strips to this measurement. Join these border strips to the top and bottom of the quilt (**Diagram 5**). Our top and bottom borders measure $48^1/_4$ inches and the side borders measure 62 inches — but do check your own measurements before cutting.

Finishing Cut a piece of batting to fit the quilt top and baste to the wrong side of the top around all edges.

Remaining indigo fabric will probably not be wide enough for quilt backing, so you will need to join two pieces, or add borders as for quilt front. Whichever method you use, add seam allowance on all sides.

With right sides together, stitch the completed backing to the quilt top, leaving an opening in the center of one seam for turning. Trim seam, turn quilt right side out and slipstitch opening closed.

Completed quilt can be quilted by hand or machine, whichever you prefer, or all three layers can be fastened or tied together at points marked on **Diagram 5**.

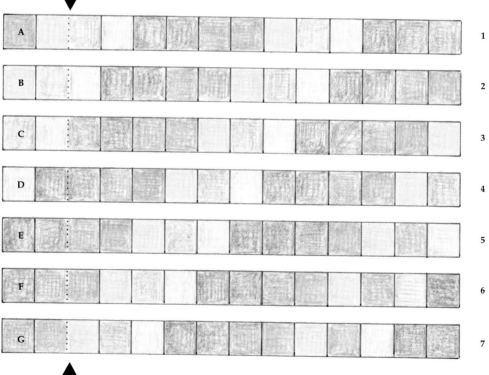

DIAGRAM 3

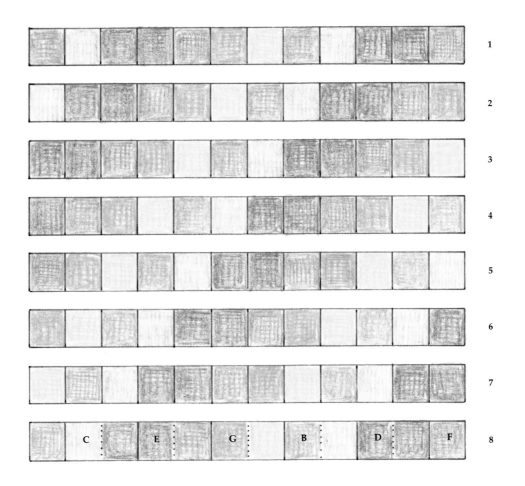

DIAGRAM 4

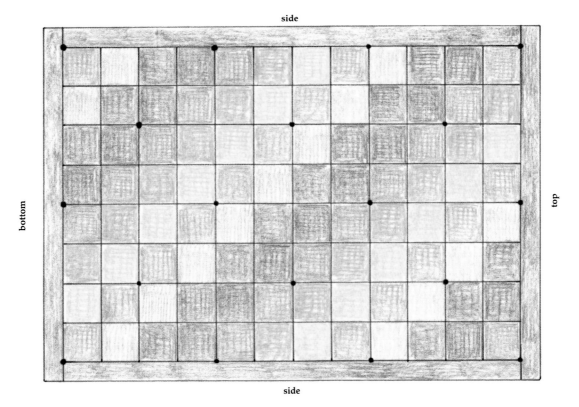

DIAGRAM 5

NASTURTIUM APPLIQUÉ PILLOW AND QUILT

T*he nasturtium, with its brilliant colors and sculptural leaves, is a perfect subject for artistic interpretation. Here, its colorful cheer is preserved on an appliquéd quilt and matching pillow, the bold flower shapes showing up beautifully on the plain green cotton quilt and, for variation, the fresh green and white gingham pillow. Equally at home indoors or tossed on the lawn for an alfresco lunch, these items will bring a happy touch of color to the dullest day.*

Pillow and quilt designed and stitched by Vivien Prince
Photography by Andre Martin
Styling by Lisa Hilton

Pillow

MEASUREMENTS
Finished pillow measures approximately $19^1/4$" square.

MATERIALS
- $^1/_4$ yard x 45" each of cream, pale yellow, gold-yellow and orange fabrics
- $^1/_2$ yard x 45" mid-green cotton fabric
- Scrap pale green cotton fabric, for sepals
- $^1/_2$ yard x 36" double-sided fusible webbing
- $^2/_3$ yard x 45" green and white gingham
- Tailor's chalk or carbon paper
- Thin brown paper or waxed paper
- Scrap cotton fabric (for practice)
- Threads to match appliqué fabrics
- 20" square Fusible Fleece bonded batting
- 24" square white lawn or similar fabric
- $16^1/2$" zipper
- 18–20" pillow form

Note: *Useful but not essential accessories are an appliqué or open embroidery foot, which makes it easier to see the work area, and a walking foot or dual feed option on sewing machine, which makes quilting easy.*

PATTERN PIECES

Outlines for appliqué flowers, leaves and sepals are printed on this page and opposite.

Using double-sided webbing as tracing paper, trace four A flowers, four B flowers, two D1 buds, two D2 sepals, two E leaves and two F leaves. Make sure you transfer the stitching lines as well as the outlines.

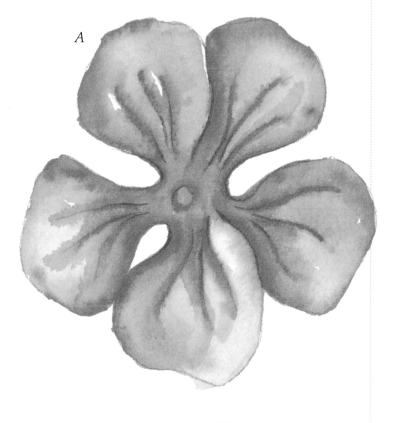

A

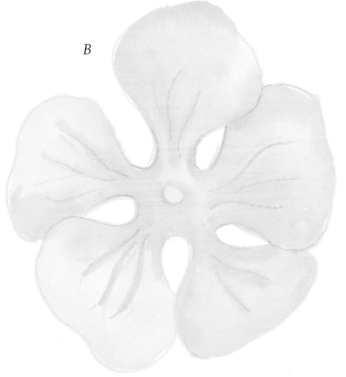

B

CUTTING

Cut out traced motifs, leaving a narrow margin around outlines. Place cut-out motif, glue side down, on wrong side of appropriate color appliqué fabric, and iron to bond. Bond colors as follows: from orange, bond one A flower and one B flower; from gold-yellow, bond one A flower, one B flower and one D1 bud; from pale yellow, bond one A flower and one B flower; from cream, bond one A flower, one B flower and one D1 bud; from pale green, bond two D2 sepals; from mid-green, bond two E leaves and two F leaves. When bonded, cut out around outlines through paper and fabric, remembering to cut out the holes at the base of the petals.

From gingham, cut one 24-inch square, and two rectangles, each 20″ x 10³/₄″.

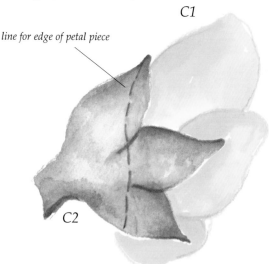

C1

line for edge of petal piece

C2

METHOD

Find center of gingham square by folding diagonally in both directions. The placement guide for the central wreath motif is printed on page 102. On a photocopier, enlarge placement guide 200 percent, then enlarge the result 113 percent. Total enlargement is 227 percent. If you are confident about working freehand, simply mark a circle with a 6-inch radius (12-inch diameter) in center of gingham using tailor's chalk, then arrange motifs around circle. If you would prefer a more specific guide, use transfer paper to copy the enlarged placement guide onto fabric.

Appliqué Read **Appliqué Hints** on page 102, and make several practice flowers until you feel confident enough to tackle the pillow front.

Place background gingham on ironing surface and arrange flowers in a circle, following placement guide if desired, and tucking leaves, bud stems and some flowers under others, as photographed. Note that where there are petals and sepals, the petal area (shown by a dotted line on the appliqué outlines) tucks under the sepals. When you are satisfied with the design,

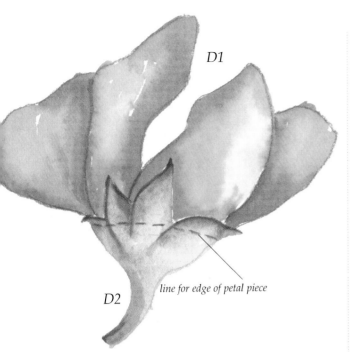

D1

D2

line for edge of petal piece

carefully peel off backing paper and iron appliqué, glue side down, to background. Mark in veins and petal divisions with pencil, or use peeled-off tracing, pencil side down, and press along pencil lines to transfer marks to flower. Pencil in any missing or too-faint lines. Pin or baste paper stabilizer behind work.

Set up machine with bobbin thread to match background and top thread to match appliqué. Start by marking veins with narrow satin stitch. Fill flower centers with open zigzag, then use a medium satin stitch to go around petals. When you reach a petal division, with or without a hole in the center, adjust to straight stitch towards center, opening out to satin stitch around hole and satin stitch back over straight stitch to edge of flower.

E

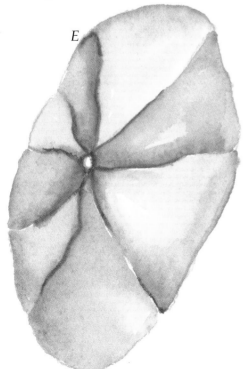

Start with underlapping leaves and flowers and finish with overlapping flowers, changing threads to match flowers as necessary. Continue in this manner until appliqué is complete.

Quilting Place 20-inch square of Fusible Fleece, glue side up, on ironing surface. Lay pillow front, right side up, on top of Fleece. Adjust iron to wool setting and use a pressing cloth to fuse batting to pillow. Press lightly for 10–12 seconds (do not glide iron back and forth), allow to cool and check adhesion. Pin 24-inch square of lawn behind Fleece, and baste all three layers securely together.

Thread machine with white or other color to blend with pillow front. Use a walking foot or dual feed, if available, or lengthen straight stitch slightly to quilt. Randomly quilt around flower circle, starting $1/4$–$3/8$" from inside edge of flower circle and stitching on the spot initially to secure threads, then lengthen stitch and "free-form" around inside of circle. Finish by knotting or tying off stitch and cutting threads close to surface. Make another row of quilting outside flower circle, using the same technique.

F

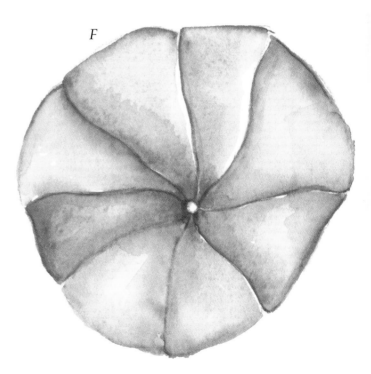

To assemble pillow With right sides together, and allowing $3/8$-inch seams, stitch gingham backing rectangles together at center seam, leaving an opening for zipper. Insert zipper in seam and leave zipper open. With right sides together, pin backing to pillow front, then stitch, allowing $3/8$-inch seams. Trim seams and corners, turn right side out through zipper and topstitch $5/8$ inch from finished edges. Insert pillow form into cover.

Quilt

MEASUREMENTS

Finished quilt measures approximately 46" square.

MATERIALS

- $1/4$ yard x 45" each of cream, pale yellow, gold-yellow and orange fabrics
- $1/2$ yard x 45" mid-green cotton fabric, for leaves and inner borders
- Scrap pale green fabric, for sepals
- $1/2$ yard x 36" double-sided fusible webbing
- $2^{1}/4$ yards x 45" dark green fabric
- 2 yards Fusible Fleece bonded batting
- 3 yards x 45" green and white gingham
- Threads to match appliqué fabrics
- Two 225-yard spools dark green cotton thread, for quilting
- Thin brown paper or waxed paper
- Scrap cotton fabric (for practice)

Note: *Useful but not essential accessories are an appliqué or open embroidery foot, which makes it easier to see the work area, and a walking foot or dual feed option on sewing machine, which makes quilting easy.*

PATTERN PIECES

Outlines for appliqué flowers, leaves and sepals are printed on pages 98 and 99. Using the double-sided webbing as tracing paper, trace 13 A flowers, 11 B flowers, four C1 buds, four C2 sepals, six D1 buds, six D2 sepals, seven E leaves and seven F leaves. Make sure that you transfer the stitching lines as well as the outlines.

CUTTING

Cut out traced motifs, leaving a narrow margin around outlines. Place cut-out motif, glue side down, on wrong side of appropriate color appliqué fabric, and iron to bond. Bond colors as follows: from orange, bond two A flowers, two B flowers, one C1 bud and one D1 bud; from gold-yellow, bond three A flowers, one B flower and two D1 buds; from pale yellow, bond three A flowers, three B flowers, one C1 bud and one D1 bud; from cream, bond five A flowers, five B flowers, two C1 buds and two D1 buds; from pale green, bond four C2 sepals and six D2 sepals; from mid-green, bond seven E leaves and seven F leaves.

From dark green fabric, cut two pieces, each 48" x 12", for the long borders, two pieces, each 26" x 12", for the short borders, and one 24-inch square for the central wreath motif.

From mid-green, cut two 24" x 2" strips and two 26" x 2" strips, for the inner border.

From gingham, remove selvages and cut two pieces, each 45" x 51", for the backing.

METHOD

Central motif and inner borders

Following instructions for the pillow, on page 98, appliqué central motif panel of quilt.

With right sides together and allowing $3/8$-inch seams, stitch 24-inch mid-green border strips to opposite sides of central square and press seams outwards. Apply longer strips to remaining two sides of square in the same way.

Outer borders

Using the **Diagram** opposite as a guide, distribute bonded flowers, buds and leaves between the border pieces — the short borders have three groups of motifs; the long borders have five. When you are satisfied with the design, press motifs in place and appliqué, as for central motif.

With right sides together, and allowing $3/8$-inch seams, stitch short borders to opposite sides of center square, press seam outwards and trim off any excess length. Attach long borders to remaining two sides in the same manner, press and trim.

To assemble quilt

Prepare large surface, such as tabletop, for ironing and lay Fusible Fleece, glue side up, on surface. Lay quilt top on top, right side up, adjusting so that edges meet. If top overhangs slightly, ensure that the excess is the same distance around — it will make the seam less bulky. Press top to Fleece, using wool setting and pressing cloth. Press lightly for 10–12 seconds (do not glide back and forth). Allow to cool and check adhesion.

Cut or tear two 4-inch-wide strips lengthwise from one piece of gingham backing fabric and stitch a strip to either side of remaining piece to make a 52-inch square, for quilt back. (Leftover gingham can be used for pillow, if desired.)

Place quilt back and padded quilt top right sides together with the gingham underneath — the gingham will extend beyond the edges of the top. Make sure it is smooth, then pin edges and stitch together, Fleece side up, allowing $3/8$-inch seams and leaving a 12-inch opening on one edge for turning right side out. Trim seams and corners, turn right side out, pushing corners out well, and slipstitch opening closed. Press edges, rolling the seams towards the back.

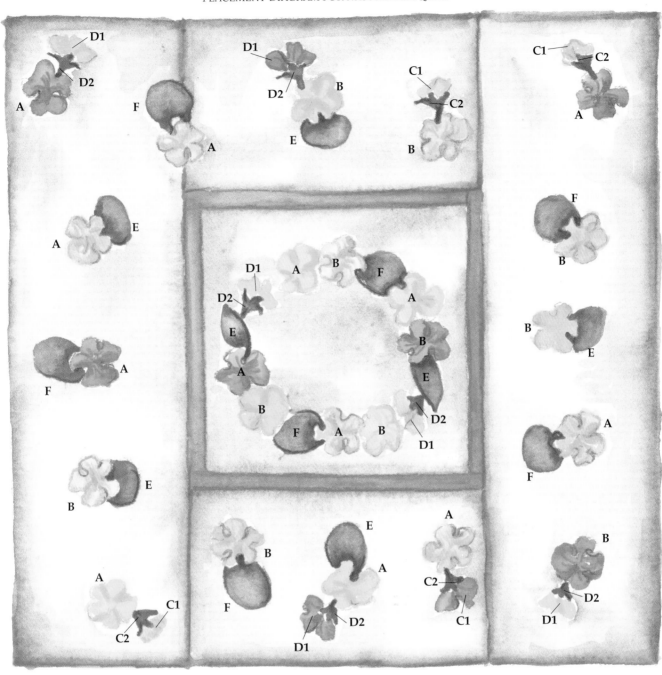

Quilting

Pin through all layers in several places to anchor backing. Set machine up for quilting and thread with cotton quilting thread.

Topstitch $^3/_8$ inch from the finished edge, keeping gingham towards back of the work. Randomly quilt around central flower circle, starting $^1/_4$–$^3/_8$" from the inside edge of the flower circle and stitching in the same place initially to secure threads, then lengthen the stitch and "free-form" around the inside of the circle. Finish by knotting or tying off the stitch and cutting threads close to the surface. Make another row of quilting a further $^1/_4$–$^3/_8$" inside the circle, then repeat two rows outside the flower circle, using the same technique. Quilt in the "ditch" inside the inner border, adjacent to mid-green strips. Finally, random quilt around both sides of the border flowers.

Central motif placement guide
enlarge 227%

Appliqué Hints

Wash all fabrics before use to ensure they are colorfast and pre-shrunk. After washing and drying calico, use spray starch when ironing before use.

MACHINE APPLIQUÉ

satin stitch If you are not used to working with the satin stitch on your machine, we strongly recommend that you practice first. Make sure machine is cleaned and oiled and fitted with a sharp size 10/12 universal needle.

Referring to your instruction book, set up machine with a medium stitch width and short stitch length. Some machines have a pre-set satin stitch in narrow, medium and wide; others have a variable stitch width so that fine points and wide swaths of stitching can be achieved.

Pin a piece of thin brown paper or waxed paper behind your work area fabric to act as a stabilizer, and work a length of satin stitch. Now check to see if bobbin thread has come through to the top; if so, tighten bobbin tension slightly — check your instruction book. Remember to adjust it back to normal after finishing the appliqué. Start another row of satin stitch by inserting and withdrawing the needle once, then pull the end of the bobbin thread through to the top. Narrow the satin stitch so that the needle stitches in the same place. Holding both thread ends towards you, adjust stitch width to satin stitch and make several stitches over thread ends before snipping them off close to surface. Knot or tie off at end of stitching by narrowing down to stitch in the same place, then cut ends of thread close to fabric.

Practice appliqué Cut a 2-inch L-shape, $^3/_4$ inch wide, from fusible webbing. Place webbing, glue (rough) side down, on back of fabric scrap and iron onto fabric with iron set to wool setting. Check for adhesion and allow to cool. Cut fabric around L-shape, then peel off paper. Place L-shape, glue side down (glue feels rubbery), onto practice fabric and iron in position. Pin stabilizing paper behind work area, then begin satin stitch over edge of appliqué (working with appliqué to left of needle), with needle just falling over the edge into the background fabric. Bobbin thread color should blend with the background and top thread should match the appliqué and be changed each time to match. Diagrams on this page show how to deal with corners, curves and points.

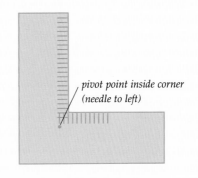

pivot point inside corner (needle to left)

INSIDE CORNER

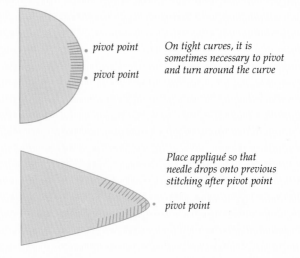

• *pivot point*

• *pivot point*

On tight curves, it is sometimes necessary to pivot and turn around the curve

Place appliqué so that needle drops onto previous stitching after pivot point

• *pivot point*

CURVES AND POINTS

HAND APPLIQUÉ

Thread your needle from the spool and knot the cut end so that your thread is less likely to tangle. To sew pieces in place, use appliqué stitch, which is like an invisible hem or small slipstitch, but a small running stitch or blanket stitch would be just as acceptable. Do not worry about small irregularities — they are all part of the charm of appliqué.

Fold under the raw edges of the appliqué pieces as you sew them to the background fabric. If you find this difficult, the edges can be turned under and basted in place before the pieces are sewn in position; $^1/_8$-inch clips around curved edges will help them to tuck under neatly.

In places where the appliqué forms a V, put extra stitches in the narrowest part to hold the unhemmed edge. At points, trim the excess fabric across the top, fold one side under and stitch almost to the point, then turn in the end and the other side, using needle to tuck in raw edges, and hold firmly in place with the thumb of your non-sewing hand while stitching in place.

Where one appliqué piece overlaps another, the edge that is underneath does not need hemming.

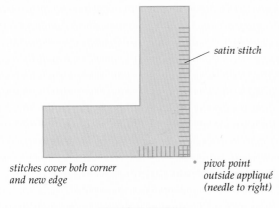

satin stitch

stitches cover both corner and new edge

• *pivot point outside appliqué (needle to right)*

OUTSIDE CORNER

TOYS

REUBEN AND ROSIE

*I*n a world of microchips and gadgetry, it's nice to see that some things don't change — small children still love the softness and comfort of knitted toys. This adorable brother and sister, each with a complete set of knitted clothes, are sure to become treasured friends.

MEASUREMENTS

Height: approximately 15". Chest: approximately 8" (undressed).

MATERIALS

For girl or boy doll

- Main Color (M — cream 055): 1 ball Panda Regal 4-ply (50g) (see **Note**)
- Small quantity bronze 261 Cleckheaton Mohair 12-ply, for Girl's Hair
- Small quantity brown 262 Cleckheaton Mohair 12-ply, for Boy's Hair
- Six-strand cotton embroidery floss, for facial embroidery: brown, white and pink
- Cream-colored cotton sewing thread
- Craft glue, for hair, if desired
- Small quantity green yarn, for Girl's Hair Ribbons
- One pair each U.S. No. 1 or English No. 12 (2.75mm); U.S. No. 2 or English No. 11 (3.0mm); and U.S. No. 5 or English No. 8 (4.0mm) knitting needles
- One pair U.S. No. 6 or English No. 7 (4.5mm) knitting needles, for Boy's Pullover
- One holder, for Bloomers and/or Shorts
- Polyester fiberfill
- Yarn needle, for sewing seams and embroidery

Dolls created by Maria Ragan
Photography by Joe Filshie
Styling by Georgina Dolling

Bloomers for Rosie
- Contrasting Color 1 (C1 — pale blue 002): 1 ball Panda Regal 4-ply (50g)
- Small quantity pink yarn, for twisted cord

Coat for Rosie
- Contrasting Color 2 (C2 — navy): 1 ball Hayfield Crushed Velvet 8-ply (50g)
- Four buttons

Dress for Rosie
- Contrasting Color 3 (C3 — gold 1884): 1 ball Cleckheaton Country 8-ply (50g)
- Contrasting Color 4 (C4 — blue 1395): 1 ball Cleckheaton Country 8-ply (50g)
- Contrasting Color 5 (C5 — pink 1840): 1 ball Cleckheaton Country 8-ply (50g)
- Three small buttons

Socks for Rosie
- Contrasting Color 6 (C6 — grey 0216): 1 ball Cleckheaton Country 8-ply (50g)

Shoes for Rosie
- Small quantity C2 from Coat
- Six-strand cotton embroidery floss for Buckle: silver

Shorts for Reuben
- Contrasting Color 1 (C1 — grey 0216): 1 ball Cleckheaton Country 8-ply (50g)
- Hat elastic

Coat for Reuben
- Contrasting Color 2 (C2 — navy): 1 ball Hayfield Crushed Velvet 8-ply (50g)
- Two buttons

Pullover for Reuben
- Contrasting Color 3 (C3 — blue 1395): 1 ball Cleckheaton Country 8-ply (50g)
- Contrasting Color 4 (C4 — cream 0050): 1 ball Cleckheaton Country 8-ply (50g)
- Two safety-pins

Socks for Reuben
- Contrasting Color 5 (C5 — gold 1884): 1 ball Cleckheaton Country 8-ply (50g)

Shoes for Reuben
- Small quantity C2 from Coat
- Six-strand cotton embroidery floss for Buckle: silver

Note: *If exact yarns are not available, consult yarn shops for suitable substitutions.*

BEFORE YOU START

See **Knitting and Crochet Notes** on page 173.

Rosie

BODY AND HEAD
(make 1, beg at base of body)

Using M and No. 1 or No. 12 (2.75mm) needles, cast on 62 sts.

Work 18 rows st st.

Shape waist. Row 19. K14, K2tog, sl 1, K1, psso, K26, K2tog, sl 1, K1, psso, K14...58 sts.

Work 3 rows st st, beg with a purl row.

Row 23. K13, K2tog, sl 1, K1, psso, K24, K2tog, sl 1, K1, psso, K13...54 sts.

Work 11 rows st st, beg with a purl row.

Shape chest. Row 35. K13, inc one st in each of next 2 sts, K24, inc one st in each of next 2 sts, K13...58 sts.

Work 11 rows st st, beg with a purl row.

Shape shoulders. Row 47. K13, K2tog, sl 1, K1, psso, K24, K2tog, sl 1, K1, psso, K13...54 sts.

Purl one row.

Row 49. K12, K2tog, sl 1, K1, psso, K22, K2tog, sl 1, K1, psso, K12...50 sts.

Purl one row.

Row 51. K8, cast off next 10 sts, knit until there are 14 sts on righthand needle, cast off next 10 sts, knit across...30 sts.

Work 3 rows st st across these 30 sts (forms neck edge), beg with a purl row.

Beg Head shaping. Row 55. *K1, inc one st in next st; rep from * across...45 sts.

Purl one row.

Row 57. K9, inc one st in next st, K1, inc one st in next st, K21, inc one st in next st, K1, inc one st in next st, K9...49 sts.

Purl one row.

Row 59. K9, inc one st in next st, K3, inc one st in next st, K21, inc one st in next st, K3, inc one st in next st, K9...53 sts.

Work 3 rows st st, beg with a purl row.

Row 63. K10, inc one st in next st, K3, inc one st in next st, K23, inc one st in next st, K3, inc one st in next st, K10...57 sts.

Work 11 rows st st, beg with a purl row.

Row 75. K10, K2tog, K3, sl 1, K1, psso, K23, K2tog, K3, sl 1, K1, psso, K10...53 sts.

Work 3 rows st st, beg with a purl row.

Row 79. K9, K2tog, K3, sl 1, K1, psso, K21, K2tog, K3, sl 1, K1, psso, K9...49 sts.

Purl one row.

Row 81. K9, K2tog, K1, sl 1, K1, psso, K21, K2tog, K1, sl 1, K1, psso, K9...45 sts.

Purl one row.

Row 83. *K1, K2tog; rep from * to end...30 sts.

Purl one row.

Row 85. K2tog to end...15 sts.

Break off yarn, thread end through rem sts, draw up and fasten off securely.

LEGS (make 2, beg at top)

Using M and No. 1 or No. 12 (2.75mm) needles, cast on 28 sts.

Work 16 rows st st.

Row 17. K1, sl 1, K1, psso, K9, sl 1, K1, psso, K2tog, K9, K2tog, K1...24 sts.

Work 9 rows st st, beg with a purl row.

Row 27. K1, sl 1, K1, psso, K18, K2tog, K1...22 sts.

Work 19 rows st st, beg with a purl row.

Row 47. K1, sl 1, K1, psso, K16, K2tog, K1...20 sts.

Work 11 rows st st, beg with a purl row.

Shape foot. Row 59. K9, inc one st in each of next 2 sts, K9...22 sts.

Purl one row.

Row 61. K10, inc one st in each of next 2 sts, K10...24 sts.

Purl one row.

Row 63. K1, sl 1, K1, psso, K8, inc one st in each of next 2 sts, K8, K2tog, K1...24 sts.

Purl one row.

Row 65. K1, sl 1, K1, psso, K18, K2tog, K1...22 sts.

Purl one row.

Row 67. K1, sl 1, K1, psso, K6, sl 1, K1, psso, K2tog, K6, K2tog, K1...18 sts.

Row 68. P1, sl 1, P1, psso, P12, P2tog, P1...16 sts.

Cast off.

ARMS (make 2, beg at top)

Using M and No. 1 or No. 12 (2.75mm) needles, cast on 14 sts.

Work 10 rows st st.

Row 11. K1, inc one st in next st, K4, inc one st in each of next 2 sts, K4, inc one st in next st, K1...18 sts.

Work 19 rows st st, beg with a purl row.

Row 31. K1, sl 1, K1, psso, K4, sl 1, K1, psso, K2tog, K4, K2tog, K1...14 sts.

Work 11 rows st st, beg with a purl row.

Shape hand. Row 43. K1, inc one st in next st, K4, inc one st in each of next 2 sts, K4, inc one st in next st, K1...18 sts.

Purl one row.

Row 45. K8, inc one st in each of next 2 sts, K8...20 sts.

Work 3 rows st st, beg with a purl row.

Row 49. K8, cast off next 4 sts, knit to end...16 sts.

Row 50. Purl across all 16 sts.
Row 51. K1, sl 1, K1, psso, K3, sl 1, K1, psso, K2tog, K3, K2tog, K1...12 sts.
Purl one row.
Cast off.

To assemble Join center seam of Body and Head. Join shoulder seams. Firmly fill Doll with polyester fiberfill; close opening at base of Body straight across. With yarn needle and length of M, stitch around neck edge, gather slightly to define neck and fasten off securely. Leaving top edges of Arms and Legs open, join back and lower edge seams. Join thumb seam. Fill Arms and Legs and close rem seam straight across. Attach Arms and Legs to Body. Using sewing thread, define knees, elbows, thumbs and feet by making small stitches through limbs, pulling thread slightly and fastening off. Using embroidery floss, embroider eyes, nose, mouth and freckles, as photographed, in straight stitch and stem stitch (see **Embroidery Stitch Guide** on page 58).***

Hair: Using Cleckheaton Mohair 12-ply, make bangs by stitching looped strands of yarn to Doll's forehead; cut loops. To make rem of hair, cut 16-inch lengths of yarn and stitch center of lengths to Head to form center part, from bangs to approximately $^3/_8$ inch from neck edge at back of Head. Stitch or glue hair to Head, divide ends of hair into pigtails and tie with Hair Ribbons (see page 110); trim as desired.

BLOOMERS
Both back and Front (make 2)

Using C1 and No. 5 or No. 8 (4.0mm) needles, cast on 20 sts for First Leg.
Work 4 rows garter st.
Work 4 rows st st.**
Cont in st st, dec one st at beg of next and foll alt row...18 sts.
Work one row.
Leave sts on a holder.
Second Leg. Work as given for First Leg to **.
Cont in st st, dec one st at end of next and foll alt row...18 sts.
Work one row.
Join Legs as folls. Next row. With right sides facing, knit across 18 sts of Second Leg, then knit across 18 sts from First Leg holder...36 sts.
Work even 15 rows st st, beg and ending with a purl row.
Work 4 rows garter st.
Cast off.

To assemble Join side seams of Bloomers, then join inside Leg seams.

Using pink yarn, make a twisted cord. Cut required number of strands of yarn 2–3 times length of finished cord; for example, 3 strands of yarn 40 inches long will produce a cord 6 strands thick and approximately 16 inches long. Knot strands together at each end, making sure all lengths are equal. Attach one end to a pin or hook, insert knitting needle through other end. Turn knitting needle clockwise until strands are twisted (**Diagram 1**). Holding center of cord, place needle and hook end together, keeping cord taut. Release center of cord so that two halves twist together. Knot, and trim both ends (**Diagram 2**).

Thread cord through Row 2 of garter st at waist edge and tie into a bow at center front.

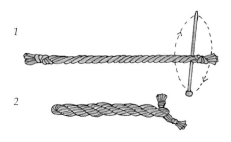

COAT

Back Using C2 and No. 5 or No. 8 (4.0mm) needles, cast on 37 sts and beg moss st patt.
Row 1. K1, *P1, K1; rep from * across.
Last row forms moss st patt.
Work another 39 rows moss st patt.
Shape armholes. Working in patt, cast off 5 sts at beg of next 2 rows...27 sts.
Work 20 rows patt.
Shape shoulders. Working in patt, cast off 8 sts at beg of next 2 rows.
Cast off rem 11 sts loosely.

Right Front Using C2 and No. 5 or No. 8 (4.0mm) needles, cast on 23 sts.
Work 41 rows moss st patt as given for Back.
Shape armhole. Next row (wrong side). Cast off 5 sts, work in patt across...18 sts.
Work 18 rows patt.
Shape neck. Next row (right side). Cast off 10 sts, work in patt...8 sts.
Work 2 rows patt.
Cast off rem 8 sts loosely (for shoulder).

Left Front Using C2 and No. 5 or No. 8 (4.0mm) needles, cast on 23 sts.
Work 4 rows moss st patt as given for Back.
Next row. Work in patt to last 4 sts, yrn (to make a st), patt 2tog, patt 2...buttonhole.
Work 17 rows patt.**
Rep from ** to ** once.
Shape armhole. Next row (right side). Cast off 5 sts, work in patt to last 4 sts, yrn (to make a st), patt 2tog, patt 2...18 sts and buttonhole.
Work 17 rows patt.
Work a buttonhole (as before) in next row...4 buttonholes in all. Work 2 rows patt.
Shape neck. Next row (wrong side). Cast off 10 sts, work in patt...8 sts. Work 2 rows patt.
Cast off rem 8 sts loosely (for shoulder).

Sleeves Using C2 and No. 5 or No. 8 (4.0mm) needles, cast on 31 sts.
Work 36 rows moss st patt as given for Back.
Cast off loosely.

Collar Using C2 and No. 2 or No. 11 (3.0mm) needles, cast on 53 sts.
Work 10 rows moss st patt as given for Back.
Cast off loosely in patt.

Pockets (make 2) Using C2 and No. 2 or No. 11 (3.0mm) needles, cast on 11 sts.
Work 10 rows moss st patt as given for Back.
Cast off loosely in patt (top of Pocket).

To assemble Join shoulder seams. Join side and Sleeve seams. Fold back ³/₄ inch of Sleeves for cuffs. Sew in Sleeves, placing center of Sleeves to shoulder seams. Sew Pockets in position. Sew Collar in position, easing fullness to Back neck, if necessary. Sew on buttons.

HAIR RIBBONS (make 2)
Using green yarn and No. 5 or No. 8 (4.0mm) needles, cast on 23 sts.
Work 3 rows moss st patt as given for Coat.
Cast off loosely in patt.
Tie into a bow around each pigtail.

DRESS
Back (beg at lower edge) Using C3 and No. 5 or No. 8 (4.0mm) needles, cast on 35 sts.
Work 3 rows moss st patt as given for Coat.
Purl one row (wrong side).
Work in st st and stripe patt as folls: 1 row C4, 1 row C3, 1 row C5, 1 row C3, 1 row C4, then 6 rows C3.
Last 11 rows form stripe patt.
Rep last 11 rows twice (33 rows stripe patt).
Change to C4 for rem and purl one row (wrong side).
Beg bodice, dec row. *K2, K2tog; rep from * to last 3 sts, K3...27 sts.**
Work 9 rows st st, beg and ending with a purl row.
Shape armholes. Cast off 3 sts at beg of next 2 rows...21 sts.
Work 8 rows.
Shape shoulders. Cast off 6 sts at beg of next 2 rows.
Cast off rem 9 sts.

Front Work as given for Back to **.
Work 5 rows st st, beg and ending with a purl row.
Divide for Front opening.
Next row. K15, *turn.*
Work even in patt for left side of Front neck.
Next row. K3, P12.
Next row. K15.
Next row. K3, P12.
Shape armhole. Cast off 3 sts, knit across...12 sts.
Work even in patt 4 more rows (without dec).
Shape neck. Cast off 3 sts, purl across...9 sts.
Dec one st at neck edge in next 3 rows...6 sts.
Work one row.
Cast off (for shoulder).

With right side facing, join C4 to rem 12 sts, cast on 3 sts (for garter st band), knit across...15 sts.
Work even in patt for right side of Front neck.
Next row. P12, K3.
Next row. Knit.
Next row. P12, K3.
Next row. Knit.
Shape armhole. Cast off 3 sts, purl to last 3 sts, K3...12 sts.
Work even in patt 2 more rows (without dec).
Shape neck. Cast off 3 sts, knit across...9 sts.
Work one row.
Dec one st at neck edge in next 3 rows...6 sts.
Work one row.
Cast off (for shoulder).

Sleeves Using C4 and No. 5 or No. 8 (4.0mm) needles, cast on 19 sts.
Work 3 rows moss st patt as given for Coat.
Purl one row (wrong side).
Join C5, knit one row; break off C5.
Join C4 for rem, work another 7 rows st st, beg and ending with a purl row.
Cast off loosely.

Neckband Join shoulder seams. With right side facing, using C4 and No. 5 or No. 8 (4.0mm) needles, knit 27 sts evenly around neck edge, incl side edge of Front opening bands.
Knit 3 rows.
Cast off loosely as to k, or knitwise.

To assemble Using duplicate stitch (see page 141) and C4 and C5, embroider vertical stripes onto skirt as photographed, noting that each "set" of stripes is 6 sts apart with one st between each vertical stripe. Beg in center to ensure stripes are even. Join side seams of Dress. Join Sleeve seams. Sew in Sleeves, placing center of Sleeves to shoulder seams. Sew 3 buttons evenly in position on right garter st band. Push buttons through knitted fabric on corresponding left band.

SOCKS
Using C6 and No. 5 or No. 8 (4.0mm) needles, cast on 21 sts.
Row 1. K2, *P1, K1; rep from * to last st, K1.
Row 2. K1, *P1, K1; rep from * across.
Rep Rows 1 and 2 8 times, dec one st in center of last row...20 sts, 18 rows ribbing.
Shape foot. Row 1. K9, inc one st in each of next 2 sts, K9...22 sts.
Row 2 and all even rows. Purl.
Row 3. K10, inc one st in each of next 2 sts, K10...24 sts.
Row 5. K1, sl 1, K1, psso, K8, inc one st in each of next 2 sts, K8, K2tog, K1...24 sts.
Row 7. K1, sl 1, K1, psso, K18, K2tog, K1...22 sts.
Row 9. K1, sl 1, K1, psso, K6, sl 1, K1, psso, K2tog, K6, K2tog, K1...18 sts.
Row 10. P1, sl 1, P1, psso, P12, P2tog, P1...16 sts.
Cast off.

To assemble Join seam and toe of Sock. Fold ribbing in half to right side.

SHOES

Foot and Ankle section (make 2)

Using C2 and No. 2 or No. 11 (3.0mm) needles, cast on 26 sts.
Work 4 rows st st.
Row 5. K11, sl 1, K1, psso, K2tog, K11...24 sts.
Purl one row.
Row 7. K10, cast off next 4 sts, knit to end...20 sts.
Next row (working on closest group of 10 sts only).
Cast off first 8 sts as to purl, or purlwise, P1 (*not incl st already on righthand needle*), *turn*.
Work even 7 rows st st in patt to form ankle strap.
Next row. Join strap to rem sts on other side of Shoe as folls. Using righthand needle, P3tog, purl to end...10 sts.
Cast off as to k, or knitwise.

Sole (make 2)

Using C2 and No. 2 or No. 11 (3.0mm) needles, cast on 6 sts.
Work 10 rows st st, inc one st at each end of Row 3...8 sts.
Dec one st at each end of next 2 rows...4 sts.
Cast off.

To assemble

Join back seam of Foot and Ankle sections. Sew in Soles. Using silver embroidery floss, embroider a French knot Buckle on one side of each Shoe (see **Embroidery Stitch Guide** on page 58).

Reuben

Foll **Body and Head**, **Legs**, **Arms** and **To assemble** instructions as given for Rosie to ***.

EARS (make 4 pieces)

Using M and No. 1 or No. 12 (2.75mm) needles, cast on 8 sts.
Work 4 rows st st.
Row 5. K1, sl 1, K1, psso, K2, K2tog, K1...6 sts.
Purl one row.
Row 7. K1, sl 1, K1, psso, K2tog, K1...4 sts.
Purl one row.
Cast off.
Stitch 2 Ear pieces tog to form one Ear. Sew an Ear to each side of Head.

HAIR

Using Cleckheaton 12-ply Mohair, make bangs by stitching looped strands of yarn to Doll's forehead; cut loops. To make rem of hair, cut 4-inch lengths of yarn and secure to Head, by stitching or gluing. Trim as desired.

SHORTS

Both Back and Front (make 2)

Using C1 and No. 2 or No. 11 (3.0mm) needles, cast on 21 sts for First Leg.
Work 4 rows moss st patt as given for Rosie's Coat.
Work 10 rows st st, dec one st in center of first row...20 sts.**
Cont in st st, dec one st at beg of next and foll alt row...18 sts.
Work one row. Leave sts on a holder.
Second Leg. Work as given for First Leg to **.

Cont in st st, dec one st at end of next and foll alt row...18 sts.
Work one row.
Join Legs as folls. Next row. With right sides facing, knit across 18 Second Leg sts, then knit across 18 sts from First Leg holder...36 sts.
Work 15 rows st st on these 36 sts, beg and ending with a purl row, and dec one st in center of last row...35 sts.
Work 4 rows moss st patt.
Cast off loosely in patt.

To assemble

Join side seams of Shorts, then join inside Leg seams. Thread a length of hat elastic through moss st band at waist edge, draw up slightly and fasten off.

COAT

Back

Using C2 and No. 5 or No. 8 (4.0mm) needles, cast on 37 sts.
Row 1. K1, *P1, K1; rep from * across.
Last row forms moss st patt.
Work 23 more rows in moss st patt.
Shape armholes. Working in patt, cast off 5 sts at beg of next 2 rows...27 sts.
Work 20 rows moss st patt.
Shape shoulders. Working in patt, cast off 8 sts at beg of next 2 rows.
Cast off rem 11 sts loosely.

Right Front

Using C2 and No. 5 or No. 8 (4.0mm) needles, cast on 23 sts.
Work 25 rows moss st patt as for Back.
Shape armhole. Next row (wrong side). Cast off 5 sts, work in patt across...18 sts.
Work 18 rows patt.
Shape neck. Next row (right side). Cast off 10 sts, work in patt across...8 sts.
Work 2 rows patt.
Cast off rem 8 sts loosely (for shoulder).

Left Front

Using C2 and No. 5 or No. 8 (4.0mm) needles, cast on 23 sts. Work 6 rows moss st patt as given for Back.
Next row. Work in patt to last 4 sts, yrn (to make a st), patt 2tog, patt 2...buttonhole.
Work 18 rows patt.
Shape armhole. Next row (right side). Cast off 5 sts, work in patt to last 4 sts, yrn (to make a st), patt 2tog, patt 2...18 sts and buttonhole. Work 17 rows patt.
Shape neck. Next row (wrong side). Cast off 10 sts, work in patt across...8 sts. Work 2 rows patt. Cast off rem 8 sts loosely (for shoulder).

Sleeves Work as given for **Rosie's Coat.**

Pockets Work as given for **Rosie's Coat.**

Hood Using C2 and No. 2 or No. 11 (3.0mm) needles, cast on 53 sts.
Work 36 rows moss st patt as given for Back.
Cast off loosely in patt.
Fold Hood in half and stitch across cast-off seam. Turn inside out and stitch across top of Hood, 3/4 inch from point, so that Hood is not pointed. Turn to right side and fold back 5/8 inch at base of Hood to form a brim. Slipstitch brim at side edges to hold in place.

To assemble Join shoulder seams. Join side and Sleeve seams. Fold back 3/4 inch of Sleeves for cuffs. Sew in Sleeves, placing center of Sleeves to shoulder seams. Sew Pockets in position. Sew Hood evenly into position, easing fullness to Back neck if necessary and noting to stitch through both thicknesses at brim. Sew on buttons.

SOCKS

Work as given for **Rosie's Socks,** using C5.

SHOES

Work as given for **Rosie's Shoes.**

PULLOVER

Back Using C3 and No. 5 or No. 8 (4.0mm) needles, cast on 33 sts.
Row 1. K2, *P1, K1; rep from * to last st, K1.
Row 2. K1, *P1, K1; rep from * across.
Rep Rows 1 and 2 twice (6 rows ribbing in all).
Using C3, work 3 rows st st.
Using C4, purl one row.
Using C3, knit one row.
Using C4, purl one row.
Change to No. 6 or No. 7 (4.5mm) needles and beg Fair Isle patt.
Note. Do not weave colors in Fair Isle patt.

Carry color not in use loosely across on wrong side of work. Always carry colors to end of rows and fasten at side edge. Always carry C3 above C4.
Row 1. K1 C4, *K3 C3, K1 C4; rep from * across.
Row 2. P1 C3, *P1 C4, P1 C3; rep from * across.
Row 3. K2 C3, *K1 C4, K3 C3; rep from * to last 3 sts, K1 C4, K2 C3.
Row 4. Repeat Row 2.
Rows 1 to 4 incl form Fair Isle patt.
Work 6 more rows patt.
Shape armholes. Working in patt, cast off 3 sts at beg of next 2 rows...27 sts.****
Work 8 rows patt.
Shape shoulders. Working in patt, cast off 7 sts at beg of next 2 rows.
Leave rem 13 sts on a holder.

Front Work as given for Back to ****.
Work 4 rows patt.
Shape neck. Next row. Patt 9 sts, *turn.*
**Working even in patt for 9 sts, dec one st at neck edge in next 2 rows...7 sts.
Work one row patt.**
Cast off (for shoulder).
With right side facing, slip next 9 sts on a holder and set aside. Join appropriate color to rem 9 sts and work in patt across.
Work as from ** to **.
Work one row patt.
Cast off (for shoulder).

Sleeves Using C3 and No. 5 or No. 8 (4.0mm) needles, cast on 25 sts.
Work 6 rows ribbing as given for Back.
Using C3, work 3 rows st st.
Using C4, purl one row.
Using C3, knit one row.
Using C4, purl one row.
Change to No. 6 or No. 7 (4.5mm) needles and beg Fair Isle patt.
Work 16 rows Fair Isle patt as given for Back.

Cast off loosely.

Neckband Join right shoulder seam. Using C3 and No. 5 or No. 8 (4.0mm) needles, knit up 35 sts evenly around neck edge, incl sts from holders. Work 9 rows ribbing as given for Back, beg with Row 2.
Cast off loosely in rib st.

To assemble Join left shoulder and Neckband seam. Fold Neckband in half to wrong side and slipstitch loosely in place. Join side and Sleeve seams. Sew in Sleeves, placing center of Sleeves to shoulder seams.

BAA BAA PATCH SHEEP

This cute little fellow, made from a patched and quilted piece of fabric, is a great project for both patchwork novice and expert alike. Use the simple pinwheel pattern to make the fabric, in coordinated colors for a softly old-fashioned look or from random scraps left over from other projects. We added a simple bell around our Sheep's neck, but remember, if making a gift for a baby, the bell should be omitted.

Sheep designed and stitched by Lisa Johnson
Photography by Joe Filshie
Styling by Georgina Dolling

MEASUREMENTS

Finished Sheep measures approximately $10^{1}/_{4}$" long x $6^{3}/_{4}$" high.

MATERIALS

- $^{1}/_{4}$ yard x 45" blue patterned fabric, or a mix of several blue prints
- $^{1}/_{4}$ yard x 45" beige fabric
- $^{1}/_{4}$ yard square black cotton fabric
- Two 16" squares homespun
- Two 16" squares fine batting
- Polyester fiberfill
- Black sewing thread
- Écru quilting thread
- Quilting needle
- Cardboard or plastic, for template
- $^{1}/_{4}$ yard x $^{1}/_{3}$"-wide velvet ribbon
- Small brass bell (optional)

PATTERN PIECES

All pattern pieces are printed on opposite page. Trace Body, Foot, Ear, Muzzle and Tail.

CUTTING

Note: *$^{1}/_{4}$-inch seam allowance is **included** on all pattern pieces. Construct the patchwork fabric for the Body before cutting pattern pieces.*

From black cotton fabric, cut four Ears, four Feet, two Muzzles and two Tails.

METHOD

To make patchwork fabric

From cardboard or plastic, cut one 3-inch square template.

Using the template, cut 24 squares of each of the blue patterned and beige fabrics (48 squares in total). Cut half of the blue patterned squares into halves with the diagonal running from bottom left to top right, and the other half with the diagonal running from bottom right to top left. Repeat for the beige squares (48 triangles of each fabric).

Referring to the **Diagram** on this page, which shows a completed pinwheel, with right sides together, machine- or hand-stitch one blue and one beige fabric triangle together along the diagonal to form a square. Repeat to form a second square.

Join the two squares together to form the top half of the pinwheel, then repeat the process for the bottom half. Join both sections together to complete the pinwheel.

Continue with remaining triangles (12 complete pinwheels in total).

With right sides together, stitch pinwheels into two separate pieces of patchwork fabric, each three pinwheels wide by two deep.

Lay one homespun square down flat, then center one piece of batting on top. Place one patched piece on top of batting, right side up. Pin then baste all layers together. Repeat for other side.

Lay Body pattern on top of one piece to determine the triangles that require quilting, then outline-quilt the appropriate triangles $^{1}/_{4}$ inch from each seam line. Repeat with remaining piece, flipping body outline over to form a reverse image.

Cut Body pattern from first piece of quilted fabric, then reverse pattern and cut second Body piece.

To assemble sheep

With right sides together, stitch two Feet and one Muzzle in position on each patched Body.

With right sides together, stitch Tails together, leaving lower edge open. Turn right side out, press and fold. With raw edges even, pin and stitch Tail onto one Body piece where marked on pattern.

With right sides together, stitch Ears together in pairs around curved edges, leaving open between small dots. Turn right side out, fold raw edges to inside and hand-stitch firmly onto each side of Body as indicated on pattern.

With right sides together, stitch the two Bodies together, leaving an opening at rear as indicated. Clip curves, turn right side out, lightly fill with polyester fiberfill (overfilling will distort the shape) and stitch opening closed.

Place ribbon around Sheep's neck, stitch ends together and stitch bell in place.

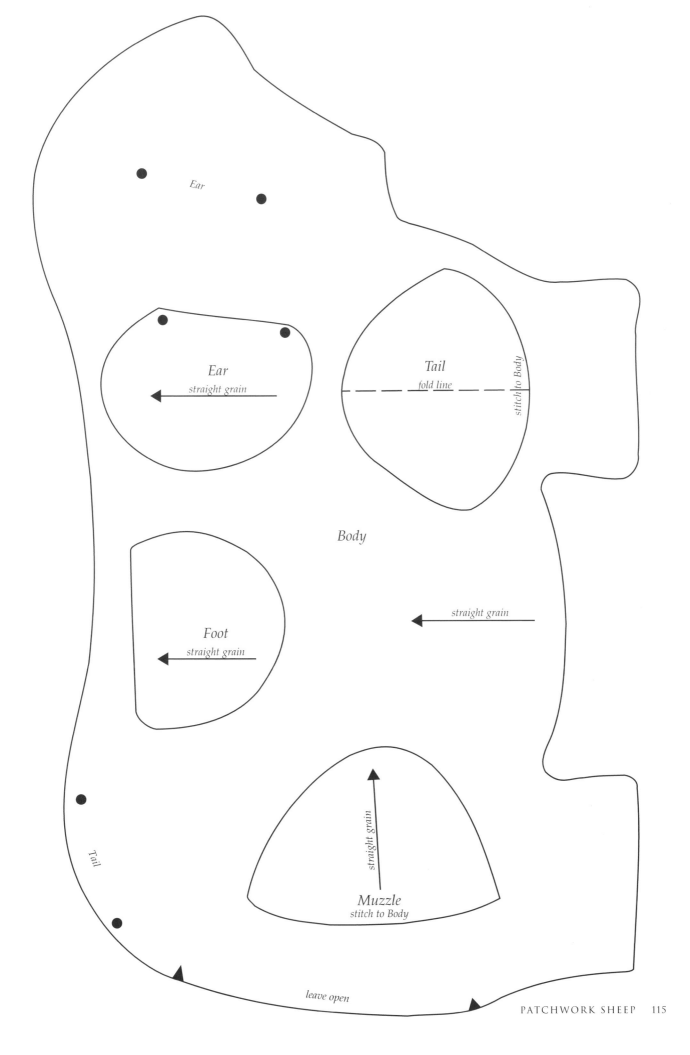

Ear

Ear
straight grain

Tail
fold line
stitch to Body

Body

Foot
straight grain

straight grain

Tail

Muzzle
stitch to Body

straight grain

leave open

TWO BY TWO

With Mr. and Mrs. Noah on board, plus two of every animal safely in the hold, this little wooden Ark can pull up its drawbridge and weather out the wildest storm for 40 days and nights. This captivating toy will provide hours of imaginative play for young children and can then be carefully packed away for the next generation, and the next...

MEASUREMENTS

Finished Ark measures approximately 10" long x 7^1/$_2$" high. Each figure is around 2" tall.

MATERIALS

- Noah's Ark Wooden Set (see **Note**)
- Sanding block or sandpaper
- Artist-quality background paints, such as Jo Sonja's: Pale Beige, Straw, Pimento and Ritz Blue, or equivalent
- Artist-quality flow formula acrylics, such as Jo Sonja's: Paynes Grey, Titanium White, Dioxazine Purple, Antique Blue, Phthalo Blue, Skin Tone Deep, Skin Tone Mid, Skin Tone Light, Yellow Mid, Raw Sienna, Yellow Oxide and Terracotta, or equivalent

Wooden Ark and figures designed by Timber Turn, and painted by Lynda Maker
Photography by Andre Martin
Styling by Vicki Liley

- Brushes: flat, 00 liner and small sponge
- Crackle medium, such as Jo Sonja's or Delta (optional)
- Ruler and pencil
- Transfer paper
- Water-based antiquing medium, such as ChemTek or Jo Sonja's
- Water-based satin varnish, such as Jo Sonja's, Liquitex, or Palmers
- Furniture wax
- PVA glue, archival quality
- ^{3}/$_4$ yard homemade or purchased twisted cord
- Small brass eye hook

Note: *Wooden Ark and craftwood animals are produced by Timber Turn, 63 Boothby Street, Panorama, SA 5041, Australia, ph 618 8277 5056 or fax 618 8277 5540.*

METHOD

Ark Lightly sand the pieces of the Ark and the animals to remove any rough edges. Remove Ark's door and set aside hinges and screws.

Basecoat the hull of the boat inside and out with Pale Beige, using the sponge brush. The cabin is basecoated in Straw, while the cabin roof is basecoated using Pimento.

Paint a second coat on the cabin using Pimento, and mix Paynes Grey with a little Titanium White for the roof. Give the eaves another coat of Pale Beige.

Paint inside the hull (remember the inside of the door) and the inside of the rails on the deck in Straw.

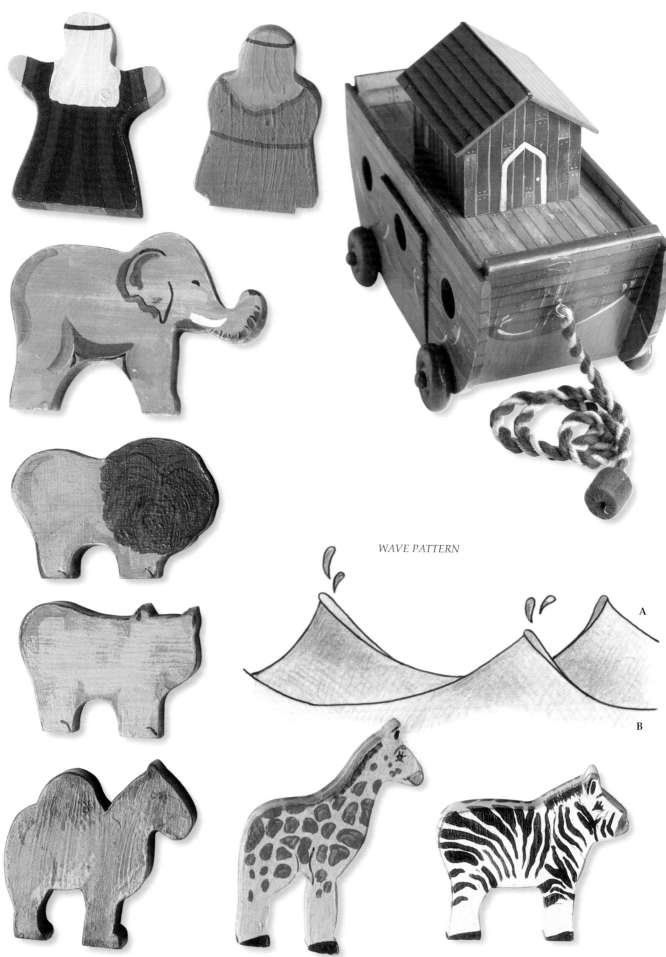

WAVE PATTERN

A

B

Figures and animals are actual size, showing both sides of the painting. Trace the features and details from both sides and transfer them to the figures, or use your own imagination with the photographs as a guide. Remember to continue the markings around the edges of each animal. Both ends of the Ark are shown, revealing the door of the cabin at one end and the window at the other. Join the two halves of the wave pattern (below) together before transferring the pattern to the Ark.

A

B

If you want your Ark to have an antique, crackled finish, you need to add a coat of crackle medium before you add the finish coat. Follow manufacturer's instructions for this step, remembering that the thicker the finish coat of paint, the larger the cracks will be.

Paint the deck with a mixture of Straw and Pimento to give a mellow orange (make sure it's not too close to the Pimento of the cabin). For the outside of the boat, mix together a concoction of Ritz Blue, a small amount of Pimento, some Dioxazine Purple and a little Titanium White, to end up with a grape color; you can make it warmer by adding a little more Pimento, or cooler by adding Dioxazine Purple.

Give the wheel rims a coat of Pimento, paint the hubs with the mellow orange, and give the spokes a coat of grape.

When dry, lightly sand finish coat to reveal basecoat and to give a worn, well-used look.

Rule pencil lines, $3/8$ inch apart, along the front and back of the boat hull to make the wood panelling (it is a good idea to reattach the hinges with just one screw at this point to make it easier to continue the lines). Again, rule lines on the ends of the hull and, freehand, join lines around the ridges. Make nailed "joints" in the wood randomly.

Use wave pattern (on pages 118 and 119), or simply draw two sets of wave lines around the hull, one slightly lower than the other.

Add a little water to some Paynes Grey and side-load a damp flat brush. Squeeze out excess water from unloaded side and paint along pencil wood lines. This will produce a shaded line, which helps to make the wood panels appear to be overlapping.

Continue the shaded lines around the boat. Paint wood paneling joints and nails using liner brush. Tint some Titanium White with a tiny amount of the grape color, and thin with water. Using the flat brush, run along some wood panels using this watery wash to give the effect that not all panels are the same.

The "back" set of waves can now be filled in using Antique Blue mixed with a little Titanium White and a bit of Phthalo Blue.

The "front" waves are filled in using an equal mix of Antique Blue and White. Add highlights in Titanium White.

Paint a lip around the port holes using Pimento, and outline in Paynes Grey. Divide the inside panels of the upper deck into wood panels and shade as for the hull.

Divide inside of hull door into $3/8$-inch panels and shade as for the outside. Divide the deck into $5/16$-inch panels. (It's easier to mark $5/16$-inch increments on a piece of paper and lay it on the deck than to use a ruler.)

Outline wood using a liner brush and Skin Tone Deep, and divide some lengths to make joints, as before.

Using a watery Titanium White and a small flat brush, wash over some panels.

Divide the roof of the cabin into $5/16$-inch panels and shade as for the hull using Paynes Grey.

Divide the walls of the cabin into $5/16$-inch vertical panels. Paint panel lines and joints using Skin Tone Mid or Yellow Oxide. Highlight some panels using the flat brush in the same color.

Paint the door and window using Titanium White tinted with a little Skin Tone Mid, and outline in Paynes Grey. Fill in window using Paynes Grey.

If desired, lightly sand the waves to distress. Remove hinges again. Cover the whole of the Ark with one coat of water-based satin varnish. When dry, mix a little Raw Sienna with antiquing medium and rub over the boat, then rub off excess to give a mellow, antiquated look.

When dry, rub lightly with furniture wax and buff to a shine.

Use PVA glue to attach the cabin to the deck and glue the wheels in place. Reattach the hinges.

To finish, we attached a twisted cotton cord to the Ark using a small brass eye hook.

Figures Mr. and Mrs. Noah and all the animals are photographed actual size on pages 118 and 119. Trace the features (from both sides) and transfer to wooden figures, using transfer paper, remembering to continue the marking around the edges of each creature. Or simply use the photographs as a guide to painting the figures.

Elephant: Basecoat in Pale Beige; finish coat in equal parts Titanium White and Paynes Grey. Paint tusks in Titanium White; eyes, ears and outlines in Paynes Grey; shade areas in Paynes Grey mixed with a little Titanium White; feet in Skin Tone Light mixed with a little Paynes Grey. Tail is painted on back edge and continues to one side.

Zebra: Basecoat in two coats of Titanium White. Paint all stripes and features in Paynes Grey, continuing stripes and mane on to top edge of Zebra. Paint muzzle in Paynes Grey mixed with a little Titanium White. Tail is painted on the back and continues to one side.

Giraffe: Basecoat in Pale Beige, finish coat in Yellow Mid mixed with a little Titanium White. Paint spots in Yellow Oxide; mane in Skin Tone Deep mixed with Yellow Oxide; eyes, ears and feet in Paynes Grey. Tail is painted on back edge; continue mane and spots onto back edge as well.

Camel: Basecoat in Pale Beige; finish coat in Terracotta mixed with a little Titanium White. Paint feet, ears, eyes and mouth in Skin Tone Deep; shade top of humps in a wash of Skin Tone Deep; shade under belly and chest in Terracotta mixed with Titanium White.

Lion and Lioness: Basecoat in Pale Beige; finish coat in Straw. Paint tail and features in Skin Tone Deep; mane in Terracotta; mane highlights in Skin Tone Deep. Tail starts on back edge and continues to front. Fill in mane shape completely on back. Use same colors for the Lioness, omitting mane.

Mr. Noah: Basecoat in Pale Beige, then trace the features. Paint face and hands in Skin Tone Light mixed with a little Titanium White; coat in stripes of Terracotta and Phthalo Blue; gown in Yellow Oxide; outlines in Paynes Grey; beard in Titanium White; head shawl in Titanium White mixed with a small amount of Paynes Grey.

Mrs. Noah: Basecoat in Pale Beige, then trace the features. Paint gown in Phthalo Blue mixed with a little Terracotta; outline in Paynes Grey; face and hands in Skin Tone Light mixed with a little Titanium White; scarf in Yellow Oxide mixed with a little Titanium White; edge of scarf in Terracotta; hair in Skin Tone Deep.

Finish off all figures with a coat of varnish.

EASTER BILBY

Apart from the bad press that rabbits receive in Australia, there is an even better reason to introduce small believers to the Easter Bilby. Bilbies are now on the endangered list, found only in Australia's most inaccessible desert regions. By raising awareness of this little marsupial, we can perhaps ensure that its plight does not go unheeded and that, for future generations, the Easter Bilby will not have become just a childhood myth.

MEASUREMENTS

Height approximately 12$^{1}/_{4}$".

MATERIALS

Fingering, baby, or sportweight knitting yarn to give gauge (50g) (see **Note**):

- Main Color (M — grey): 3 balls
- Contrasting Color 1 (C1 — cream): 1 ball
- Contrasting Color 2 (C2 — pink): 1 ball
- Contrasting Color 3 (C3 — black): 1 ball
- One pair U.S. No. 2 or English No. 11 (3.0mm) knitting needles
- Washable polyester fiberfill
- Two small safety eyes

Bilby created by Maria Ragan
Photography by Jaime Plaza

- One U.S. C/2 or D/3 or English No. 10 or No. 11 (3.0mm) crochet hook

Note: *We used Patons Pure Spun 8-ply for M and C1, Patons Wool Rich Chambray 8-ply for C2, and Patons Fireside 8-ply for C3. If using a different yarn, knit a pattern swatch before starting Bilby. See **Knitting and Crochet Notes** on page 173 for equivalents and conversions.*

STITCH GAUGE

See **Knitting and Crochet Notes** on page 173. 27 sts and 36 rows = 4 inches st st, using No. 2 or No. 11 (3.0mm) needles and M. This toy has been knitted on a tighter tension than normally recommended.

SPECIAL ABBREVIATION

Purl fabric: reverse st st (purl all sts on right side of work, knit all sts on wrong side of work).

BACK/SIDE BODY (make 2)

Using M and No. 2 or No. 11 (3.0mm) needles, cast on 6 sts.
Knit 2 rows garter st.
Row 3 (wrong side). (Inc one st in next st, K1) 3 times...9 sts.
Row 4. Purl.
Row 5. Inc one st in each of next 9 sts...18 sts.
Work 5 rows purl fabric, beg with a purl row.
Row 11. (Inc one st in next st, K1) 9 times...27 sts.
Work 5 rows purl fabric.
Row 17. (K2, inc one st in next st) 9 times...36 sts.
Work 31 rows purl fabric.
Row 49. K5, (K2tog, K4) 4 times, K2tog, K5...31 sts.
Work 5 rows purl fabric.

Row 55. K3, (K2tog, K4) 4 times, K2tog, K2...26 sts.
Work 5 rows purl fabric.
Row 61. K2, (K2tog, K3) 4 times, K2tog, K2...21 sts.
Work 5 rows purl fabric.
Row 67. K2, (K2tog, K2) 4 times, K2tog, K1...16 sts.
Work 3 rows purl fabric.
Row 71. (K1, K2tog) 5 times, K1...11 sts.
Row 72. Purl.
Cast off.

FRONT GUSSET

Using C1 and No. 2 or No. 11 (3.0mm) needles, cast on 4 sts. Knit 2 rows garter st.
Row 3 (wrong side). (Inc one st in next st, K1) twice...6 sts.
Row 4. Purl.
Row 5. Inc one st in each of next 6 sts...12 sts.
Work 5 rows purl fabric.
Row 11. (Inc one st in next st, K1) 6 times...18 sts.
Work 5 rows purl fabric.
Row 17. K5, inc one st in next st, K6, inc one st in next st, K5...20 sts.
Work 31 rows purl fabric.
Row 49. K3, (K2tog, K2) 3 times, K2tog, K3...16 sts.
Work 5 rows purl fabric.
Row 55. K3, (K2tog, K2) 3 times, K1...13 sts.
Work 5 rows purl fabric.
Row 61. (K1, K2tog) 4 times, K1...9 sts.
Work 5 rows purl fabric.
Row 67. (K1, K2tog) 3 times...6 sts.
Work 5 rows purl fabric.
Cast off.

HEAD

Using M and No. 2 or No. 11 (3.0mm) needles, cast on 25 sts. Knit 2 rows garter st.
Row 3 (wrong side). (K2, inc one st in next st, K2) 5 times...30 sts.
Row 4. Purl.
Row 5. (K2, inc one st in next st, K2) 6 times...36 sts.
Row 6. Purl.
Row 7. (K2, inc one st in next st, K3) 6 times...42 sts.
Row 8. Purl.
Work 8 rows purl fabric (beg with a knit row), inc one st at each end of every row...58 sts.
Work 8 more rows purl fabric, beg with a knit row.
Divide Head. Row 25. Cast off 2 sts, knit until there are 22 sts on righthand needle, *turn* and work even 22 sts for Right Side of Head.
Row 26. P2tog, purl across.
Row 27. Cast off 2 sts, knit across. Rep last 2 rows 3 times.
Row 34. Cast off 2 sts, purl across. Cast off rem 8 sts.
With wrong side facing, join M to rem 34 sts.

Next row. K10, *turn* and work even 10 sts for Gusset.
Work 11 rows purl fabric.
Work 2 rows, dec one st at beg of each row...8 sts.
Work 8 rows purl fabric, beg with a knit row.
Rep last 10 rows twice more...4 sts.
Cast off.
With wrong side facing, join M to rem 24 sts for Left Side of Head.
Next row. K2tog, knit across.
Next row. Cast off 2 sts, purl across.
Rep last 2 rows 3 times.
Next row. Cast off 2 sts, knit across.
Next row. Cast off 2 sts, purl across.
Cast off rem 8 sts.

SNOUT

Using a flat seam, join Head Gusset and Head Side Pieces. With right side facing (purl fabric) and using C2 and No. 2 or No. 11 (3.0mm) needles, knit 8 sts evenly along Right Side of Head, 4 sts evenly across Gusset, then 8 sts evenly along Left Side of Head...20 sts.
Row 1 (wrong side). Knit.
Row 2. Purl.
Row 3. K3, (K2tog, K2) 3 times, K2tog, K3...16 sts.
Work 3 rows purl fabric.
Row 7. K3, (K2tog, K2) twice, K2tog, K3...13 sts.
Work 3 rows purl fabric.
Row 11. (K1, K2tog) 4 times, K1...9 sts.
Row 12. Purl.
Row 13. (K1, K2tog) 3 times...6 sts.
Row 14. Purl.
Break off yarn, run end through rem sts, draw up and fasten off securely.

LEFT OUTER ARM

Using M and No. 2 or No. 11 (3.0mm) needles, cast on 16 sts.
Row 1. Knit.
Row 2. Inc one st in first st, purl across...17 sts.
Work 8 rows purl fabric, beg with a knit row.
Row 11. Cast off 10 sts, knit across...7 sts.
Work 2 rows purl fabric.
Work 4 more rows purl fabric, inc one st at beg of each row...11 sts.
Work 3 rows purl fabric.
Work 3 more rows purl fabric, dec one st at each end of each row...5 sts.
Cast off.
With wrong side facing (knit side) and using C1 and No. 2 or No. 11 (3.0mm) needles, knit up 8 sts evenly along side (wrist) edge of Arm.
Next row. Purl.
Next row. Inc one st in first st, knit to last 2 sts, K2tog.
Rep last 2 rows 3 times...8 sts.

Next row. Purl.

Next row. (K2tog) 4 times...4 sts.

Break off yarn, run end through rem sts, draw up and fasten off securely.

RIGHT OUTER ARM

Work to correspond with Left Outer Arm, working purl for knit and knit for purl, thus reversing all shaping.

LEFT INNER ARM

Work as for Right Outer Arm.

RIGHT INNER ARM

Work as for Left Outer Arm.

LEGS (make 2)

Using C1 and No. 2 or No. 11 (3.0mm) needles, cast on 24 sts.

Row 1 (wrong side). Knit.

Row 2. Inc one st in each of next 24 sts...48 sts.

Row 3. (K1, inc one st in next st) twice, K16, (K1, inc st in next st) 4 times, K16, (inc one st in next st, K1) twice...56 sts.

Row 4. Purl.

Work 4 rows purl fabric, beg with a knit row.

Row 9. K25, K2tog, K2, K2tog, K25...54 sts.

Row 10. Purl.

Row 11. K24, K2tog, K2, K2tog, K24...52 sts.

Row 12. Purl.

Row 13. K7, cast off next 38 sts, knit across...14 sts.

Row 14. Purl across all 14 sts. Break off C1. Join M.

Row 15. Purl.

Row 16. Purl.

Row 17. (Inc one st in next st, K4, inc one st in next st, K1) twice...18 sts.

Row 18. (Inc one st in next st, P6, inc one st in next st, P1) twice...22 sts.

Row 19. (Inc one st in next st, K8, inc one st in next st, K1) twice...26 sts.

Cont inc in this manner until the row "(Inc one st in next st, K16, inc one st in next st, K1) twice.. .42 sts" has been completed.

Row 24. Purl.

Row 25. (Inc one st in next st, K18, inc one st in next st, K1) twice...46 sts.

Row 26. Purl.

Row 27. (Inc one st in next st, K20, inc one st in next st, K1) twice...50 sts.

Work 5 rows purl fabric.

Row 33. (K2tog, K20, K2tog, K1) twice...46 sts.

Row 34. (P2tog, P18, P2tog, P1) twice...42 sts.

Row 35. (K2tog, K16, K2tog, K1) twice...38 sts.

Cont dec in this manner until 14 sts rem.

Cast off.

OUTER EARS (make 2)

Using M and No. 2 or No. 11 (3.0mm) needles, cast on 19 sts. Work 10 rows purl fabric.

Work 2 rows, dec one st at beg of each row...17 sts.

Work 8 rows purl fabric.

Work 2 rows, dec one st at beg of each row...15 sts.

Work 8 rows purl fabric.

Work 8 rows, dec one st at beg of each row...7 sts.

Dec one st at each end of next 2 rows...3 sts.

Cast off.

INNER EARS (make 2)

Using C2 and No. 2 or No. 11 (3.0mm) needles, cast on 19 sts. Work to correspond with Outer Ears, noting to work in st st throughout.

TAIL

Using M and No. 2 or No. 11 (3.0mm) needles, cast on 15 sts.

Work 6 rows purl fabric.

Break off M.

Using C3, work 20 rows st st.

Next row. K2tog, knit to last 2 sts, K2tog...13 sts.

Work 8 rows st st, beg with a purl row.

Next row. P2tog, purl to last 2 sts, P2tog...11 sts.

Work 2 rows st st.

Break off C3.

Using C1, work 6 rows st st.

Dec one st at beg of next 4 rows...7 sts.

Work 2 rows.

Next row. (K2tog) 3 times, K1...4 sts.

Cast off.

TO ASSEMBLE

Using a flat seam, stitch Body pieces tog, leaving an opening at back. Fill firmly and close opening. Stitch Head and Snout seam, leaving an opening. Fill Head firmly and attach to Body. Secure eyes to Head as photographed. Join Inner Ear pieces to Outer Ear pieces, fold and stitch Ears in place as photographed. Fold Tail in half lengthwise and stitch to join. Place a small amount of filling in Tail and attach Tail to Body. Cut $1/2$-inch lengths of C1 and fold in half. Using hook, thread lengths through C1 section of Tail as photographed. Brush end of Tail. Fold Legs and stitch seams, leaving an opening. Fill Legs and close opening. Attach Legs to Body as photographed. Join Arm pieces tog, leaving an opening. Fill Arms, close opening and stitch Arms to Body.

LIZZIE THE RAG DOLL

*O*ur Lizzie is absolutely everything a real rag doll should be — cute as a button, very soft and cuddly, and wearing lots of layers of pretty lace-trimmed clothes. Lizzie is sure to become dearly loved by the delighted small child who first makes her acquaintance.

MEASUREMENTS
Finished doll is approximately 20" tall.

MATERIALS

- $^2/_3$ yard x 45" calico
- $^2/_3$ yard x 36" white fabric, for underclothes
- $^2/_3$ yard x 36" fabric, for Dress
- $^1/_2$ yard x 36" fabric, for Pinafore
- $^3/_4$ yard x 36" fabric, for Hat
- $^1/_2$ yard x 36" iron-on interfacing
- 12" square felt, for Shoes
- Polyester fiberfill
- Two $^5/_8$"-diameter buttons
- Doll needle
- Strong thread
- $1^2/_3$ yards x $1^1/_8$"-wide lace edging

- 1 yard x $^3/_{16}$"-wide elastic
- Small amount very narrow, round elastic
- Bias binding, for Collar piping (optional)
- $1^1/_2$ yards x $1^1/_8$"-wide pre-gathered eyelet lace
- Five small snaps
- $^2/_3$ yard x $^3/_8$"-wide lace edging, for Handkerchief
- Two $^1/_4$"-diameter pearl beads, for Shoes
- Pair of purchased smallest size baby socks
- Two $^1/_2$"-diameter shank-style black buttons, for eyes
- Small amount dusty pink six-strand cotton embroidery floss
- Blusher or red pencil
- Dark brown pencil
- Yarn for hair (you can use mohair, or substitute sport or chunky)
- Craft glue
- $1^1/_4$ yards x $^5/_8$"-wide ribbon, for hair ties

PATTERN PIECES
All pattern pieces, except rectangles, are printed on pages 131 to 133. Trace Side Head, Center Head, Front Body, Side Back Body, Center Back Body, Arm,. Leg, Foot, Bloomers, Dress Front Bodice, Dress Back Bodice, Collar, Sleeve, Pinafore Front Bodice, Pinafore Back Bodice, Pocket, Hat Crown, Hat Brim, Hat Side, Shoe Upper and Shoe Sole.

Lizzie designed and made by Georgina Bitcon
Photography by Valerie Martin

CUTTING

Note: *$1/4$-inch seam allowance and $5/8$-inch casing/hem allowance are* **included** *on all pattern pieces and in given measurements unless otherwise specified.*

From calico, cut two Side Heads, one Center Head, two Front Bodies, two Side Back Bodies, one Center Back Body, four Arms, four Legs and two Feet.

From white fabric, cut two Bloomers on the fold, one rectangle, $6^3/4''$ x 36", for Petticoat, and one $4^3/4$-inch square, for Handkerchief.

From Dress fabric, cut two Dress Front Bodices, two Dress Back Bodices on the fold, four Collars and two Sleeves on the fold. Cut also one rectangle, $7^1/4''$ x 36", for Skirt.

From Pinafore fabric, cut two Pinafore Front Bodices on the fold, two Pinafore Back Bodices on the fold and two Pockets. Cut also one rectangle, $7^1/4''$ x 32", for Skirt.

From Hat fabric, cut two Hat Crowns, two Hat Brims on bias fold and one Hat Side on bias fold.

From interfacing, cut one Hat Brim.

From felt, cut two Shoe Uppers and two Shoe Soles. Cut also two strips, each $3^3/8''$ x $^3/8''$, for Shoe Straps.

METHOD

Doll **Head:** Stitch dart in each Side Head and press dart to one side. Stitch just outside seam line of Center Head and clip to stitching. With right sides together, pin Side Heads to Center Head, matching notches, then stitch. Clip curves and turn right side out. Stuff head firmly, making sure that curves are evenly rounded. Set aside.

Body: With right sides together, stitch center front seam of Front Bodies. With right sides together, stitch a Side Back Body to each side of Center Back Body, matching small dots. With right sides together, stitch front to back at sides, leaving neck edge open. Clip curves, turn body right side out.

Stuff body firmly and evenly. Run a strong gathering thread around raw neck edge and draw up gathers tightly, lacing across any exposed stuffing. Tie off thread securely.

Joining Head to Body: Turn under raw edge on neck edge of head and baste. Center head over gathered neck edge of body and, using double thread and small, neat stitches, stitch head firmly to body, inserting more stuffing into neck, if necessary, before closing seam.

Arms: With right sides together, stitch Arms together in pairs, leaving open above notches to make turning easier. Clip curves and turn right side out. Place a small amount of stuffing into lower end of Arm, then, either by hand or by machine, stitch finger lines as shown on pattern. Tie off all threads securely and "bury" in Arm. Stuff Arm firmly as far as notches, turn in seam allowance on remaining raw edges and slipstitch neatly together.

Joining Arms to body: Thread doll needle with strong double thread and knot ends. With knot on underside of Arm, make a couple of stitches through small dot on upper Arm, emerging on outside of Arm. Thread needle through one hole of button, across into second hole then through body of doll so that top edge of Arm sets about $^5/8$ inch below neck seam. Squeeze body so that needle emerges at same position on opposite side of doll, then thread it through second Arm, through second button, and back across body to starting position. Repeat this process, then tie off thread and "bury" ends in body.

Legs and Feet: With right sides together, stitch Legs together in pairs, leaving top and bottom edges open. Clip curves. Staystitch around lower edge of each Leg and clip to stitching.

With right sides together, pin Feet to lower edges of Legs, matching dots to center front and back seams. Baste and stitch. Clip curves and turn right side out.

Joining Legs to body: Stuff Legs firmly and evenly. Turn in seam allowance on upper edges and slipstitch edges together, matching center front and back seams. Position Legs on lower edge of body, along front/back seam line, and stitch firmly in place with small, neat stitches, taking slight tucks in upper edge where necessary so that each Leg fits between side edge and center front seam.

It is easier to dress doll before adding face and hair.

Underclothes **Bloomers:** Press under $^1/4$ inch on leg edge of each Bloomer piece. Cut a piece of $1^1/8$-inch-wide lace to fit each leg edge and, with edge of lace even with turned-in raw edge of Bloomers, stitch lace to inside edge, about $^1/8$ inch from fold. Cut a piece of very narrow, round elastic to fit along leg edge. Set machine to a wide zigzag stitch. Lay elastic along inside edge of lace and zigzag in place, stitching carefully so that elastic is encased within zigzag but not sewn in place. Leave elastic ends extending.

With right sides together, stitch inside leg seams, stitching across lace edging at the same time. Neaten seam with zigzag or knotting. Pull up elastic to fit doll's legs and knot ends firmly to hold. Trim excess elastic.

With right sides together, stitch crotch seam from center front to center back, matching inside leg seams. Neaten seam.

Press under $^1/4$ inch on upper raw edge, then turn under another $^3/8$ inch and stitch to form casing, leaving an opening at center back to thread elastic. Cut a piece of $^3/16$-inch elastic to fit doll's waist, thread through casing, adjust to fit, secure ends, then stitch opening closed.

Petticoat: With right sides together, stitch short ends of Petticoat together to form center back seam. Neaten edges and press seam open.

Press under $^1/4$ inch on lower edge, then turn under another $^3/8$ inch and stitch to form hem. Cut a piece of

$^1/_8$-inch-wide lace to fit lower edge of Petticoat, plus hem allowance, and stitch in place on inside, as close as possible to lower edge. Neaten raw edges of lace by hand.

Press under $^1/_4$ inch on waist edge, then turn under another $^3/_8$ inch and stitch to form casing, leaving an opening at center back to thread elastic. Cut a piece of $^3/_{16}$-inch elastic to fit doll's waist, thread through casing, adjust to fit, secure ends, then stitch opening closed.

Dress

Collar: If you are piping the Collar, cut two pieces of bias binding to fit around outside edge of Collar, allowing easing for curves, and press each in half lengthwise. With right sides together, baste binding to outer edge of Collar so that folded edge of binding will extend $^1/_8$ inch beyond seam when Collar is complete. With right sides together, stitch remaining Collar sections to piped sections, enclosing raw edges of binding. Clip curves, turn Collars right side out and press. (If you are not using piping, simply stitch the Collars together in pairs, turn right side out and press.)

Bodice: With right sides together, join one Front Bodice to one Back Bodice at lefthand shoulder seam. Join same Front to second Back Bodice at righthand shoulder seam. Repeat with second Front Bodice, joining remaining shoulder seams, to form one continuous piece. Press seams open and press Back Bodices in half along center back fold lines so that one Front/Back Bodice section now forms bodice lining.

Baste Collars to Front Bodice, raw edges even and matching center fronts. With right sides together, stitch bodice and bodice lining together at neck edge, sandwiching Collars at the same time. Clip curves, turn bodice lining back to inside and press. Baste remaining raw edges of bodice and bodice lining together, matching shoulder seams.

Sleeves: Run a gathering thread around upper edge of Sleeves. Test length of Sleeve on doll's arm and trim shorter if desired. (Pattern allows for a full-length sleeve.)

Press under $1^1/_2$ inches on lower edge of Sleeve and baste close to raw edge to hold. Cut eyelet lace to fit lower edge and stitch to Sleeve, close to folded edge. Cut a piece of $^3/_{16}$-inch elastic to fit doll's arm, plus seam allowance and, using zigzag and stretching elastic as you sew, stitch elastic to inside of Sleeve, covering raw edge of Sleeve hem at the same time. Remove basting.

With right sides together, pin Sleeve to armhole edge, draw up gathers to fit and stitch. Neaten seam. Repeat for remaining Sleeve.

With right sides together, stitch side and Sleeve seams in one operation, stitching across eyelet lace and securing ends of elastic at same time. Neaten seam.

Skirt: With right sides together, stitch short ends of Skirt together to form center back seam, leaving $2^3/_8$ inches open at waist edge. Press seam open, including edges of opening.

Press under $^1/_4$ inch on lower edge of Skirt, turn under another $^3/_8$ inch to form hem, stitch. Cut a piece of eyelet lace to fit lower edge of Skirt, plus hem allowance, and stitch in position, turning under raw ends at center back and neatening by hand.

Run two gathering threads around waist edge and draw up gathers to fit bodice.

With right sides together, pin Skirt to bodice and stitch, allowing a $^3/_8$-inch seam. Trim and neaten seam.

Finishing: Sew three small snaps to center back to close.

Pinafore **Bodice:** With right sides together, join one Front Bodice to one Back Bodice at lefthand shoulder seam. Join same Front to second Back Bodice at righthand shoulder seam. Repeat with second Front Bodice, joining remaining shoulder seams, to form one continuous piece. Press seams open and press Back Bodices in half along center back fold lines so that one Front/Back Bodice section now forms bodice lining.

With right sides together, stitch bodice and bodice lining together around neck and armhole edges, leaving side seams open. Clip curves, turn right side out and press. Open out sides so that underarm seams and waist edges match on each side and stitch side seam in one long seam.

Skirt: Press under $1/4$ inch on each short edge of Skirt, then turn under another $3/8$ inch and stitch. Make a similar hem on one long edge of Skirt. Run two gathering threads along remaining raw edge of Skirt and draw up gathers to fit bodice. With right sides together, pin bodice to Skirt, keeping bodice lining free, adjust gathers and stitch, allowing a $3/8$-inch seam. Turn under raw edge of bodice lining and slipstitch in place over seam.

Pockets: Press $5/8$-inch facing allowance to outside on upper edge of each Pocket and stitch at sides, continuing stitching around Pocket on seam line. Turn facing back to inside, clip across seam allowance to stitching and press seam allowance under on stitching line. Position Pockets on front of Pinafore and topstitch in place. Using a close, narrow zigzag, stitch $3/8$-inch-wide lace to edges of $4^3/4$-inch white square, mitering corners as you go. Neaten miters and raw edges of lace by hand. Fold Handkerchief and place in pocket of Pinafore.

Finishing: Sew two small snaps to center back edge of bodice.

Hat **Side:** With right sides together, stitch short ends of Hat Side and press seam open. Press Side in half lengthwise, wrong sides together, matching seams, and baste raw edges to hold. Run a line of ease stitching around raw edges of Hat Side.

Crown: With wrong sides facing, baste Hat Crowns together. With right sides facing, baste and stitch Crown to raw edges (not folded edge) of Hat Side, pulling up ease stitching to accommodate fullness, and distributing fullness evenly so that there are no tucks in seam line. Neaten seam.

Brim: Apply interfacing to wrong side of one Brim piece. With right sides together, join short ends of Brim and press seam open. Repeat for remaining Brim piece, which becomes Brim Lining.

With right sides together, stitch Brim to Brim Lining around outer edge. Turn right side out and press. Stitch raw edges of Brim and Lining together, following seam line. Clip across seam allowance to stitching around inner edge of Brim. Position folded edge of Hat Side over inner edge of Brim, using stitching line as a guide, and baste. Topstitch close to folded edge of Side. Neaten seam and press towards Side, then topstitch again, about $1/4$ inch above first row of topstitching.

Shoes With rights sides together, stitch center back seam of Shoe Upper, stitching $1/8$ inch from edge. With right sides together, stitch Sole into Upper — it may be easier to do this by hand, as it's rather fiddly. Round one end of each Strap, fold the tip back on itself and cut a tiny nick with scissors, to form buttonhole. Stitch remaining end of Strap to inside of shoe, positioning it slightly diagonally so that it will sit snugly across doll's instep. Sew a small pearl to each outer side so that the Strap can be buttoned.

Face Using a doll needle and strong thread, and anchoring thread at back of head, stitch black buttons to face for eyes, pulling them slightly to create eye sockets. Tie off threads securely. Ends will be hidden by hair. Using two strands of dusty pink embroidery floss, work a simple curved mouth in stem stitch. Using one strand of dusty pink, work a smaller curve in backstitch as a nose. Rub a little blusher or red pencil onto cheek areas, and dot lightly across nose and below eyes with a sharp brown pencil for freckles.

Hair Cut a piece of calico on the bias, about $5^1/4''$ x $2^1/2''$. Lay this strip across the top of doll's head at bangs level, and mark head seam lines with a pencil. Cut a number of 10-inch lengths of yarn and fold in half. The exact number will depend on how thick you want the bangs to be, but you need enough to fit side by side along the length of your bias strip, between the pencil lines. Using a little craft glue, position folded yarn lengths across bias strip, having loops even with one long edge, and the other ends extending beyond the opposite edge. Using a matching sewing thread, stitch along the center of the bias strip, to secure yarn, then stitch again a couple more times, close to the first line of stitching — this will ensure that yarn is securely held (**Diagram 1**). Set aside.

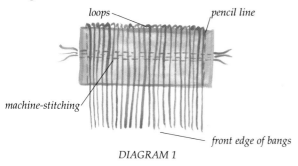

DIAGRAM 1

Now cut another calico bias strip, about $2^{1}/_{4}"$ x 8", and mark pencil lines across each end of strip, about $^{3}/_{4}$ inch from the end. Cut the remainder of yarn into 28-inch lengths and arrange across strip, between pencil lines, this time so that strip lies in center of yarn and yarn ends extend evenly on each side. Glue and stitch as before (**Diagram 2**).

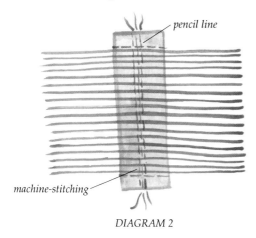

DIAGRAM 2

Fold under and glue front raw edge of bangs strip almost back to the stitching line. Spread craft glue thoroughly over underside of strip and glue in position across top of head so that folded edge sits approximately where you imagine the hairline would be, and matching pencil lines to seams. The bangs will probably be too long at this stage, but can be trimmed later. Allow this to dry.

Fold under extending raw edges at each end of longer strip so that they are completely concealed, and glue in place. Position this strip down center back of doll's head so that the top edge is even with the bangs stitching line and completely covers the looped ends, and the lower edge sets about $1^{1}/_{2}$ inches above the nape of the neck. Glue firmly in place. Lift hair out of the way and lightly pencil a hairline around sides and lower back of head.

Spread glue fairly liberally over head, following hairline, and press hair firmly into glue. When dry, trim bangs (not too evenly) and arrange hair into braids, trimming ends even and tying with matching hair ribbons.

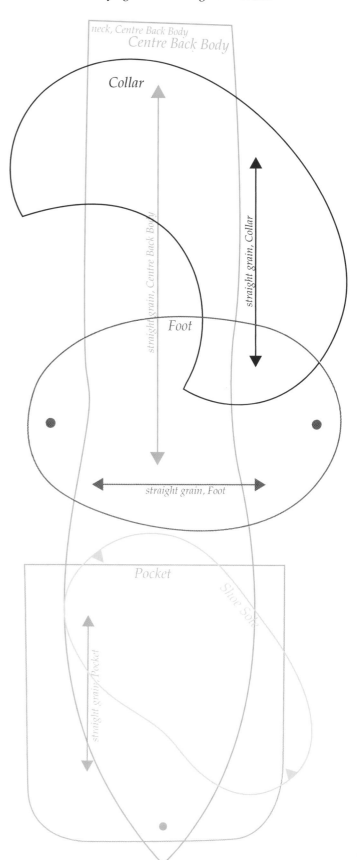

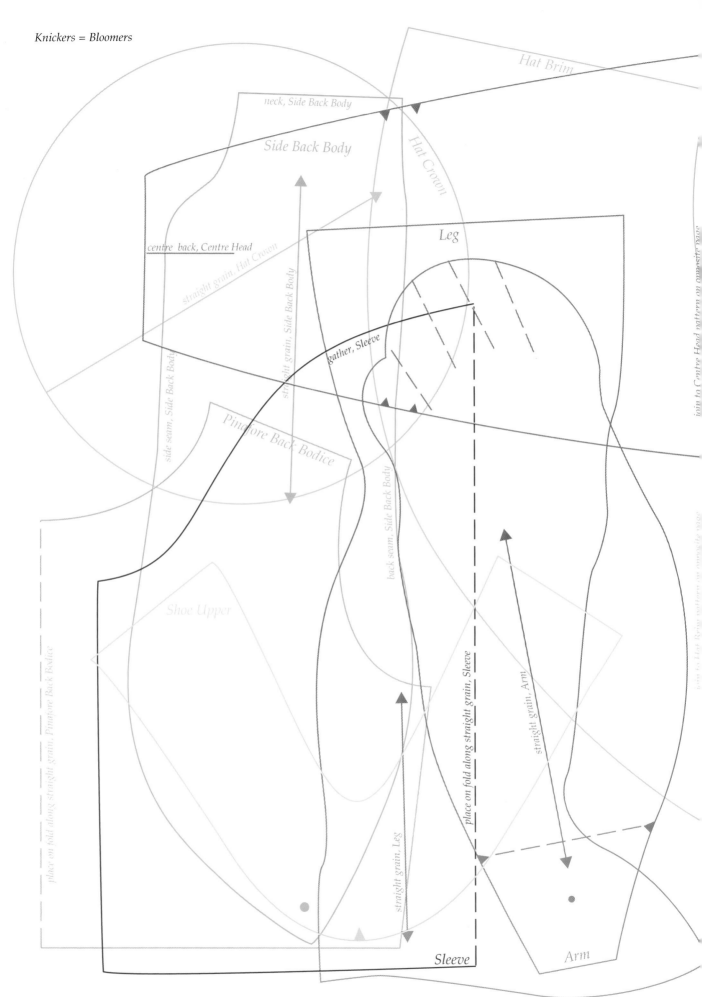

neck, Side Back Body

Hat Brim

Side Back Body

Hat Crown

Leg

centre back, Centre Head

straight grain, Hat Crown

straight grain, Side Back Body

gather, Sleeve

side seam, Side Back Body

Pinafore Back Bodice

back seam, Side Back Body

Shoe Upper

place on fold along straight grain, Pinafore Back Bodice

straight grain, Leg

place on fold along straight grain, Sleeve

straight grain, Arm

Sleeve

Arm

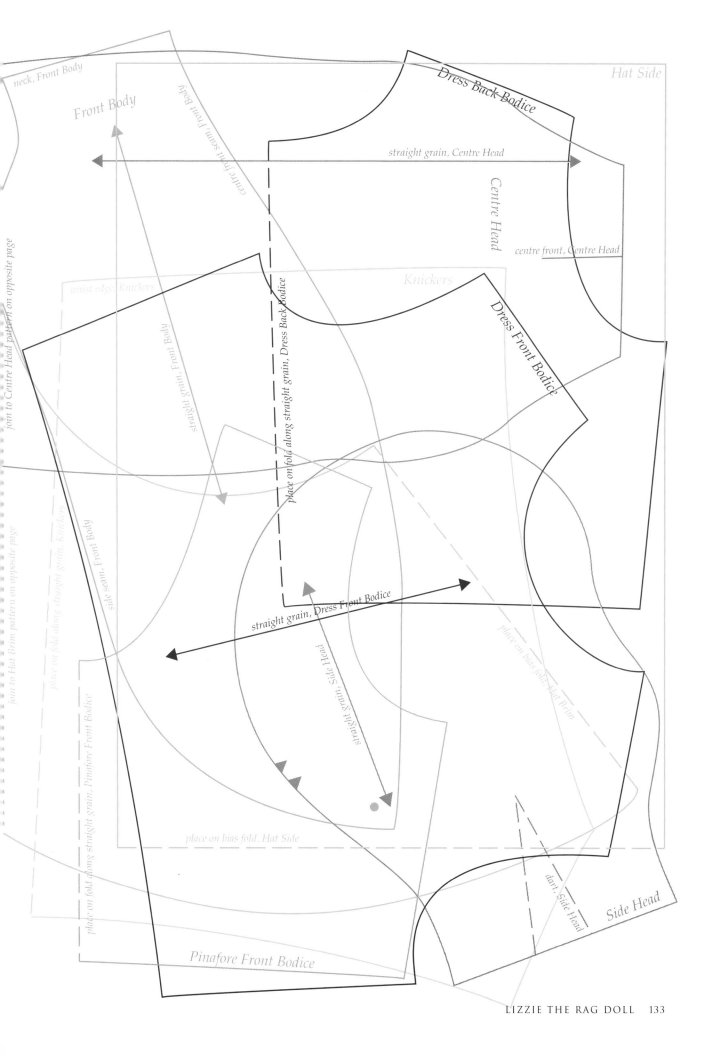

neck, Front Body

Front Body

centre front seam, Front Body

Dress Back Bodice

Hat Side

straight grain, Centre Head

Centre Head

centre front, Centre Head

join to Centre Head pattern on opposite page

waist edge, Knickers

Knickers

Dress Front Bodice

place on fold along straight grain, Dress Back Bodice

straight grain, Front Body

join to Hat Brim pattern on opposite page

place on fold along straight grain, Knickers

side seam, Front Body

straight grain, Dress Front Bodice

straight grain, Side Head

place on bias fold, Hat Brim

place on fold along straight grain, Pinafore Front Bodice

place on bias fold, Hat Side

dart, Side Head

Side Head

Pinafore Front Bodice

KNITTING AND CROCHET

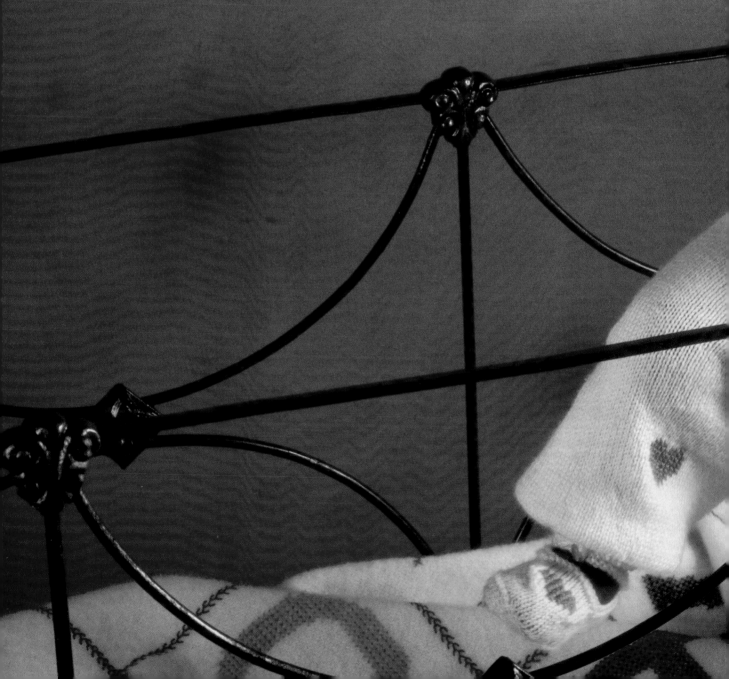

JUST FOR FUN KIDS KNITS

T*ake three children, a collection of wonderful picture knits and a sunny day at the park and the result, as you can see on these pages, is enchanting. This is a series of pullovers that youngsters will adore — and moms and grannies will love to knit.*

Basic Instructions

Follow instructions for Basic Pullover Pattern 1 or 2 in conjunction with the directions for the variation you have chosen. When working motifs from graphs, use the wool-wind method (page 140) to knit them in as you go along, or embroider them afterwards using duplicate stitch (page 141). We suggest that the best results may be achieved by knitting-in any large areas, then embroidering the smaller, more intricate areas on completion. Work the duplicate stitch embroidery before pressing or sewing your garment.

Basic Pullover Pattern 1 knits designed by Coats Patons
Photography by Scott Cameron
Styling by Mary-Anne Danaher
Where's Spot? pullover designed and knitted by Helen Fowler
Photography for Where's Spot? by Catherine Muscat

Basic Pullover Pattern 1

MEASUREMENTS

To fit size: A (**B**, C, **D**, E). Fits age: 1 (**2**, 3, **4**, 5) years. Fits underarm: $20^3/4''$ (**$21^3/4''$**, $22^3/4''$, **$24^3/4''$**, $24^3/4''$). Garment measures (approximately): $24^1/2''$ (**$26''$**, $27''$, **$28^3/4''$**, $30^1/2''$). Length (approximately): $15^3/4''$ (**$16^1/2''$**, $17^1/2''$, **$18^1/4''$**, $19''$). Sleeve seam (approximately): $8^1/4''$ (**$9''$**, $10''$, **$11''$**, $12''$).

MATERIALS

- Fingering, baby, or sportweight knitting yarn to give gauge (see **Note**, below)
- One pair U.S. No. 5 or English No. 8 (4.0mm) knitting needles
- One set U.S. No. 3 or English No. 10 (3.25mm) knitting needles
- Three holders
- Two buttons
- Yarn needle, for sewing seams and embroidery

Note: *We used Patons. See individual patterns for yarn types, colors and amounts. If using a different yarn, knit a pattern swatch before starting garment.*

STITCH GAUGE

See **Knitting and Crochet Notes** on page 173.
22.5 sts and 30 rows = 4 inches st st, using U.S. No. 5 or English No. 8 (4.0mm) needles and the specified yarn.

GRAPHS

All graphs are printed on pages 146–157.

PATTERN

Back Using No. 5 or No. 8 (4.0mm) needles, cast on 70 (**74**, 78, **82**, 86) sts.

Row 1. K2, *P2, K2; rep from * across.

Row 2. P2, *K2, P2; rep from * across.

Rep Rows 1 and 2 5 (**5**, 6, **7**, 7) times, inc 2 sts evenly across last row...72 (**76**, 80, **84**, 88) sts, 12 (**12**, 14, **16**, 16) rows ribbing.

Work 66 (**70**, 70, **72**, 76) rows st st.

Tie a colored thread at each end of last row to mark beg of armholes as there is no armhole shaping.**

Work 36 (**40**, 42, **46**, 48) more rows.

Divide for Back opening. Row 1. K36 (**38**, 40, **42**, 44), *turn* and cont in patt.

Row 2. K2, purl across.

Row 3. Knit.

Row 4. Repeat Row 2.

Shape shoulder. ***Cont in garter st patt for border, cast off 6 (**6**, 7, **7**, 8) sts at beg of next and foll alt rows 3 times. Work one row.

Cast off 6 (**7**, 6, **7**, 6) sts at beg of next row.***

Work one row.

Leave rem 12 (**13**, 13, **14**, 14) sts on a holder.

With right side facing, join yarn to rem 36 (**38**, 40, **42**, 44) sts and knit across.

Row 2. Purl to last 2 sts, K2.

Row 3. Knit.

Rep Rows 2 and 3 once.

Shape shoulder. Work as from *** to ***. Leave rem 12 (**13**, 13, **14**, 14) sts on a holder.

Front Work as for Back to **.

Work 22 (**24**, 26, **28**, 30) more rows.

Shape neck. Next row. K29 (**31**, 33, **35**, 37), *turn* and work even in patt. Dec one st at neck edge in alt rows until 24 (**25**, 27, **28**, 30) sts rem.

Work 7 rows.

Shape shoulder. Cast off 6 (**6**, 7, **7**, 8) sts at beg of next and every other row 3 times.

Work one row.

Cast off rem 6 (**7**, 6, **7**, 6) sts.

With right side facing, slip next 14 sts on a holder and set aside. Join yarn to rem 29 (**31**, 33, **35**, 37) sts and knit across. Complete to correspond with other side of neck, reversing shaping.

Sleeves Using No. 5 or No. 8 (4.0mm) needles, cast on 42 (**46**, 46, **50**, 50) sts.

Work 25 (**25**, 29, **33**, 33) rows ribbing as for Back.

Working in st st (beg with a knit row), inc one st at each end of 5th and foll alt (**4th**, alt, **4th**, **4th**) row/s until there are 46 (**60**, 50, **70**, 72) sts, then in foll 4th (**6th**, 4th, **6th**, 6th) rows until there are 60 (**64**, 70, **74**, 78) sts.

Work 15 rows.

Cast off loosely.

Neckband Using backstitch, join shoulder seams. With right side facing and using set of No. 3 or No. 10 (3.75mm) needles, knit 78 (**86**, 86, **90**, 90) sts evenly around neck, incl sts from holders.

Note. Work in rows not rnds.

Work 9 rows rib as for Back, beg with Row 2.

Work 10 rows st st.

Cast off loosely as to k, or knitwise.

To assemble With a slightly damp cloth and warm iron, press Patons Totem 8-ply or Patons Fireside 8-ply lightly. Do not press Patons Supersaver 8-ply or Patons Neon 8-ply.

Using backstitch, sew in Sleeves evenly between colored threads, placing center of Sleeves to shoulder seams. Join side and Sleeve seams, noting to reverse seam on Sleeves for three-quarters of ribbing for cuffs. Turn back cuffs. Make two buttonloops and attach to top of Back opening in first and last row of ribbing on Neckband. Sew on buttons. Press seams.

Wool-wind Method

This is the simplest method of knitting-in motifs. It must not be interchanged with Fair Isle. When changing colors in the middle of a row, twist color to be used (on wrong side) underneath and to right of the color, giving a gentle tug to even up loose stitches. Use a separate quantity of yarn for each section of color. To minimize tangles, wind small amounts of yarn onto yarn bobbins. Unwind only enough yarn to knit required stitches, keeping bobbin close to work.

For ease of reading, enlarge graph by photocopying. Color each section of graph in color to be used.

When working from graphs, knit all sts on right-side rows, reading graphs from right to left, and purl all sts on wrong-side rows, reading graphs from left to right.

Duplicate Stitch

Duplicate, or knitting, stitch is worked over each knitted stitch using yarn of same thickness as knitted garment but in contrasting color. Do not pull stitch too tightly, and it will cover existing stitch. Finished stitch looks like a "V". Each square on graph represents one stitch. For ease of reading, enlarge graph on photocopier and color in each section in color to be used.

Begin at lower edge of graph, on righthand side. Using tapestry or yarn needle, bring needle from back through center of stitch below one to be covered.

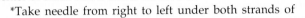

*Take needle from right to left under both strands of stitch above one to be covered. Bring needle back to start of stitch, take needle behind two strands in row below and across into center of next stitch. You have worked one duplicate stitch.

Repeat from * following graph for required number of stitches. To finish, bring needle back to the start of the stitch and through to the back of the work.

To begin second row, bring needle from back to center of stitch below one to be covered. Working from left to right, pick up both strands of stitch in row above one to be covered. Take needle back to beginning of stitch, pick up two strands, which brings needle across into center of next stitch. When working stitch above one worked in previous row, needle will come up in center of this worked stitch. Repeat this, following graph for number of stitches to be worked.

Basic Pullover Pattern 2

MEASUREMENTS

To fit size: A (**B**, C, **D**, E). Fits age: 1 (**2**, 3, **4**, 5) years. Fits underarm: $20^3/_4''$ (**$21^3/_4''$**, $22^3/_4''$, **$24^3/_4''$**, $24^3/_4''$). Garment measures: $23^1/_2''$ (**$24^3/_4''$**, 26", **$27^3/_4''$**, 29"). Length : $14^1/_4''$ (**15"**, $15^3/_4''$, **$16^1/_2''$**, $17^1/_2''$). Sleeve seam: $8^1/_4''$ (**9"**, 10", **11"**, 12").

MATERIALS

- Fingering, baby or sportweight knitting yarn to give gauge (see **Note**, below)

- One pair U.S. No. 5 or English No. 8 (4.0mm) knitting needles

- One set U.S. No. 3 or English No. 10 (3.75mm) knitting needles

- Two holders

- Yarn needle, for sewing seams and embroidery

Note: *We used Patons 8-ply Totem. If using a different yarn, knit a pattern swatch before starting garment.*

TENSION

See **Knitting and Crochet Notes** on page 173.
22.5 sts and 30 rows = 4 inches st st, using U.S. No. 5 or English No. 8 (4.0mm) needles.

PATTERN

Back Using No. 3 or No. 10 (3.75mm) needles, cast on 69 (**73**, 77, **81**, 85) sts.
Row 1. K2, *P1, K1; rep from * to last st, K1.
Row 2. K1, *P1, K1; rep from * across.
Rep Rows 1 and 2 4 (**4**, 5, **6**, 6) times...10 (**10**, 12, **14**, 14) rows ribbing.
Change to No. 5 or No. 8 (4.0mm) needles.
Work 56 (**60**, 62, **64**, 68) rows st st.
Tie a colored thread at each end of last row to mark beg of armholes, as there is no armhole shaping.**

Work 40 (**42**, 44, **46**, 48) more rows st st.
Shape shoulders. Cont in st st, cast off 5 sts loosely at beg of next 8 rows, then 3 (**4**, 5, **6**, 7) sts at beg of foll 2 rows. Leave rem 23 (**25**, 27, **29**, 31) sts on a holder.

Front Work as for Back to **.
Work 24 (**24**, 26, **28**, 30) more rows st st.
Shape neck. Next row. K29 (**31**, 32, **33**, 34), *turn.*
Work even in patt 29 (**31**, 32, **33**, 34) sts, dec one st at neck edge in alt rows until 23 (**24**, 25, **26**, 27) sts rem. Work 3 rows st st.
Shape shoulder. Cont in st st, cast off 5 sts loosely at beg of next row and foll alt rows 4 times.
Work one row.
Cast off rem 3 (**4**, 5, **6**, 7) sts.
With right side facing, st next 11 (**11**, 13, **15**, 17) sts on a holder and set aside. Join yarn to rem 29 (**31**, 32, **33**, 34) sts and work to correspond with side just completed, reversing shaping.

Sleeves Using No. 3 or No. 10 (3.75mm) needles, cast on 35 (**35**, 37, **39**, 41) sts.
Work 10 (**10**, 12, **14**, 14) rows ribbing as for Back, inc 6 (**8**, 8, **8**, 8) sts evenly across last row...41 (**43**, 45, **47**, 49) sts.
Change to No. 5 or No. 8 (4.0mm) needles.
Cont in st st, inc one st at each end of 5th and foll 6th rows until there are 53 (**57**, 59, **63**, 67) sts. Work 13 (**13**, 15, **17**, 17) rows st st. Cast off very loosely.

Neckband Using backstitch, join right shoulder seam. With right side facing and using No. 3 or No. 10 (3.75mm) needles, knit 83 (**89**, 93, **97**, 101) sts evenly around neck, incl sts from holders.
Work 9 rows ribbing as for Back, beg with a Row 2.
Cast off loosely in ribbing.

To assemble With damp cloth and warm iron, press lightly. Using backstitch, join left shoulder and Neckband seam (if desired, for smaller sizes, leave an opening and fasten with buttons and loops). Join Sleeves and side seams to colored threads. Sew in Sleeves. Press seams.

Miffy

MATERIALS

Fingering, baby, or sportweight knitting yarn to give gauge (100g) (we used Patons Supersaver):

- Main Color (M — blue): 2 (**2**, 3, **3**, 4) balls
- One ball each of 4 contrasting colors (C1 — white, C2 — yellow, C3 — orange, C4 — black)

DIRECTIONS

Foll Basic Pullover Patt 1 (page 136), working garment in M throughout and working Front from Graph 1 on page 146.

© Yoram Gross
Film Studio Pty Limited

Toy Train

MATERIALS

Fingering, baby, or sportweight knitting yarn to give gauge (50g) (we used Patons Totem):

- Main Color (M — light grey): 5 (**5**, 6, **6**, 7) balls
- Contrasting Color 1 (C1 — dark grey): 2 (**2**, 2, **3**, 3) balls
- One ball each of 5 contrasting colors (C2 — red, C3 — yellow, C4 — blue, C5 — black, C6 — white)

DIRECTIONS

Foll Basic Pullover Patt 1 (page 136), noting to work lower bands and first 14 (**18**, 18, **20**, 24) rows of st st in C1 for Back and Front then rem in M, and noting to work train motif to Front from Graph 3 on page 148. Work Sleeve cuffs in C1, then rem of Sleeve in M. Work Neckband in M.

Illustrations Dick Bruna
© Mercis bv, 1953–1999

Blinky Bill

MATERIALS

Fingering, baby, or sportweight knitting yarn to give gauge (50g) (we used Patons Totem):

- Main Color (M — magnolia): 5 (**6**, 6, **7**, 7) balls
- One ball each of 5 contrasting colors (C1 — brown, C2 — red, C3 — gold, C4 — dark brown, C5 — charcoal)

DIRECTIONS

Foll Basic Pullover Patt 1 (page 136), working garment in M throughout and working Front from Graph 2 on page 147.

snowflakes

MATERIALS

Fingering, baby, or sportweight knitting yarn to give gauge (50g) (we used Patons Totem):

- Main Color (M — maroon): 6 (**7**, 7, **8**, 9) balls
- One ball each of 2 contrasting colors (C1 — cream, C2 — natural), for embroidery

DIRECTIONS

Foll Basic Pullover Patt 1 (page 136), working garment in M throughout. Using duplicate stitch and C1 and C2, embroider motifs from Graphs 4a, 4b, 4c and 4d on page 149 at random on Back, Front and Sleeves, as photographed.

Dalmation

MATERIALS

Fingering, baby, or sportweight knitting yarn to give gauge (50g) (we used Patons Neon):

- Main Color (M — red): 4 (**4**, 5, **5**, 6) balls
- Contrasting Color 1 (C1 — black): 2 balls (all sizes)
- Contrasting Color 2 (C2 — white): 1 ball (all sizes)

DIRECTIONS

Foll Basic Pullover Patt 1 (page 136), working all ribbing bands and Neckband in C1 and rem of garment in M, and noting to work Front from Graph 5 on page 150. Using C1 and backstitch, outline Dalmatian, then embroider areas indicated on graph for backstitch.

Lion

MATERIALS

Fingering, baby, or sportweight knitting yarn to give gauge (100g) (we used Patons Supersaver):

- Main Color (M — red): 2 (**2**, 2, **3**, 3) balls
- One ball each of 2 contrasting colors (C1 — yellow, C2 — dark brown)

DIRECTIONS

Foll Basic Pullover Patt 1 (page 136), working garment in M throughout and working lion motif to Front from Graph 6 on page 151.

seaside

MATERIALS

Fingering, baby, or sportweight knitting yarn to give gauge (50g) (we used Patons Fireside):

- Main Color (M — green): 6 (**7**, 7, **8**, 8) balls
- One ball each of 4 contrasting colors (C1 — yellow, C2 — blue, C3 — red, C4 — white)

DIRECTIONS

Foll Basic Pullover Patt 1 (page 136), working garment in M throughout. Using duplicate stitch and colors as indicated on key, embroider design from Graph 7 on page 152 to Front, then embroider a C1 fish and a starfish to each Sleeve, as photographed.

Barnyard Patches

MATERIALS

Fingering, baby, or sportweight knitting yarn to give gauge (50g) (we used Patons Totem):

- Main Color (M — cream): 6 (**6**, 7, **7**, 8) balls
- One ball each of 4 contrasting colors (C1 — blue, C2 — burgundy, C3 — camel, C4 — olive)

DIRECTIONS

Foll Basic Pullover Patt 1 (page 136), working garment in M throughout and working Front from Graph 8 on page 153. Using C3, work French knots for cow's eyes, then outline cow's ear in backstitch, as photographed.

BABAR

MATERIALS

Fingering, baby, or sportweight knitting yarn to give gauge (100g) (we used Patons Supersaver):

- Main Color (M — orange): 2 (**2**, 3, **3**, 4) balls
- One ball each of 2 contrasting colors (C1 — green, C2 — grey)
- One skein each of 4 contrasting colors of Anchor Tapisserie Wool (C3 — black, C4 — white, C5 — yellow, C6 — red)

DIRECTIONS

Foll Basic Pullover Patt 1 (page 136), working garment in M throughout and working Front from Graph 9 on page 154.

Teddy Bears

MATERIALS

Fingering, baby, or sportweight knitting yarn to give gauge (50g) (we used Patons Totem):

- Main Color (M — rose): 6 (**6**, 7, **7**, 8) balls
- One ball each of 8 contrasting colors (C1 — brown, C2 — beige, C3 — pink, C4 — maroon, C5 — blue, C6 — navy, C7 — cream, C8 — black)

DIRECTIONS

Foll Basic Pullover Patt 1 (page 136), working garment in M throughout and working Front from Graph 10 on page 155. Using C8 and satin stitch, embroider eyes and noses to bears, as photographed. Remaining details are worked in stem stitch, using colors as photographed.

Rocket ship

MATERIALS

Fingering, baby, or sportweight knitting yarn to give gauge (50g) (we used Patons Neon):

- Main Color (M — black): 5 (**5**, 6, **6**, 7) balls
- One ball each of 4 contrasting colors (C1 — white, C2 — yellow, C3 — red, C4 — blue)

DIRECTIONS

Foll Basic Pullover Patt 1 (page 136), working garment in M throughout and working Front from Graph 11 on page 156.

Where's Spot?

MATERIALS

Fingering, baby, or sportweight knitting yarn to give gauge (50g) (we used Patons Totem):

- Main Color (M — red): 5 (**5**, 6, **6**, 7) balls
- Contrasting Color 1 (C1 — yellow): 1 ball (all sizes)
- One skein each of 2 contrasting colors of Anchor Tapisserie Wool (C2 — black, C3 — brown)

DIRECTIONS

Foll Basic Pullover Patt 2 (page 141), working garment in M throughout. For Front, work 15 (**19**, 21, **23**, 27) rows st st, then work rows 2 to 48 incl from Graph 12 on page 157. Using M for rem, work 18 (**18**, 20, **22**, 24) rows st st, then shape Front neck and complete as for Basic Pullover Patt 2. Embroider features as described on graph.

Where's Spot?
©Eric Hill/Salspot
Limited 1999

Graph 1
Miffy

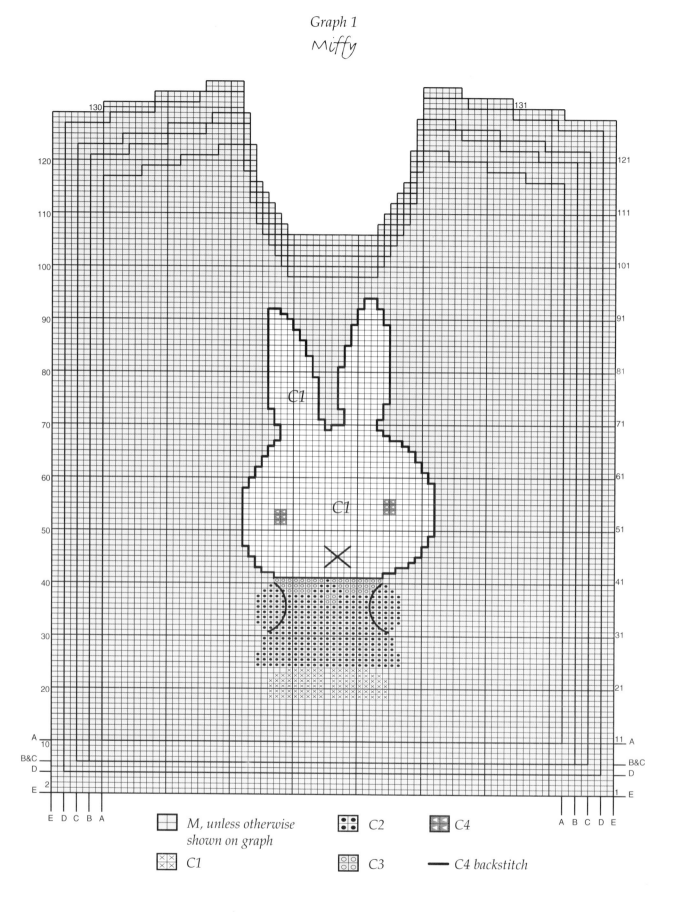

	M, unless otherwise shown on graph		C2		C4
	C1		C3	—	C4 backstitch

Note: *When working from graph, read odd-numbered rows (knit rows) from right to left, and even-numbered rows (purl rows) from left to right. Heavy lines represent changes in color.*

Graph 2
Blinky Bill

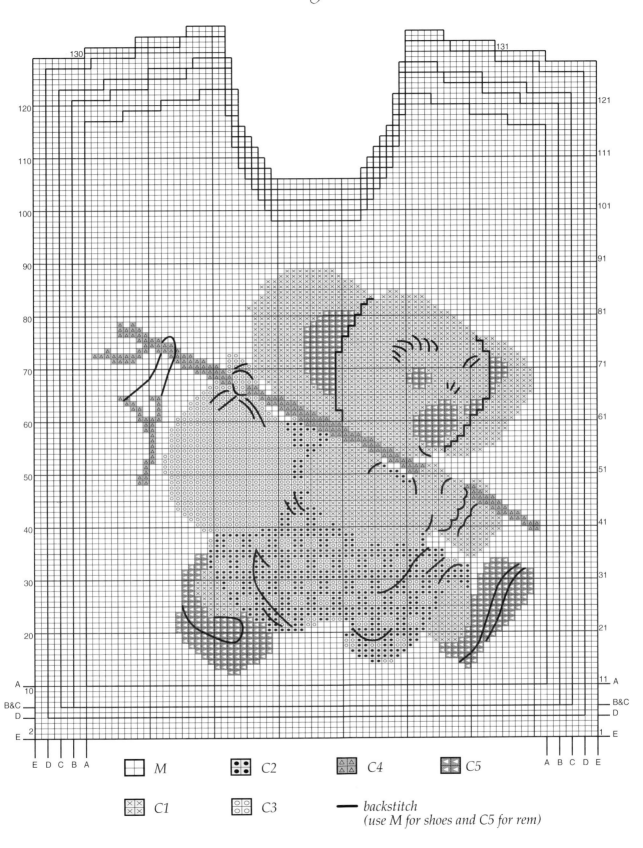

	M		C2		C4		C5
	C1		C3		backstitch (use M for shoes and C5 for rem)		

Note: *When working from graph, read odd-numbered rows (knit rows) from right to left,*
and even-numbered rows (purl rows) from left to right.

Graph 3
Toy Train

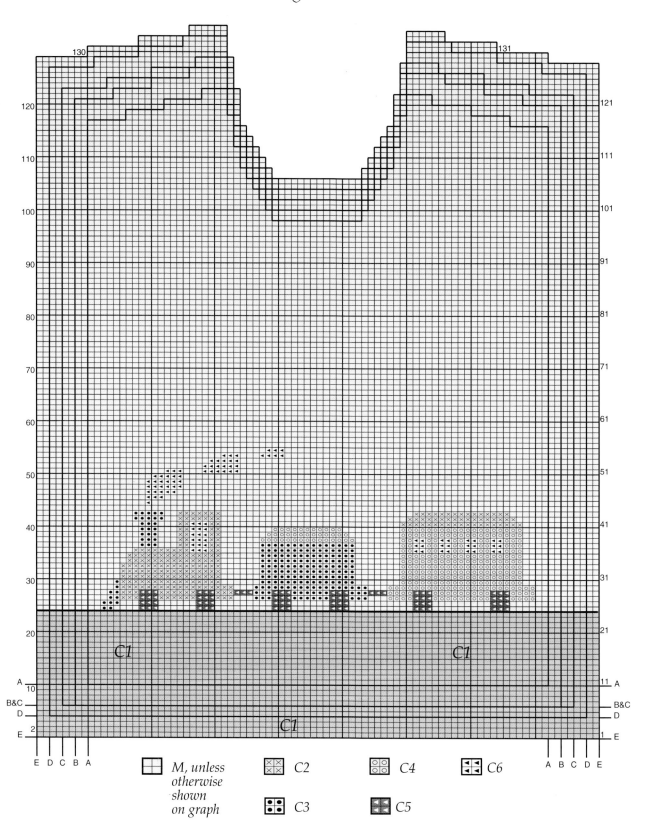

M, unless otherwise shown on graph

C2

C3

C4

C5

C6

Note: *When working from graph, read odd-numbered rows (knit rows) from right to left, and even-numbered rows (purl rows) from left to right. Heavy lines represent changes in color.*

Graph 4
Snowflakes

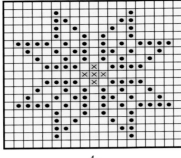

4a

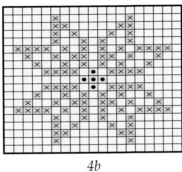

4b

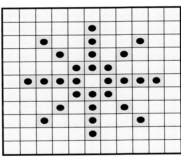

4c

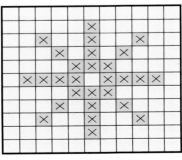

4d

 M   C1 knitting stitch   C2 knitting stitch

Graph 5
Dalmation

Note: *When working from graph, read odd-numbered rows (knit rows) from right to left, and even-numbered rows (purl rows) from left to right. Heavy lines represent changes in color.*

Graph 6
Lion

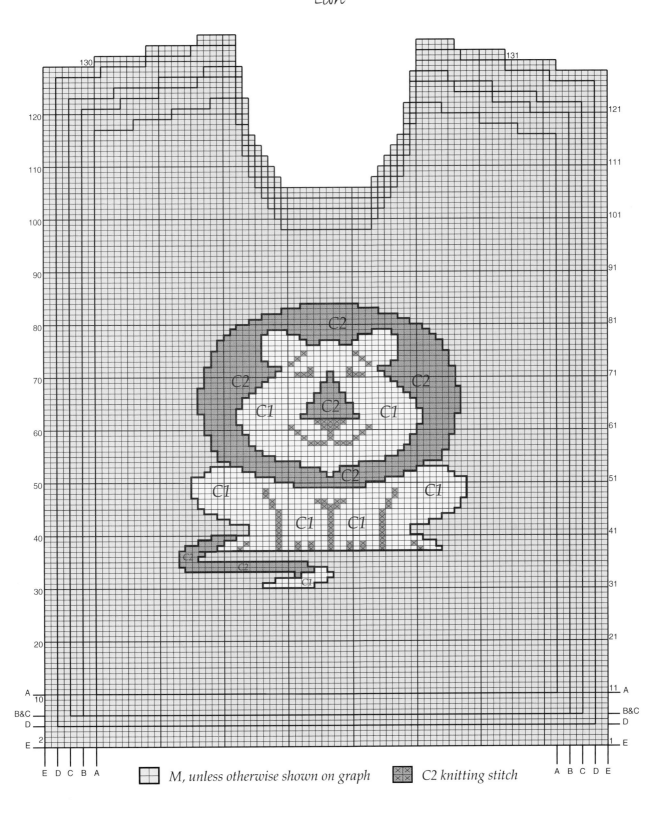

Note: *When working from graph, read odd-numbered rows (knit rows) from right to left, and even-numbered rows (purl rows) from left to right. Heavy lines represent changes in color.*

Graph 7
seaside

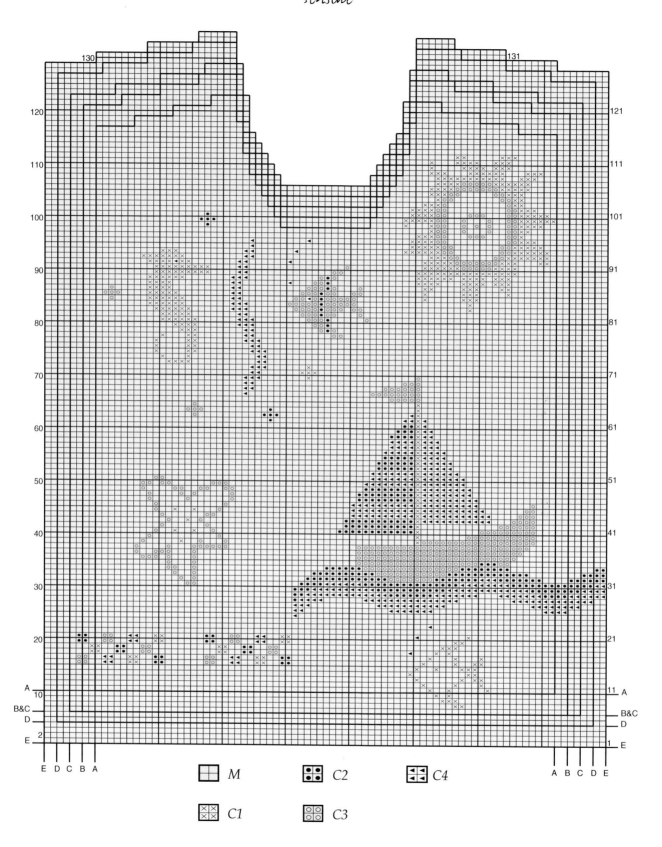

	M			C2			C4
	C1			C3			

Graph 8
Barnyard Patches

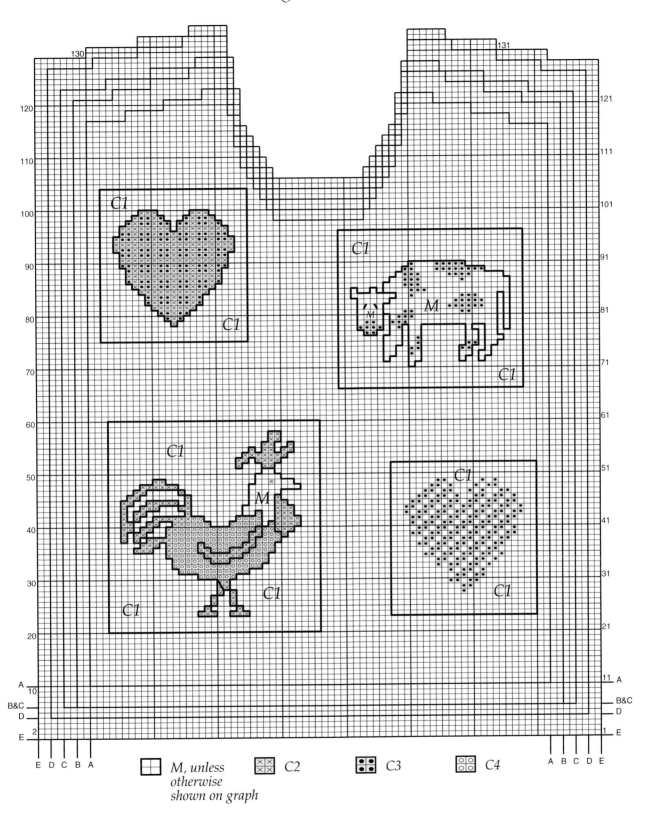

Note: *When working from graph, read odd-numbered rows (knit rows) from right to left, and even-numbered rows (purl rows) from left to right. Heavy lines represent changes in color.*

Graph 9
BABAR

Work eyes and buttons in C3 satin stitch

Note: *When working from graph, read odd-numbered rows (knit rows) from right to left, and even-numbered rows (purl rows) from left to right. Heavy lines represent changes in color.*

Graph 10
Teddy Bears

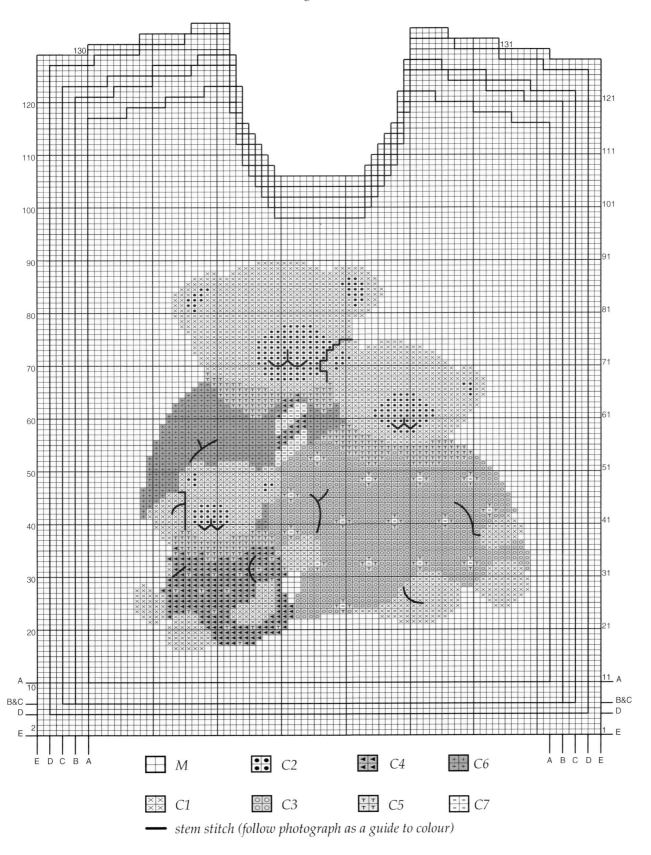

	M		C2		C4		C6
	C1		C3		C5		C7

— *stem stitch (follow photograph as a guide to colour)*

Note: *When working from graph, read odd-numbered rows (knit rows) from right to left,
and even-numbered rows (purl rows) from left to right.*

Graph 11
Rocket ship

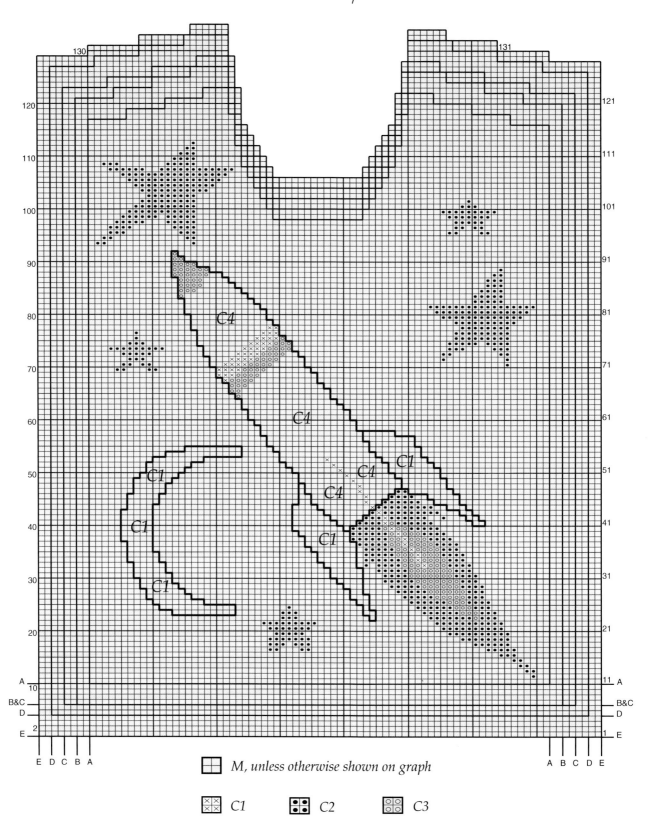

M, unless otherwise shown on graph

C1   C2   C3

Note: *When working from graph, read odd-numbered rows (knit rows) from right to left, and even-numbered rows (purl rows) from left to right. Heavy lines represent changes in color.*

Graph 12
Where's Spot?

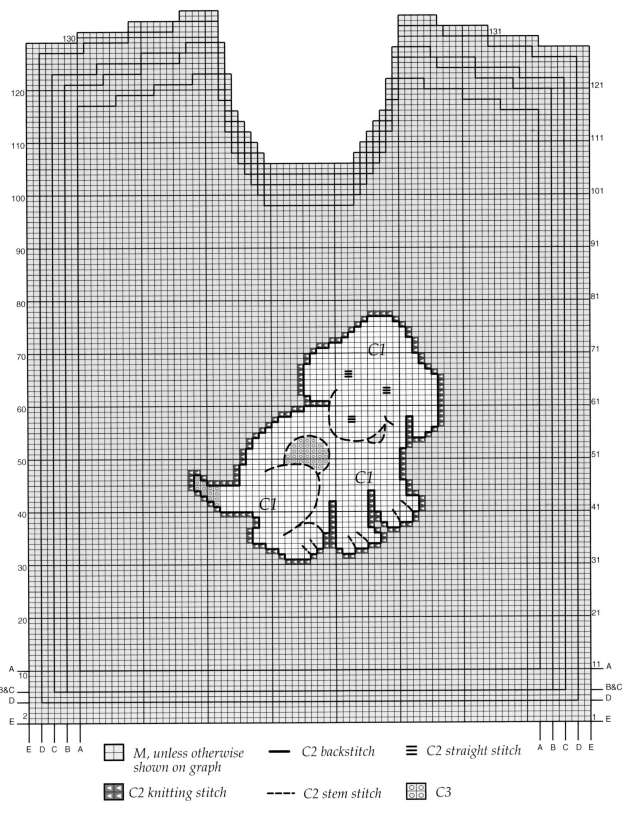

	M, unless otherwise shown on graph	— C2 backstitch	≡ C2 straight stitch
	C2 knitting stitch	---- C2 stem stitch	C3

Embroider tongue in red satin stitch

Note: *When working from graph, read odd-numbered rows (knit rows) from right to left, and even-numbered rows (purl rows) from left to right. Heavy lines represent changes in color.*

A FOR ADORABLE

B *for Baby and C for these Cute knitted clothes for babies from newborn to 12 months. Comprising pullover, pants, bootees and a winsome hat, and decorated with simple cross stitch, this outfit involves no-nonsense knitting that a beginner could manage.*

MEASUREMENTS

To fit age: approximately 3 (**6**, 12) months. **Pullover:** fits underarm $15^3/4''$ (**$17^3/4''$**, $19^3/4''$); garment measures $17^1/2''$ (**$19^3/4''$**, 22″); length $9^1/2''$ (**$10^3/4''$**, $12^1/4''$); sleeve fits 5″ (**$6^1/4''$**, $7^1/2''$), or length desired. **Pants:** length at side (with cuff turned back) approximately $12^3/4''$ (**$14^1/2''$**, $16^1/2''$). **Hat:** fits head $15^3/4''$ (**$17^3/4''$**, 19″). **Bootees:** fit foot $3^1/4''$ (**$3^3/4''$**, $4^1/4''$).

MATERIALS

Fingering, baby, or sportweight knitting yarn to give gauge (25g) (see **Note**):

- Pullover: 4 (**5**, 6) balls
- Pants: 4 (**5**, 6) balls
- Hat: 2 balls (all sizes)
- Bootees: 1 ball (all sizes)
- One pair U.S. No. 1 or English No. 12 (2.75mm) (No 12) knitting needles, for Pullover, Pants and Hat

Outfit designed by Coats Patons
Photography by Joe Filshie
Styling by Georgina Dolling

- One pair U.S. No. 3 or English No. 10 (3.25mm) knitting needles, for Pullover, Pants, Hat and Bootees
- Three holders and three buttons, for Pullover
- Round elastic, for Pants
- Small piece of cardboard, for Hat
- Two buttons, for Bootees
- Two skeins six-strand cotton embroidery floss, for embroidery
- Tapestry or yarn needle, for sewing seams and embroidery

Note: *We used Patons Dreamtime 4-ply. If using a different yarn, knit a pattern swatch before starting garment.*

TENSION

See **Knitting and Crochet Notes** on page 173. 29 sts and 38.5 rows = 4 inches st st, using U.S. No. 3 or English No. 10 (3.25mm) needles.

Pullover

BACK

Using No. 1 or No. 12 (2.75mm) needles, cast on 67 (**75**, 83) sts.
Row 1. K2, *P1, K1; rep from * to last st, K1.
Row 2. K1, *P1, K1; rep from * across.
Rep last 2 rows 4 times...10 rows ribbing in all.
Change to No. 3 or No. 10 (3.25mm) needles.
Work even in st st until work measures 6″ (**$6^3/4''$**, 8″) from beg, ending with a purl row.
Tie a colored thread at each end of last row to mark beg of armholes as there is no armhole shaping.**
Work 6 (**10**, 14) rows st st.

Divide for Back opening. Row 1. K36 (**40**, 44), *turn* and work even.

Row 2. K5, purl across.

Row 3. Knit.

Rep Rows 2 and 3 4 times, then Row 2 once.

Row 13. Knit to last 3 sts, yfwd, K2tog (buttonhole), K1. Rep Rows 2–13 once, then Row 2 once.

Shape shoulder. Working border in garter st, cast off 8 (**9**, 10) sts at beg of next row and foll alt row, then 7 (**8**, 9) sts at beg of foll alt row.

Work one row.

Leave rem 13 (**14**, 15) sts on a holder.

With right side facing, join yarn to rem 31 (**35**, 39) sts, cast on 5 sts for Placket and knit across...36 (**40**, 44) sts.

Row 2. Purl to last 5 sts, K5.

Row 3. Knit.

Rep Rows 2 and 3 12 times.

Shape shoulder. Working border in garter st, cast off 8 (**9**, 10) sts at beg of next row and foll alt row, then 7 (**8**, 9) sts at beg of foll alt row.

Leave rem 13 (**14**, 15) sts on a holder.

FRONT

Work as for Back to **.

Work 18 (**22**, 24) rows st st.

Shape neck. Next row. K28 (**31**, 35), *turn* and work even in patt.

***Dec one st at neck edge in alt rows until 23 (**26**, 29) sts rem.

Work 3 rows.

Shape shoulder. Cast off 8 (**9**, 10) sts at beg of next row and foll alt row.

Work one row.

Cast off rem 7 (**8**, 9) sts.***

With right side facing, sl next 11 (**13**, 13) sts on a holder and set aside. Join yarn to rem 28 (**31**, 35) sts; knit across. Work as from *** to ***, working 4 rows instead of 3 before shoulder shaping.

SLEEVES

Using No. 1 or No. 12 (2.75mm) needles, cast on 41 (**43**, 47) sts.

Work 14 rows ribbing as for Back.

Change to No. 3 or No. 10 (3.25mm) needles.

Work in st st, inc one st at each end of 5th and foll 6th row/s until there are 45 (**51**, 51) sts, then in foll 8th rows until there are 49 (**55**, 61) sts.

Work even in st st until work measures 5" (**6¼"**, 7½") (or length desired) from beg, ending with a purl row.

Cast off.

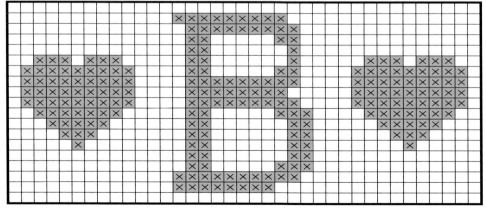

GRAPH A

NECKBAND

Using backstitch, join shoulder seams. With right side facing and using No. 1 or No. 12 (2.75mm) needles, knit 69 (**73**, 79) sts evenly around neck, incl sts from holders.

Row 1. K5, *P1, K1; rep from * to last 4 sts, K4.

Row 2. K6, *P1, K1; rep from * to last 5 sts, K5.

Row 3. Repeat Row 1.

Row 4. K6, rib st to last 5 sts, K2, yfwd, K2tog (buttonhole), K1.

Rep Rows 1 and 2 twice, then Row 1 once.

Cast off loosely in rib st.

TO ASSEMBLE

With a slightly damp cloth and warm iron, press lightly. Using embroidery floss and cross stitch (see **Embroidery Stitch Guide** on page 58), embroider the hearts and letter from Graph A, page 160, to Front (or letter of choice from letters on page 163). Using backstitch, sew in Sleeves evenly between colored threads, placing center of Sleeves to shoulder seams. Join side and Sleeve seams. Sew Placket in position. Sew on buttons. Press seams.

Pants

LEFT LEG

Using No. 1 or No. 12 (2.75mm) needles, cast on 43 (**45**, 49) sts.

Work 28 rows ribbing as for Back of Pullover (Row 1 is right side when Cuff is turned back).

Row 29. Work 2 (**0**, 2) rib st, inc one st in each st to last st, 1 rib st...83 (**89**, 95) sts.

Change to No. 3 or No. 10 (3.25mm) needles.

Cont in st st (beg with a knit row) until work measures 5$\frac{1}{4}$″ (**6$\frac{3}{4}$″**, 8$\frac{1}{2}$″) from center row of ribbing, ending with a purl row.

Shape crotch. Cast on 2 (**3**, 4) sts at beg of next 2 rows...87 (**95**, 103) sts.

Dec one st at each end of 5th and foll 8th rows until 73 (**79**, 87) sts rem.**

Work 5 (**1**, 5) row/s.

Shape Back. Note. Before *turning*, take yarn under needle to right side of work, sl next st onto righthand needle, take yarn under needle to wrong side of work, sl st back onto lefthand needle, then *turn* and proceed as instructed (this avoids leaving holes in work).

Row 1. K42 (**48**, 54), *turn.*

Row 2 and all even rows. Purl across.

Row 3. K35 (**40**, 45), *turn.*

Row 5. K28 (**32**, 36), *turn.*

Row 7. K21 (**24**, 27), *turn.*

Row 9. K14 (**16**, 18), *turn.*

Row 10. Purl across.

Change to No. 1 or No. 12 (2.75mm) needles.

Work even 14 rows ribbing as before.

Cast off loosely in rib st.

RIGHT LEG

Work as for Left Leg to **.

Work 4 (**0**, 4) rows.

Shape Back. Work Rows 1–10 as for Left Leg, working purl for knit and knit for purl throughout.

Next row. Purl across.

Change to No. 1 or No. 12 (2.75mm) needles.

Work 14 rows ribbing as before.

Cast off loosely in rib st.

TO MAKE UP

With a slightly damp cloth and warm iron, press lightly. Using embroidery floss and cross stitch, embroider one heart from Graph A, page 160, to each knee of Pants as photographed. Using backstitch, join front, back and Leg seams, reversing seam for first 18 rows of ribbing on leg for Cuff. With wrong side facing, thread round elastic through Rows 2, 7 and 12 of ribbing at waist and draw up to desired measurement. Turn up Cuffs. Press seams.

Hat
(make 2 pieces)

Using No. 1 or No. 12 (2.75mm) needles, cast on 61
(**67**, 73) sts.
Work 12 rows ribbing as for Back of Pullover.
Change to No. 3 or No. 10 (3.25mm) needles.
Cont in st st until work measures 5¹/₂″ (**6¹/₄″**, 7″) from
beg, ending with a purl row.
Cast off.

TO ASSEMBLE

With a slightly damp cloth and warm iron, press lightly.
Using embroidery floss and cross stitch, embroider
three hearts from Graph A, page 160, to front of Hat as
photographed. Using backstitch, join side and crown
seams. Press seams. Using a 1″-diameter circle of
cardboard with a ¹/₂″ hole, make two pompoms and
attach to corners of Hat.

Bootees
(beg at sole)

Using No. 3 or No. 10 (3.25mm) needles, cast on 31
(**39**, 47) sts.
Row 1 and odd-numbered rows (wrong side). Knit.
Row 2. *Inc one st in next st, K13 (**17**, 21), inc one st in
next st, rep from * once, K1.
Row 4. *Inc one st in next st, K15 (**19**, 23), inc one st in
next st, rep from * once, K1.
Row 6. *Inc one st in next st, K17 (**21**, 25), inc one st in
next st, rep from * once, K1.
Row 8. *Inc one st in next st, K19 (**23**, 27), inc one st in
next st, rep from * once, K1.
Row 10. *Inc one st in next st, K21 (**25**, 29), inc one st in
next st, rep from * once, K1...51 (**59**, 67) sts.
Row 12. Knit.
Row 13. K1, purl to last st, K1.
Rep Rows 12 and 13 2 (**3**, 4) times.

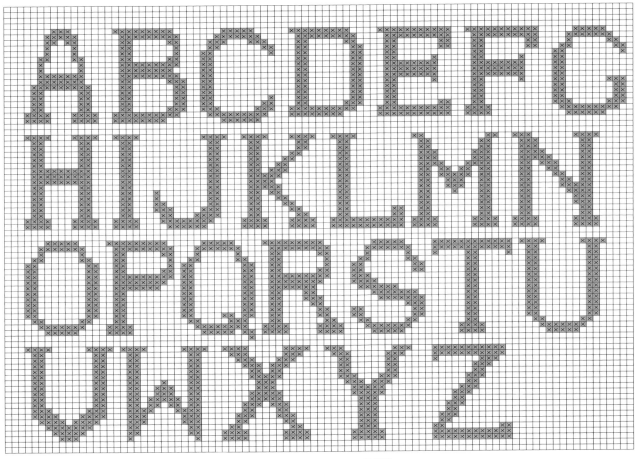

ALPHABET FOR BABY KNITS

Shape instep. When *turning*, foll instructions given in Left Leg of Pants **"Shape Back. Note"**, on page 161.

Row 1. K28 (**32**, 36), 1 sl as to k, or knitwise, K1, psso, K1, *turn*.

Row 2. P7, P2tog, P1, *turn*.

Row 3. K8, sl 1, K1, psso, K1, *turn*.

Row 4. P9, P2tog, P1, *turn*.

Row 5. K10, sl 1, K1, psso, *turn*.

Row 6. P10, P2tog, *turn*.

Rep Rows 5 and 6 2 (**3**, 4) times.

Next row. Knit across...41 (**47**, 53) sts.

Next row. Knit across.

Next row. K14 (**17**, 20), K2tog, K9, sl 1, K1, psso, K14 (**17**, 20).

Cast off loosely as to k, or knitwise.

STRAP

Using No. 3 or No. 10 (3.25mm) needles, cast on 35 (**38**, 41) sts.

Row 1 (wrong side). Knit.

Row 2. K2, yfwd, K2tog (buttonhole), knit across.

Cast off loosely as to k, or knitwise.

TO MAKE UP

With a slightly damp cloth and warm iron, press lightly. Using embroidery floss and cross stitch, embroider a heart from Graph B, on this page, to front of each Bootee

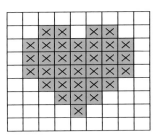

GRAPH B

as photographed. Using a flat seam, join leg and foot seams. Sew center of Strap to back of Bootee for $^3/_4$ inch each side of seam (taking care to reverse Strap on second Bootee so that buttonhole is at other end). Sew on buttons. Press seams.

CROCHETED MEDALLION AFGHAN

H*ere's a new version of an old favorite, created in a palette of subtly toning colors.*

MEASUREMENTS
Finished afghan measures approximately 47" x 59".

MATERIALS
Fingering, baby, or sportweight knitting yarn to give gauge (50g) (see **Note**, below):

- Main Color (M — white): 24 balls
- Contrasting Color 1 (C1 — olive green): 4 balls
- Contrasting Color 2 (C2 — lilac): 2 balls
- Contrasting Color 3 (C3 — light olive green): 3 balls
- Contrasting Color 4 (C4 — pale blue): 2 balls
- Contrasting Color 5 (C5 — plum pink): 3 balls
- Contrasting Color 6 (C6 — mauve-pink): 2 balls
- Contrasting Color 7 (C7 — gold): 2 balls
- Contrasting Color 8 (C8 — blue): 2 balls
- Contrasting Color 9 (C9 — aqua): 3 balls
- One U.S. F/5 or English No. 8 (4.0mm) crochet hook
- Yarn needle, for sewing seams

Note: *We used Cleckheaton Country 8-ply. If using a different yarn, crochet a pattern swatch before starting afghan.*

STITCH GAUGE
See **Knitting and Crochet Notes** on page 173.
One motif measures 4$\frac{1}{2}$ inches across, using U.S. F/5 or English No. 8 (4.0mm) hook.

Photography by Andrew Elton
Styling by Lisa Hilton

SPECIAL ABBREVIATIONS
Cl2: Cluster 2 (work 2tr, leaving last loop of each tr on hook, yo, and draw yarn through all 3 lps on hook).
Cl3: Cluster 3 (work 3tr, leaving last loop of each tr on hook, yo, and draw yarn through all 4 lps on hook).
htr Cluster: work 2htr into corner, leaving last loop of each htr on hook, yo, and draw yarn through all 3 lps on hook.

MOTIFS

C1 Motif (make 18) Using hook and M, ch4, join with a sl st to form a ring.
Round 1: Ch3, Cl2 into ring, (ch3, Cl3) 5 times into ring, ch1, 1tr in top of Cl2. Fasten off.
Round 2: Join C1 with a sl st in tr from last round, ch3, Cl2 in tr, *ch3, (Cl3, ch3, Cl3) in next ch3 space, rep from * 4 times, ch3, (Cl3, ch1) in tr at end of last round, 1tr in top of ch3 at beg of round.
Round 3: Ch3, Cl2 in last tr from last round, *ch3, (Cl3, ch3, Cl3) in next ch3 space, ch3, Cl3 in next ch3 space, rep from * 4 times, ch3, (Cl3, ch3, Cl3) in next ch3 sp, ch1, 1tr in top of ch3 at beg of round. Fasten off.
Round 4: Join M with a sl st in last tr from last round, ch3, 1tr in tr, 3tr in next ch3 space, *(3tr, ch2, 3tr) in next ch3 space, (3tr in next ch3 space) twice, rep from * 4 times, (3tr, ch2, 3tr) in next ch3 space, 1tr in tr at end of last round.
Round 5: Sl st into 3rd ch at beg of last round, 1dc into each st across, sl st into 1st dc at beg, fasten off.

C2 Motif (make 18) Rep same rounds as C1 Motif, using C2 instead of C1.

C3 Motif (make 22) Rep same rounds as C1 Motif, using C3 instead of C1.

C4 Motif (make 18) Rep same rounds as C1 Motif, using C4 instead of C1.

C5 Motif (make 23) Rep same rounds as C1 Motif, using C5 instead of C1.

C6 Motif (make 18) Rep same rounds as C1 Motif, using C6 instead of C1.

C7 Motif (make 18) Rep same rounds as C1 Motif, using C7 instead of C1.

C8 Motif (make 18) Rep same rounds as C1 Motif, using C8 instead of C1.

C9 Motif (make 23) Rep same rounds as C1 Motif, using C9 instead of C1.

TO ASSEMBLE

Refer to diagram below, and join motifs as illustrated, using yarn needle.

Using hook and C1, work 1 row tr evenly around edge of afghan, dec as necessary to keep work flat and working 1tr, ch2, 1tr into each outer corner of motifs and "htr Cluster" into each inner corner of motifs.

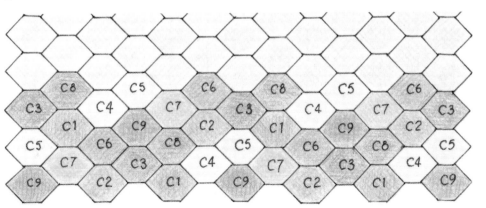

Rep these 3 rows for patt

CHECK IT OUT

You don't have to be Scottish to fall for these terrific crocheted plaid afghans! Both the Stewart and the Black Watch plaids combine simple crochet and weaving — a technique that a beginner could master — resulting in practical car blankets that are wonderfully light and warm.

Black Watch Plaid Afghan

MEASUREMENTS
Finished afghan measures approximately 51" square.

MATERIALS
Sportweight or worsted weight acrylic yarn to give gauge (100g) (see **Note**, below):

- 4 balls each black and royal blue, 3 balls dark green
- One U.S. F/5 or English No. 8 (4.0mm) and one U.S. I/9 or English No. 5 (5.5mm) crochet hook
- Yarn needle

Note: *Whichever yarn you choose, crochet a pattern swatch before starting afghan.*

STITCH GAUGE
See **Knitting and Crochet Notes** on page 173.
18.5 sts and 9 rows = 4 inches, using F/5 or No. 8 (4.0mm) hook.

Afghans designed and crocheted by Kath Baker
Photography by Andre Martin
Styling by Lisa Hilton

ABBREVIATIONS
See **Knitting and Crochet Notes** on page 173.

AFGHAN
Foundation row. Using blue yarn and F/5 or No. 8 (4.0mm) hook, ch246 loosely.
Row 1. Skip 5ch, 1tr in 6th ch from hook, *ch1, skip 1ch, 1tr in next ch; rep from * across...121 spaces.
Row 2. Ch4, *1tr in next tr, ch1; rep from * across, 1tr in 2nd turning ch.

Rep last row to make a total **5 rows blue, 1 row black, 1 row blue, 1 row black, 1 row blue, 4 rows black, 4 rows green, 1 row black, 4 rows green, 4 rows black, 4 rows blue, 1 row black, 1 row blue, 1 row black, 4 rows blue, 4 rows black, 4 rows green, 1 row black, 4 rows green, 4 rows black, 1 row blue, 1 row black, 1 row blue, 1 row black.**
Rep from ** to ** twice, then work 5 rows blue...121 rows. Fasten off (**Pic 1**).

WEAVING
Work lengths of ch the length of afghan, leaving 3 inches of yarn at each end for weaving in. Chain should be long enough to weave through spaces without being too tight.

Work chains as follows: 48 black, 41 blue, 32 green.
Thread chain from top to bottom of afghan, beg at side edge (**Pics 2 & 3**) and securing at each end as follows: 5 rows blue, 1 row black, 1 row blue, 1 row black, 1 row blue, 4 rows black, 4 rows green, 1 row black, 4 rows green, 4 rows black, 4 rows blue, 1 row black, 1 row blue, 1 row black, 4 rows blue, 4 rows black, 4 rows green, 1 row black, 4 rows green, 4 rows black, 1 row blue, 1 row black, 1 row blue, 1 row black;

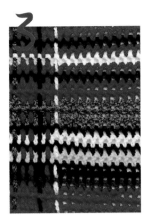

rep twice more, ending with 5 rows blue...all spaces filled. With yarn needle, weave all ends and trim neatly.

EDGING

Using blue yarn and I/9 or No. 5 (5.5mm) hook, work 1 rnd dc, then 1 rnd crab st evenly around afghan, working extra sts in each corner. Fasten off.

S.tewart Plaid Afghan

MEASUREMENTS

Finished afghan measures approximately 47" square.

MATERIALS

Sportweight or worsted weight acrylic yarn to give gauge (100g) (see **Note**, below):

- 4 balls red, 3 balls black, 2 balls dark green, 1 ball each royal blue, white and yellow

- One U.S. F/5 or English No. 8 (4.0mm) and one U.S. I/9 or English No. 5 (5.5mm) crochet hook

- Yarn needle

Note: *Whichever yarn you choose, crochet a pattern swatch before starting afghan.*

STITCH GAUGE

See **Knitting and Crochet Notes** on page 173. 18.5 sts and 9 rows = 4 inches, using F/5 or No. 8 (4.0mm) hook.

ABBREVIATIONS

See **Knitting and Crochet Notes** on page 173.

AFGHAN

Afghan begins and ends with 5 rows of red.
Foundation row. Using red yarn and hook, ch218 loosely.
Row 1. 1tr in 6th ch from hook, *ch1, skip 1ch, 1tr in next ch; rep from * across...107 spaces.
Row 2. Ch4, *1tr in next tr, ch1; rep from * across, 1tr in 2nd turning ch.
Rep last row to make a total **5 rows red, 1 row blue, 2 rows black, 1 row yellow, 1 row black, 1 row white, 1 row black, 3 rows green, 2 rows red, 1 row black, 1 row red, 1 row

white, 1 row red, 1 row black, 2 rows red, 3 rows green, 1 row black, 1 row white, 1 row black, 1 row yellow, 2 rows black, 1 row blue.**
Rep from ** to ** twice, then work 5 rows red...107 rows. Fasten off (**Pic 1**).

WEAVING

Work lengths of chain the length of afghan, leaving 3 inches of yarn at each end for weaving in before fastening off. Chains should be long enough to weave through spaces without being too tight. Work chains as follows: 38 red, 6 blue, 9 white, 6 yellow, 18 green, 30 black.

Thread chain from top to bottom of afghan, beg at side edge (**Pics 2 & 3**) and securing at each end as follows: 5 red, 1 blue, 2 black, 1 yellow, 1 black, 1 white, 1 black, 3 green, 2 red, 1 black, 1 red, 1 white, 1 red, 1 black, 2 red, 3 green, 1 black, 1 white, 1 black, 1 yellow, 2 black, 1 blue; rep twice more, ending with 5 red...all spaces filled. With yarn needle, weave all ends and trim neatly.

EDGING

Using red yarn and I/9 or No. 5 (5.5mm) hook, work 1 rnd dc, then 1 rnd crab st evenly around afghan, working extra sts in each corner. Fasten off.

HOT
FAVORITES

They might be old-fashioned, but our knitted slippers and hotwater bottle cover are a whole lot prettier and more environmentally friendly than an electric blanket. Knitted in pure wool, each has been decorated with a soft spray of wool-embroidered lazy daisies and French knots in beautifully subtle autumnal shades.

Hotwater Bottle Cover

MEASUREMENTS

To fit standard hotwater bottle: approximately 9" x 12^1/$_4$".

MATERIALS

Fingering, baby, or sportweight knitting yarn to give gauge (50g) (see **Note**, below):

- 3 balls
- One pair U.S. No. 5 or English No. 8 (4.0mm) knitting needles

Hotwater bottle and slippers designed and made by Lynda Maker
Photography by Andrew Elton
Styling by Lisa Hilton

- Yarn needle, for sewing seams
- Four buttons
- One skein Paterna Persian Yarn in each of the following colors: red-brown A870, orange-brown A871, apricot-brown A873, pale pink A846, light brown D123, olive green A641, light olive green D531, yellow ocher A732, gold A725, or equivalent
- One skein DMC Medici Wool, very dark olive green 8309, or equivalent
- One skein Patina Rayon Thread, red-brown PA252, or equivalent
- ^{2}/$_3$ yard x ^{3}/$_{16}$"-wide silk ribbon, in desired color
- Small amount six-strand cotton embroidery floss, to match ribbon
- Candlewicking and embroidery needle

Note: *We used Cleckheaton Country 8-ply. If using a different yarn, knit a pattern swatch before starting cover.*

STITCH GAUGE

See **Knitting and Crochet Notes** on page 173. 23.5 sts and 36 rows = 4 inches, using No. 5 or No. 8 (4.0mm) needles.

FRONT

Using No. 5 or No. 8 (4.0mm) needles, cast on 58 sts.
Beg patt. Row 1. K5, *P4, K4; rep from * to last 5 sts, P5.
Rep last row 3 times.
Row 5. P5, *K4, P4; rep from * to last 5 sts, K5.
Rep Row 5 3 times.
Last 8 rows form patt.

Cont in patt until the work measures approximately 10³/₄ inches from beg, ending with a 4th or 8th patt row (a complete check).

Note. When *turning*, take yarn under needle and onto other side of work, slip next st onto righthand needle, take yarn under needle and back to original position, slip st back onto lefthand needle, then *turn* and proceed as instructed. This avoids holes in the work.

Shape for opening. Row 1. Work patt 25 times, *turn.*

Row 2 and even-numbered rows. Work in patt across.

Row 3. Work patt 22 times, *turn.*

Row 5. Work patt 19 times, *turn.*

Row 7. Work patt 16 times, *turn.*

Row 9. K25, work in patt across.

Rep Rows 1–7 once.

Next row. Work in patt across.

Next row. Working even, knit across.

Knit 2 rows garter st.

Next row. K6, (yfwd, K2tog, K6) twice, knit to last 16 sts, (K2tog, yfwd, K6) twice...4 buttonholes.

Knit 3 rows garter st.

Cast off loosely as to k, or knitwise.

BACK

Work as for Front, omitting buttonholes.

TO ASSEMBLE

Work embroidery (see instructions below) before assembling cover, as it is easier to manipulate needle.

When embroidery is complete, lap garter st rows at top of Front over garter st rows on Back and whipstitch at side edge. Join lower edge and side seams, leaving a 1¹/₂-inch opening in center of lower edge. Sew on buttons.

EMBROIDERY

It is almost impossible to trace an embroidery pattern onto a knitted item. It is easier to trace pattern (printed actual size on page 172) onto tissue paper, lay it in desired position and make small basting stitches to mark centers

of large flowers. Tear paper away, leaving stitches as markers, then work embroidery, referring to photograph below and **Embroidery Stitch Guide** on page 58.

Dahlia-type flowers: Using a double strand of A870, make 7–8 lazy daisy stitches in a circle. Use a double strand of A871 to make a second circle of stitches over the top of the first circle, making the points of the petals fall between those underneath. Use a double strand of A873 to make a third circle of lazy daisy stitches, slightly smaller than previous circles, to reveal colors below. This top row of stitches does not require the needle to go directly through the knitted fabric: simply pass the needle through the stitches below. This allows the flowers to "stand up". Work centers of flowers in French knots using one strand of A732. (When working French knots on knitted fabric, bring the needle up through the yarn itself, rather than in spaces between knitted stitches. This allows the knot to sit on top of the knitted fabric and prevents it from disappearing.)

Work the lighter flowers using A871 as the base circle, A873 as the middle circle and A846 as the top circle. Work leaves in a double strand of green in lazy daisy. Work buds in straight stitch, using a double strand of D531.

Five-petal flowers: These flowers are worked using a double strand of either A732 or A725, making five small lazy daisy stitches in a tight circle. Centers are worked

in Medici 8309, using one French knot, wrapping thread around needle three times. Leaves are worked in a double strand of D531 using lazy daisy.

Purple sprays: Work these using a single strand of D123, using French knots, wrapping thread twice around needle. Add lazy daisy leaves in A641.

Finish the bouquet by adding random French knots, using Patina Rayon thread. Stems are added in straight stitch, using all the greens.

Thread needle with silk ribbon and thread beneath stems, leaving half the ribbon on either side. Tie a bow around stems and secure using French knots of one strand of matching embroidery floss. Take ribbon ends through to back of embroidery and secure.

Lady's slippers

MEASUREMENTS
To fit average lady's foot: $8^3/_4$–$10^1/_4$″.

MATERIALS
Fingering, baby, or sportweight knitting yarn to give gauge (50g) (see **Note**):

• 3 balls
• One pair U.S. No. 3 or English No. 10 or 11 (3.25mm) knitting needles

• Yarn needle, for sewing seams
• Embroidery wools and needles, as for Hotwater Bottle Cover

Note: *We used Cleckheaton Country 8-ply. If using a different yarn, knit a pattern swatch before starting slippers.*

STITCH GAUGE
See **Knitting and Crochet Notes** on page 173.
23 sts and 28 rows = 4 inches, using No. 3 or No. 10 or 11 (3.25mm) needles.

LOWER HALF
Using No. 3 or No. 10 or 11 (3.25mm) needles, cast on 4 sts.
Working in garter st (every row knit), shape point as folls.
Row 1. K1, inc one st in next st, knit to last 2 sts, inc one st in next st, K1.
Row 2. Knit.
Rep last 2 rows 10 times...26 sts. Work even 5 rows knit.
Row 28. *K1, P1; rep from * across.
Row 29. *K1, P1; rep from * across.
Row 30. *K1, P1, yrn, P2tog; rep from * to last 2 sts, K1, P1. Work 3 rows in K1, P1 ribbing, then knit 2 rows garter st.
Rep Row 1 3 times...32 sts.
Row 39. Knit.
Note. When *turning*, take yarn under needle and onto other side of work, slip next st onto righthand needle, take yarn under needle and back to original position, slip st back onto lefthand needle, then *turn* and proceed as instructed (to avoid holes in work).
Shape Heel. Row 1. Knit to last 4 sts, *turn*.
Row 2. Repeat Row 1.
Row 3. Knit to last 6 sts, *turn*.
Row 4. Repeat Row 3.
Row 5. Knit to last 8 sts, *turn*.
Row 6. Repeat Row 5.
Row 7. Knit to last 10 sts, *turn*.
Row 8. Repeat Row 7.
Row 9. Knit to last 12 sts, *turn*.
Row 10. Knit to last 10 sts, *turn*.
Row 11. K11, *turn*.
Row 12. K13, *turn*.

Cont in this manner, working 2 sts more in each row until the end of Row 19.

Row 20. K29.

Row 21. Knit across...32sts.

Cont in garter st, dec one st at each end of 9th and foll 12th rows until 26 sts rem, then at each end of every foll 6th row until 20 sts rem.

Work 3 rows.

Shape Toe. Working in garter st, dec one st at each end of next and every alt row until 10 sts rem.

Cast off.

Embroidery outline for slippers

Embroidery outline for Hotwater Bottle Cover

UPPER HALF

Using No. 3 or No. 11 (3.25mm) needles, cast on 4 sts.

Work Rows 1 and 2 as for Lower Half until there are 20 sts.

Work even 5 rows knit.

Next row. *K1, P1; rep from * across.

Next row. *K1, P1; rep from * across.

Next row. *K1, P1, yrn, P2tog; rep from * across.

Work 3 rows in K1, P1 ribbing.

Work even in garter st until Upper Half matches Lower Half to beg of Shape Toe.

Shape Toe. Work as for Lower Half.

TO ASSEMBLE

Work embroidery (see the instructions under Hotwater Bottle Cover, on page 170, ignoring reference to stalks and silk ribbon) before assembling, as it is easier to manipulate the needle. Place traced tissue pattern onto slipper, baste through large flower centers, then carefully remove pattern and *turn over* before placing on second slipper so that pattern will be a mirror image of the first. When the embroidery is complete, join side and toe seams. Make a 2-foot-long twisted cord and thread through holes at ankle.

Knitting and Crochet Notes

Read each pattern thoroughly before purchasing materials and beginning the project you have chosen.

STITCH GAUGE

Correct tension is essential. If your tension is not exactly as specified in the pattern, your garment will be the wrong size. Before starting any pattern, make a pattern swatch, at least 4 inches square. If you have more stitches equal to 4 inches in width than recommended, use larger needles or hook. If you have fewer stitches equal to 4 inches than recommended, use smaller needles or hook.

KNITTING ABBREVIATIONS

Alt: alternate
beg: begin/ning
cont: continue
dec: decrease, decreasing
foll: following
garter st: knit every row
inc: increase, increasing
incl: including, inclusive
K: knit
mm: millimeters
0: no rows, stitches or times
patt: pattern
P: purl
psso: pass slipped stitch over
p2sso: pass 2 sts over
rem: remain/s, remaining, remainder
rep: repeat
rnd/s: round/s
sl: slip
st/s: stitch/es
st st: stockinette st (knit row on right side, purl row on wrong side)
tbl: through back of loop
tog: together
ybk: yarn back (take yarn back under needle from purling position)

yft: yarn front (bring yarn under needle from knitting position to purling position)
yfwd: yarn forward (bring yarn under needle then over into knitting position again, thus making a stitch)
yrn: yarn around needle (take yarn around needle into the purling position, thus making a stitch)

KNITTING GRAPHS

Knit odd-numbered (right side) rows and purl even-numbered (wrong side) rows unless it is otherwise stated.

KNITTING NEEDLE SIZES

Metric (mm)	British	U.S.
9–10	000	15
8.5	00	13
8	0	12
7.5	1	11
7	2	10$\frac{1}{2}$
6.5	3	10
6	4	9
5.5	5	8
5	6	7
4.5	7	6
4	8	5
3.75	9	4
3.5	9	4
3.25	10	3
3	11	2
2.5	12	1
2.25	13	0
2	14	–

CROCHET ABBREVIATIONS

Bl: block = 3tr
ch: chain
crab st: work as for dc, working from left to right instead of from right to left; reverse double crochet
dc: double crochet
dec: decrease (insert hook into first st, draw through and leave on hook, insert hook into next st, draw yarn through, yo and draw through all 3 lps)
dtr: double treble
htr: half treble
lp/s: loop/s
rep: repeat
rnd/s: round/s
sl st: slipstitch
sp: space
st/s: stitch/es
tr: treble
yo: yarn over hook

CROCHET HOOK SIZES

Metric (mm)	British	U.S.
.6	7	14 steel
2.00	13/14	B/1
2.50	12	C/2
3.00	10/11	D/3
3.50	9	E/4
4.00	8	F/5
4.50	7	G/6
5.00	6	H/8
5.50	5	I/9
6.00	4	J/10
7.00	2	K/10$\frac{1}{2}$

YARN EQUIVALENTS

fingering: baby yarn
double knit: sportweight
aran: 4-ply worsted weight
chunky: bulky

Grams	Ounces
30	1
60	2
90	3
120	4
150	5
180	6
210	7
240	8
270	9
300	10

PAINTING
AND
STENCILING

TIN CAN ALLEY

Making do, recycling and home decorating on a shoestring — all are the hallmarks of the country homemaker, and these canisters and plates are stamped (or rather stenciled) with this traditional style. The canisters began life as ordinary tea and coffee cans, while the plate is the inexpensive enamel variety available from outdoor supply stores. With their cheerful blue sponged borders and simple barnyard stencils, they would make charming and low-cost additions to an old cabinet or cupboard shelf of a country kitchen.

Tin cans and plate stenciled by Pamela Worsdall
Photography by Andre Martin
Styling by Lisa Hilton

MATERIALS

- Empty tin cans with lids
- Enamel plates
- Vinegar
- Masking tape
- Spray rustproof primer, such as Krylon
- Artist-quality background paint, such as Liquitex, Blickrylic, or Jo Sonja's: White
- 1" flat brush
- Chalk pencil
- Artist-quality flow formula acrylics, such as Jo Sonja's: Cobalt Blue, Cadmium Red Medium, Red Oxide, Turner's Yellow and Black, or equivalent
- Natural sea sponge
- Mylar film
- Fine pen
- Craft blade or Xacto knife
- Cutting mat
- $^1/_2$" stencil brushes (preferably one for each color)
- Water-based satin varnish, such as Liquitex

METHOD

Wash cans and plates well with warm water and detergent, then rinse with a 1:1 water/vinegar mix, and dry thoroughly. Use masking tape and paper to cover any areas that are not to be painted — for example, inside the cans and around lid seals — as extra paint will

1

2

3

4

make them impossible to use. Spray objects with two coats of rustproof primer (**Pic 1**).

When dry, use flat brush to apply three coats of White background paint, for an opaque cover (**Pic 2**).

Using chalk pencil, roughly outline a circle or oval, depending on the shape of the can, on the side of the can or in the center of the plate.

Rinse out sea sponge in water and squeeze in a kitchen towel until just damp. Dip into Cobalt Blue paint and "pounce" the sponge onto paper towels until a distinct mottled pattern is seen. Then dab onto can or plate in a controlled manner, lifting the sponge off vertically so as not to smudge the pattern (**Pic 3**). Reloading the paint when necessary, repeat the dabbing motion all over the can or plate, except for the circled area — leave this free of paint.

Adjust size of stencil outlines (opposite) to fit your can or plate, if necessary, then trace stencils onto Mylar film using a fine pen. Cut stencils out with craft blade on a cutting mat. Cut any small or central areas first and cut towards you. Some stencils, such as the cow and pig, are cut in one piece. Others have two sections: **sheep** (body; face and ear), **goose** (body; beak and wing), **rooster and hen** (body; comb and wattle).

Position the stencil on the can or plate and secure with tape. Load a stencil brush with Black and pounce on paper until quite dry. Holding the stencil down with one hand, gently stipple around the edge to outline the shape (**Pic 4**). Add definition with patches of extra stippled color.

Paint each animal as follows: **cow** — ears, legs and tail are darker, while pattern on body is stippled; **pig** — head and backside are darker; **sheep** — feet, tail, ear and face are darker; **goose** — use Turner's Yellow for beak and feet and Black shading on inside wing; **rooster and hen** — use deeper color on feet, head and breast, and a mix of Red Oxide and Cadmium Red Medium for tail, wattle and comb.

After drying, varnish cans or plates with three coats of satin varnish. The cans can be used for storage as long as the inside is not painted; the plates are decorative only.

FRAME AND FORTUNE

Starting with two ordinary frames and a framed print, all purchased inexpensively from a local variety store, it is possible to create three totally different effects — and all look as though they cost considerably more than they did.

The First Step

With all purchased frames, it is important to remove any existing varnish or paint using a commercial paint stripper, according to the manufacturer's instructions. Wear rubber gloves, wash off under running water and use a steel wool pad to remove any residual paint stripper. Dry completely and sand well with 180 grit fine sandpaper.

Right: A wide wooden frame achieves a rich, old look with a crackle varnish treatment.

Frames painted by Pamela Worsdall
Photography by Andre Martin
Styling by Lisa Hilton

Crackled Frame

MATERIALS

- Wooden frame
- Sandpapers: P180 fine and P400 superfine
- Artist-quality background paint, such as Jo Sonja's or Liquitex: Spice, or equivalent
- All-purpose sealer, such as Jo Sonja's
- Crackle medium, such as Jo Sonja's
- Artist's acrylic gouache, such as Jo Sonja's or Winsor & Newton: Pale Gold, or equivalent
- Water-based antiquing medium, such as Jo Sonja's or ChemTek
- Brushes: 1" soft flat and varnish brush
- Tack cloth and soft, clean rag
- Satin acrylic finishing varnish, such as Jo Sonja's or Liquitex

METHOD

Prepare frame by using paint stripper (see Box at left), then sanding. Mix Spice 1:1 with sealer and give frame one coat. When dry, follow with three thick coats of Spice in quick succession. Allow each coat to dry naturally.

When last coat is dry, use flat brush to apply crackle medium in a thick coat. Do not overwork. Use a hairdryer to dry surface rapidly into ragged cracks and allow to dry overnight.

Gently sand surface using P400 sandpaper and remove dust with a tack cloth. Blow surface to remove dust from between cracks.

Mix Pale Gold with water-based antiquing medium to a medium consistency and brush over cracked surface one side at a time. Immediately wipe Pale Gold back with a soft rag, leaving most of the color between the cracks. Pick up some Pale Gold on the rag and rub along the outer edges.

Leave to dry overnight, then finish with two or three coats of satin finishing varnish.

Woodgrain Frame

MATERIALS

- Wooden frame
- P180 fine sandpaper
- Artist-quality background paint, such as Jo Sonja's Winsor & Newton or Liquitex: Primrose
- All-purpose sealer, such as Jo Sonja's
- Artist's acrylic gouache, such as Jo Sonja's or Dick Blick: Burnt Umber, Brown Earth and Rich Gold
- Kleister medium, such as Jo Sonja's
- Clear glazing medium, such as Jo Sonja's
- Water-based antiquing medium, such as Jo Sonja's
- Brushes: No. 12 flat, No. 8 flat and varnish brush
- Plastic clingwrap
- Satin acrylic finishing varnish, such as Liquitex
- Suitable print
- Soft cloth

METHOD

Frame Prepare frame by using paint stripper (see Box on page 180), then sanding.

Paint frame with two coats of Primrose mixed with all-purpose sealer (1:1). When dry, apply one coat of all-purpose sealer to give a slick surface on which to work.

Mix Burnt Umber 1:1 with kleister medium, and paint on frame, one side at a time. Dab wet paint with crumpled plastic clingwrap, which will lift some of the paint off, leaving a wrinkled pattern. Repeat on each side and allow to dry.

Carefully paint the top of one of the ridges and the inside molding with Rich Gold.

Mix Brown Earth with clear glazing medium and a few drops of antiquing medium, and paint over frame using the No. 8 flat brush. This glaze softens and enriches the colors.

Leave overnight to dry, then finish with two or three coats of satin finishing varnish.

Aged print Seal print with two coats of all-purpose sealer, allowing to dry between coats. Paint over one coat of clear glazing medium and allow to dry.

Mix Burnt Umber 1:1 with Brown Earth and add antiquing medium to ink consistency. Quickly brush a thin, even coat over the surface. Immediately begin to wipe back with the soft cloth, leaving some areas darker than others. Leave to dry.

A modern framed print is given an antique "makeover", while the frame is given a traditional woodgrain finish.

Before painting, a candle is rubbed over the wooden frame so that layers are easily rubbed back for a distressed look.

Distressed Frame

MATERIALS

- Wooden frame
- P180 fine sandpaper
- Artist-quality background paints, such as Jo Sonja's or Winsor & Newton: Soft White and Oak Moss
- Artist's acrylic gouache, such as Jo Sonja's: Raw Sienna
- All-purpose sealer, such as Bulls Eye 1-2-3 or Krylon
- No. 12 flat brush
- Colorless wax candle
- Antique pine wax, such as Black Bison or Dorland's
- Soft cloth

METHOD

Prepare frame by using paint stripper (see Box on page 180), then sanding (**Pic 1**).

Mix Soft White with a touch of Raw Sienna and mix this 1:1 with all-purpose sealer. Apply two coats of mix using the flat brush. When dry, rub candle over frame, following direction of woodgrain, along tops of ridges or in patches, wherever a worn look is required (**Pic 2**).

Apply one coat of Oak Moss over this and allow to dry (**Pic 3**).

When dry, rub top coat back with P180 sandpaper. The wax does not allow the top coat to adhere, so it is removed easily to reveal the base color. The wax will resist varnish, so apply a thin coat of antique pine wax using a soft cloth, and buff to a low sheen (**Pic 4**).

PAINTING BY NUMBERS

T he luscious fruits on these pages were produced by a technique known as "theorem painting". Once a highly popular and proper pursuit for genteel young ladies of the 19th century, theorem painting is, despite its rather forbidding name, a method of stenciling on velveteen with oil paints. The "theorem" tag comes simply from the logical numbering of the several stencils used to create the finished work. Here, we show you how to create your own example of this traditional craft, and you will be surprised at how so simple a technique can produce such pretty and professional-looking results.

MEASUREMENTS

Finished designs fit into a frame aperture or glass size of $5^3/4$" square.

Theorem paintings by Corinne Cowper
Frames created by Pamela Worsdall
Photography by Andre Martin
Styling by Vicki Liley

MATERIALS

- White cotton velveteen (size to suit frame)
- Two cups strong tea
- Mylar film
- Fine black felt-tip pen
- Craft blade or Xacto knife
- Self-healing cutting mat
- Self-adhesive vinyl
- 7" square heavy cardboard
- 4" square calico
- Oil paints (stick or tube), such as Winsor & Newton, in the following colors: Alizarin Crimson, Burnt Umber, Yellow Ocher, Olive Green and Prussian Blue
- Paper plate or palette
- No. 2 or No. 3 round brush
- Paint thinner, such as Bob Ross or Crown
- Unfinished wooden frame (see box on page 189 for how to antique your own frame)

GENERAL METHOD

Use a solution of strong tea to dye the velveteen. If the color is too strong, rinse fabric in cold water immediately. When dry, cut fabric to fit your frame.

While fabric is drying, cut Mylar film into 7-inch squares. Outlines for stencils are printed on pages 187 and 188. Each separate component for each stencil is printed in a different color. For each complete fruit, you will need to cut two or three separate stencils, depending on design. For each picture, trace the complete design onto Mylar film the required number of times, using a fine black pen. (For example, if you are stenciling the pomegranate, you will need to trace the complete design three times onto three separate pieces of film.)

Next, number each part to be removed on each stencil to avoid confusion. Then, using craft blade or Xacto knife, cut out all parts you have labeled No. 1 on Stencil 1, all parts labeled No. 2 on Stencil 2 and so on.

Cut a piece of self-adhesive vinyl a little bigger than the cardboard square. Remove backing paper from vinyl and carefully cover cardboard, sticky side out, sticking excess vinyl to itself at back. Place velveteen wrong side down on vinyl, making sure that fabric is without any wrinkles. This step is necessary to keep the fabric stable while stenciling.

Following instructions described for each individual design on pages 187 and 188, center Stencil 1 on the velveteen. Wrap calico around index finger so that there are no creases on the ball of your finger. Taking a small amount of color onto finger, dab onto a spare area of your palette so that a very light cover of paint remains on the calico. Lightly rub with a circular motion to cover exposed velveteen evenly.

Proceed as described for each individual design. When paintings are dry, remove adhesive vinyl and frame as desired (see page 189).

Pears

The Pear design consists of two stencils, which should be traced and cut according to directions under **General Method** on page 185.

Center Stencil 1 on velveteen and, using a circular motion, lightly apply Yellow Ocher to cut areas (**Pic 1**).

Rub Olive Green around edges of pears so that it blends gradually into the Yellow Ocher. Apply a small amount of Alizarin Crimson to areas outlined on diagram with a dotted line (**Pic 2**).

Carefully line up Stencil 2 so that it matches what you have already done. Use Yellow Ocher to color the leaf, then color around the edge of the leaf with Olive Green (**Pic 3**).

Using illustration as a guide, load the round brush with Burnt Umber thinned with a little paint thinner, and paint in stalks, outlines and veins of leaves and bases of pears. Also outline the bottom edge of the branch (**Pic 4**).

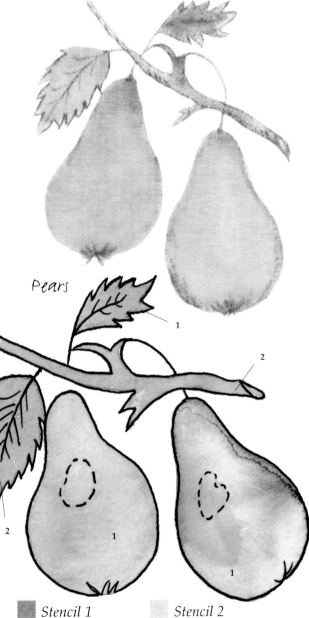

Pears

Stencil 1   Stencil 2

Apples

The Apple design consists of two stencils, which should be traced and cut according to directions under **General Method** on page 185.

Center Stencil 1 on velveteen, and apply Yellow Ocher to cut areas. Pick up a little Alizarin Crimson and apply gently to cut apple and whole apple, leaving a lighter patch in area outlined by broken line. Using Burnt Umber, rub color into the base and side of whole apple and into cut apple to create shadows.

Carefully line up Stencil 2 so that it matches what you have already done. Use Yellow Ocher to color leaves. Color cut apple very lightly with yellow. Color around edges with Olive Green.

Using the illustration as a guide, load the round brush with Burnt Umber diluted with a little paint thinner, and paint apple stalk, outlines of leaves, cut edge of apple, veins of leaves, and seeds and interior markings of cut apple.

Apples

Stencil 1

Stencil 2

Pomegranates

The Pomegranate design consists of three stencils, which should be traced and cut according to the directions under **General Method** on page 185.

Center Stencil 1 on velveteen, and apply Yellow Ocher to leaves. Color edges of leaves with Olive Green. Apply Alizarin Crimson to base of the cut pomegranate, seeds and sepal at top of rear pomegranate. Rub Burnt Umber into sepal at top of rear pomegranate, seeds and bottom edge of cut pomegranate, for shading.

Carefully align Stencil 2, and rub Alizarin Crimson into rear pomegranate — make the coverage very light. Rub Burnt Umber into edges of rear pomegranate and (using illustration as a guide) in a line down the fruit.

Align Stencil 3, and very lightly apply Alizarin Crimson unevenly to cut face of pomegranate.

Load the round brush with Burnt Umber diluted with thinner, and paint in outlines and veins of leaves, the broken line on the face of the cut fruit and all the edges of the fruit to sharpen the image.

Raspberries

The Raspberry design consists of three stencils, which should be traced and cut according to the directions under **General Method** on page 185.

Center Stencil 1 on velveteen, and apply Yellow Ocher to leaves. Color edges of leaves in Olive Green, making bottom leaf darker than others. Color raspberries in Alizarin Crimson, leaving a lighter area for highlight.

Align Stencil 2, and apply Yellow Ocher to leaves and branch. Color edges of leaves and berry sepals in Olive Green. Use Burnt Umber to color bottom edge of branch. Color remaining raspberries with Alizarin Crimson, as before.

Align Stencil 3, and apply Yellow Ocher to leaf and sepals. Darken edges of leaf and sepals with Olive Green.

Load the round brush with Burnt Umber diluted with a little thinner and paint in outlines, veins, stems of leaves, branch and sepals. Mix Alizarin Crimson with a little Prussian Blue, dilute with thinner and paint in divisions of raspberries.

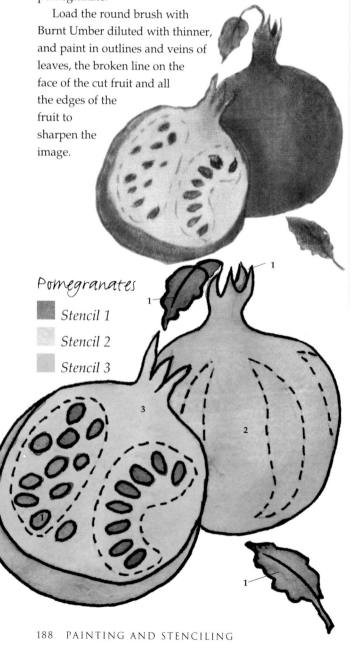

Pomegranates

Stencil 1

Stencil 2

Stencil 3

Raspberries

Stencil 1

Stencil 2

Stencil 3

Antiqued frames

Using plain inexpensive wooden frames, you can create just the right antique look to complement the traditional style of the theorem paintings.

MATERIALS

- Unfinished wood frame (ours measures 11" square; glass size $5^3/4$" square)
- P180 fine sandpaper
- Artist's acrylic gouache, such as Jo Sonja's, Dick Blick, or The French School: Brown Earth and Burnt Umber
- Water-based antiquing medium, such as Jo Sonja's
- Clear glazing medium, such as Jo Sonja's or Dick Blick
- 1" flat brush
- Old toothbrush
- Oil-based antiquing patina, such as Modern Options
- Oil paint, such as Winsor & Newton: Burnt Umber
- Disposable gloves
- Lint-free rag
- Furniture wax and polishing cloth
- 0000 or very fine artist-grade steel wool

METHOD

Sand frames with P180 grit to smooth any rough areas, and remove dust with a dampened rag.

Mix Brown Earth and Burnt Umber 2:1, to make a rich, warm brown.

The glaze/stain is prepared by adding antiquing medium to clear glazing medium (1:3), then mixing up to one part of the brown paint into this. Add just enough paint to make a transparent stain, not an opaque color. Test your mix on the back of the frame.

Using the flat brush, brush the stain onto one side of the frame, quickly covering the entire side, then immediately wipe off the excess with a damp cloth. Repeat this process on the remaining three sides. Allow frame to dry.

Dilute Burnt Umber acrylic with water to an ink consistency and use an old toothbrush to spatter frame as follows: Load the toothbrush, tap it over paper to remove excess paint and large drops, then hold it in one hand and stroke the bristles with the forefinger of the other hand, allowing fine droplets to fall on the frame.

For the antiquing process, work in a well-ventilated area and wear disposable gloves. Moisten lint-free rag with oil-based antiquing patina and wipe over surface of frame. Pick up some Burnt Umber oil paint with the patina-soaked rag, and rub this over the frame, with extra shading on the inner and outer edges, along the joints and recessed edges — anywhere dust or dirt would normally collect over time. If any area starts to dry out during this process, moisten with more patina and continue. Set frame aside to dry for two days.

Finish frame by waxing. Rub the first coat of wax in using 0000 steel wool and a circular motion. Leave to set (about 20 minutes), then polish with a soft cloth. Apply a second layer with a soft cloth and buff the frame to a low sheen.

THE FLOWERING VINE

Painted in an early American folk art style, a small chest of drawers has been transformed from the merely useful to an elegant piece that will grace any room. The simple flowering vine motif is one that even a non-painter can work with perfect ease. Adapted from the style of furniture decorated by Robert Crossman of Taunton, Massachusetts, in the 1700s, the design can be easily scaled up or down to accommodate different sized objects, ranging from this small, inexpensive chest of drawers, to a full-size dresser, or even cabinet doors.

Chest of drawers painted by Pamela Worsdall
Photography by Andre Martin
Styling by Vicki Liley

MEASUREMENTS

Our chest of drawers measures $16^1/2''$ wide x $11^1/2''$ high x 8" deep. To enlarge the design to fit these measurements, photocopy at 118 percent, or enlarge or reduce to fit the piece you wish to paint.

MATERIALS

- Unfinished pine chest of drawers
- P180 fine sandpaper
- Tack cloth
- Artist's acrylic gouache, such as Jo Sonja's: Burnt Umber, Brown Earth, Warm White and Raw Sienna
- Clear glazing medium, such as Jo Sonja's or Liquitex
- Water-based antiquing medium, such as Jo Sonja's
- Brushes: 1" foam, 00 liner and No. 2 round
- Tracing paper
- Transfer paper
- Stylus
- Flow medium, such as Jo Sonja's or Winsor & Newton
- Old toothbrush
- Artist-quality odorless lean medium
- Oil paint, such as Winsor & Newton: Burnt Umber
- Disposable gloves
- Lint-free rag
- Satin solvent finishing varnish, such as Grumbacher

METHOD

Gently sand all the drawers and the box and remove any dust with a tack cloth.

Mix Burnt Umber with Brown Earth (1:2) and add a small amount of this to a mixture of clear glazing medium plus antiquing medium (3:1) to produce a transparent mid-brown stain.

Using the foam brush, paint one side of the box, following the grain, then wipe off excess with a damp cloth. Repeat on each side, and then on all the drawers. If the stain appears too light, repeat the process — it is better to build up layers of light color than to apply one heavy coat that would mask the grain of the wood. Allow to dry, and lightly sand again.

The folk art design is printed on the opposite page. Adjust the design to fit your piece and trace it onto tracing paper. Transfer complete design to chest using transfer paper and stylus, noting that you will need to flip the design for second half of chest so that one half is the mirror image of the other.

Mix Warm White with a touch of Raw Sienna to produce a light cream; thin this with flow medium and a little water, and then use the liner brush to outline the entire design with this mix. With the round brush, and a mix of Raw Sienna and Warm White (1:1), fill in selected flower petals, as well as wings, tails and breasts of birds, as photographed. Apply two coats, allowing to dry in between.

Add any decorative lines with the 00 liner brush and light cream, and paint the dots with the No. 2 round brush.

When dry, distress the design by sanding gently. Spatter the box and drawers with a watery mix of Burnt Umber, using the old toothbrush to flick the paint. Allow project to dry thoroughly — for 24 hours.

To antique, wear disposable gloves and work in a well-ventilated area. Use lint-free rag to wipe lean medium over the box and drawers. Pick up some Burnt Umber oil paint with the medium-soaked rag, and wipe the color over the surface. Remove excess color with a clean cloth, and if the surface starts to dry out, just add more lean medium. Leave the edges of the drawers darker than the centers.

When antiquing is absolutely dry (up to several days), apply three coats of finishing varnish, leaving to dry for 24 hours between each coat. If the drawers stick, sand gently and rub some candle wax along the sides.

Folk art
design outline
enlarge 118%

A NEST
OF BOXES

These painted Easter boxes would make a wonderful gift. Not only can they be used to package Easter goodies, but as a set they also make a great display.

MEASUREMENTS

We used a set of four boxes — 4″, 5″, 6″ and 7″ in diameter — but designs can be adapted to fit any size box.

MATERIALS

- Balsa wood boxes of various sizes, or any round wooden or papier mâché boxes (available from art materials suppliers)
- Sandpaper
- Artist-quality background paints, such as Jo Sonja's: Pale Beige, Pimento, Heritage Blue and Straw, or equivalent
- Artist-quality flow formula acrylics, such as Jo Sonja's: Antique White, Yellow Oxide, Red Oxide, Burnt Sienna, Hookers Green, Napthol Scarlet, Burnt Umber, Metallic Gold, Pthalo Blue and Cadmium Yellow Medium, or equivalent
- Brushes: sponge, bristle, round and liner
- Tracing paper and pattern transfer paper
- Stylus or sharp pencil
- Spray sealer (gloss or matte), such as Shiva

Project designed and painted by Linda Maker
Photography by Valerie Martin

- Oil-based antiquing patina, such as Trichem or Modern Options
- Lint-free rag
- Oil paint, such as Winsor & Newton, Grumbacher, or Rembrandt: Burnt Umber
- Beeswax (optional)
- Raffia or straw, to fill
- Assorted eggs (we painted daisy patterns on ours, using edible food dye)

Large Box with Chicken

Paint inside of both box and lid using sponge brush and Pimento background paint. (Some background paints include a built-in sealer; if not included, you may need to seal balsa first with an all-purpose sealer.)

Paint outside of box using bristle brush. This gives a strong "grained" effect to the finished product, so do not be too careful. Brush on quickly, using Pimento on the box and Pale Beige on the lid. Allow to dry.

Using the sponge brush, paint outside of box again in Pale Beige and give the outside lid a coat of Straw. Allow to dry. Sand all over. The grain of the bottom coat will easily come through and create an antique look.

Trace the chicken design, printed on following page, and enlarge or reduce to the lid size of your box. Tape design in position on lid, slide transfer paper between design and lid, and use stylus or sharp pencil to trace design onto lid.

Paint the chicken in Antique White, loading the round brush quite heavily and pressing it very flat. This will give the chicken a three-dimensional look. Mix a little Burnt Sienna with White to darken feathers slightly around the edges. Comb and "eye mask" are painted in Napthol Scarlet and beak in Yellow Oxide. Add detail lines around feathers or beak using a liner brush and watered-down Burnt Sienna or Burnt Umber. Pupil of eye is undiluted Burnt Umber. Paint the hen's nest using the liner brush and any combination of earthy colors.

The window frame is painted in a mix of Burnt Sienna and a little Burnt Umber, while the sky is Pthalo Blue mixed with a little Burnt Umber to give a steely blue. Mix a greyish color from your palette for the farmhouse. Paint the windows in a mix of Cadmium Yellow and a touch of Antique White.

Using any darker earth tones left on the palette, darken any background areas to highlight the hen.

Use Pimento to add the border to the lid and finish with a thin line of Metallic Gold. Add gold dots around the side of the lid using the tip of the paintbrush handle.

When dry, transfer the daisies printed at the bottom of this page to the side of the box so that they are evenly spaced. The easiest way to do this is to cut a piece of tracing paper the height of the box and the length of the circumference. Mark on the paper a line for the depth of the lid, then a line halfway between this mark and the base. This gives you the "halfway point" that you see when the lid is on. Divide the length into sections and evenly space daisies on the paper. Then wrap tracing paper around the box, slide the transfer paper between the tracing paper and the box, and trace.

Paint daisy petals using Yellow Oxide, and paint centers in Red Oxide, with a tiny Metallic Gold dot in the center of each.

Pthalo Blue with a little Burnt Umber

Burnt Sienna with a little Burnt Umber

Cadmium Yellow with a little Antique White

Antique White

Use combination of earthy browns

Metallic Gold

Grey mix

Napthol Scarlet

Yellow Oxide

Add detail in Burnt Sienna or Burnt Umber

Red Oxide with Metallic Gold center   *Yellow Oxide*

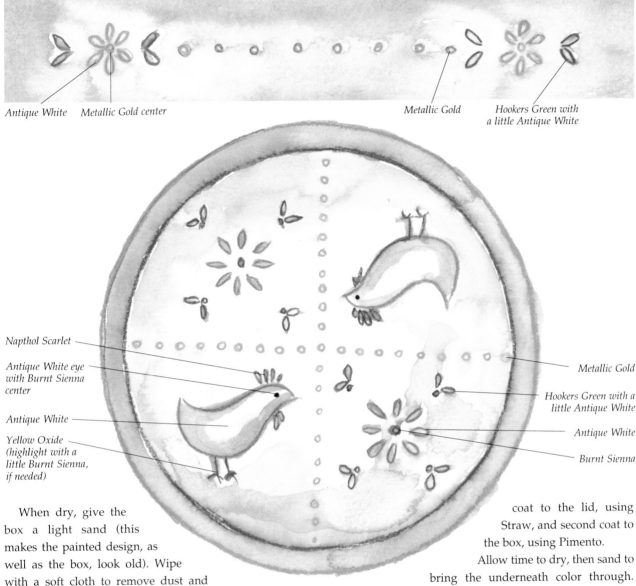

Antique White   Metallic Gold center   Metallic Gold   Hookers Green with a little Antique White

Napthol Scarlet

Antique White eye
with Burnt Sienna
center

Antique White

Yellow Oxide
(highlight with a
little Burnt Sienna,
if needed)

Metallic Gold

Hookers Green with a
little Antique White

Antique White

Burnt Sienna

When dry, give the box a light sand (this makes the painted design, as well as the box, look old). Wipe with a soft cloth to remove dust and spray lightly with sealer.

To antique the box, apply a small amount of antiquing patina on a lint-free rag. Use the same rag to spread Burnt Umber oil paint over the surface, then use a clean cloth to remove the desired amount of paint, leaving the color of the box slightly deeper and more mellow.

Apply a coat of beeswax, if desired, to give a beautiful luster.

Box with Two Chickens

Paint the inside of the box and lid in Pale Beige, using the sponge brush.

Using the bristle brush, paint the outside of the lid using Pale Beige and the outside of the box using Straw. Using the sponge brush again, apply a second coat to the lid, using Straw, and second coat to the box, using Pimento.

Allow time to dry, then sand to bring the underneath color through. Transfer the design above to the lid, as for the Large Box.

Use the lid design as a color reference for painting. Each chicken can be worked in three long strokes. Start with the round brush on a point at the beak end, flatten the brush out as you move to the center of the body, then lift it again to a point to finish at the tail.

Work the daisy petals by flattening the brush at the outer edge of the petal and lifting the brush inwards to the point.

When dry, transfer the design at the top of this page to the side of the box. Use the method described for the Large Box on the opposite page to make sure the daisies are evenly spaced. When painting, use the design for color reference.

When dry, give the box a light sand and a coat of spray sealer. Antique, if desired, following instructions for the Large Box, and finish with beeswax.

Box with Four Chickens

Paint the inside of the lid and box in Heritage Blue, using the sponge brush.

Using the bristle brush, paint the outside of the lid in Straw, and the outside of the box in Heritage Blue. Using the sponge brush again, apply a second coat of Heritage Blue to the lid, and a second coat of Straw to the box.

Referring to the method for the Large Box, trace the circular border only onto the lid. Remove tracing paper and paint the inner circle using Pale Beige. Allow to dry, and sand to bring base colors through. Now trace remaining (inner) design onto lid.

Using the lid design for color reference, paint the four chickens using the same method as for the Box with Two Chickens.

Transfer the side design below as for the Large Box, and paint, using the design as a color reference.

Finish as for the Large Box.

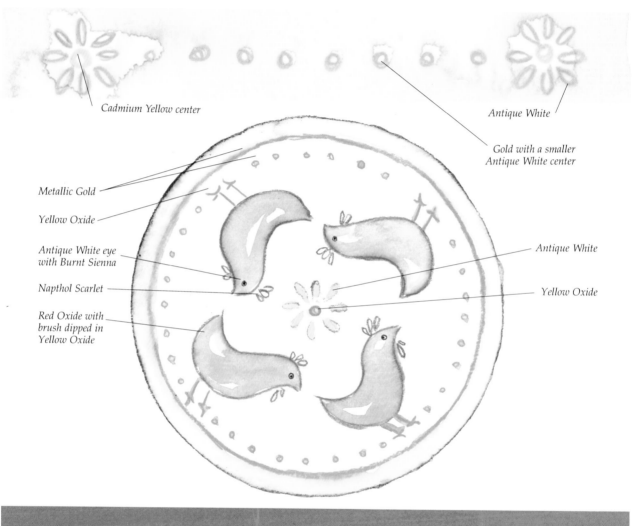

Cadmium Yellow center

Antique White

Gold with a smaller Antique White center

Metallic Gold

Yellow Oxide

Antique White eye with Burnt Sienna

Napthol Scarlet

Red Oxide with brush dipped in Yellow Oxide

Antique White

Yellow Oxide

These cute chicks are quick and easy potato prints, with a few strokes of paint added — just great for Easter cards or for decorating stationery.

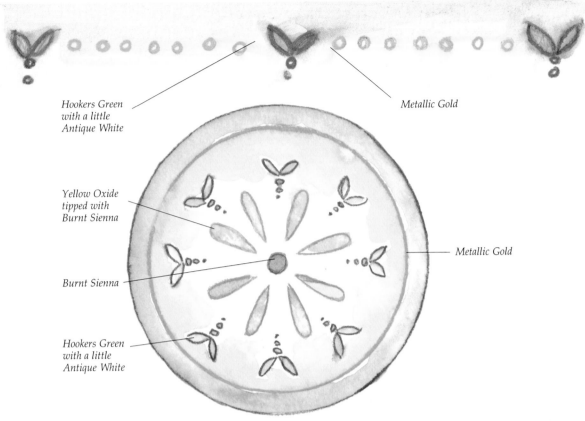

Hookers Green
with a little
Antique White

Metallic Gold

Yellow Oxide
tipped with
Burnt Sienna

Metallic Gold

Burnt Sienna

Hookers Green
with a little
Antique White

Small Box
with Flower

Paint the inside of the box and lid in Straw, using the sponge brush.

Using the bristle brush, paint the outside of the lid and box in Straw. Using the sponge brush again, give the lid a second coat of Pale Beige, and the box a second coat of Heritage Blue.

Trace the circular border only onto the lid, following the instructions for the Large Box. Remove tracing paper and paint the outer edge in Pimento. When dry, sand lightly to bring the underneath colors through. Trace remaining (inner) design onto the lid and paint the daisy pattern, using the design as a color reference.

Transfer the design at the top of the page to the side of the box, following instructions for the Large Box, and paint, using the design as a color reference.

Finish as for the Large Box.

Country colors and a coat of antiquing give a rich appearance to inexpensive balsa wood boxes. The designs are not difficult to paint and all use the same range of colors, so you could decorate several different-sized boxes for an attractive stacked display.

FRAMED
SEASHORE
COLLECTION

Quite ordinary objects often achieve a completely different status when framed for display, and this is especially true of the bits and pieces that you find when beachcombing. Small perfect shells, dried sea urchins or starfish, even an interesting bit of seaweed, are all candidates for this treatment.

The pictures shown here are stylish and very simple to assemble. Paint four simple wooden frames with a coat of Jo Sonja's Sky Blue Artists' Quality Background Color, decorate the inner edges with stripes of Soft White and Dolphin Blue and sand each frame back a little when dry to give a distressed look. Next, glue a sheet of handmade paper to each backing board and top that with a smaller square of light-colored handmade paper — torn not cut. All that you need to do now is glue little treasures in place with a glue gun.

Pictures designed and made by Lynda Maker
Photography by Louise Lister
Styling by Vicki Liley

SLICE
OF LIFE

These exquisitely shaded watercolors are actually vegetable prints, created by painting the surface of cut vegetables and using them as stamps. They are a long way from the humble potato print, but certainly not unrelated. As the moist colors blend and run on the cut surface they create a subtle effect that is enhanced by the use of artist's watercolor paper. It is really not a difficult technique — Nature provides both outline and shade card — and a little practice will produce results as beautiful as these.

MATERIALS

- Assorted vegetables (see **Note**)
- Lightweight watercolor paper, medium to rough finish
- Water squirt bottle
- Cotton dish towels or paper towel
- Small amount dishwashing detergent

- Folk art paints or watercolors
- Assorted brushes, including a liner brush
- Craft blade, ruler and pencil
- Burnishing tool (optional — available from art materials suppliers)
- Scrap cardboard
- Wooden frames to fit prints

Note: It is a good idea to experiment with a variety of vegetables. The easiest to use are those that can be cut to give a flat surface, such as eggplants, radishes, yellow squash, zucchinis, carrots (with tops) and mushrooms. Broccoli, cauliflower florets and bell peppers are also fun to try, and artichokes look beautiful but are a little more difficult to handle. Mushrooms should be used as soon as they are cut, as they tend to become more and more absorbent if left. On the other hand, if eggplant is left for a while after being cut, the cut surface starts to discolor, giving a more interesting range of shades for printing. A cut onion should also be left to dry for some hours before using so that the layers separate just slightly, resulting in a more interesting print.

Prints designed and created by Lynda Maker
Photography by Joe Filshie
Styling by Georgina Dolling

METHOD

If you are going to frame your prints, buy your frames first, then choose a perfect-sized vegetable to fit the frame. We used inexpensive frames, rubbed back and repainted using Pale Beige and Country Green.

Cut pieces of watercolor paper to frame size, then lightly rule in glass size and a border within this aperture — your design needs to fit inside these inner ruled lines.

Spray back and front of paper lightly with water (**Pic 1**) and place paper between clean dish towels or paper towel. Place a weight on top to prevent buckling and set aside while preparing vegetables.

Cut chosen vegetable in half, cutting a cross-section of the stalk as well, if appropriate. Take your time to observe the cut surface carefully, then mix various paints to match the colors of the inside of the vegetable — you may need a number of different shades of orange, green or yellow. Water the paints down with equal parts of water to paint, until the consistency is creamy.

In another container, add a few drops of dishwashing detergent to a couple of tablespoons of water. Using a fairly large brush, paint the detergent solution sparingly over the cut surface — you do not want the vegetable wet.

It is a good idea to practice the actual painting and printing on scrap paper a couple of times until you develop the technique. The same vegetables can be used several times; simply clean the surface, pat dry with paper towel and begin again.

Use an assortment of brushes to paint the surface of the vegetable with appropriate colors (**Pic 2**). Work quickly and do not be concerned as the colors blend into each other — this is what *should* happen. Blend colors on the palette as you work to create tones. To add the skin color of the vegetable, load a liner brush with color and roll around the edge of the vegetable (**Pic 3**). If you have taken a little long to paint and the vegetable appears to be drying out, spray it *very lightly* with water.

Remove damp paper from under weight; it should be limp, but not glistening. Lay paper on a clean cloth or surface, position vegetable onto paper and press (**Pic 4**).

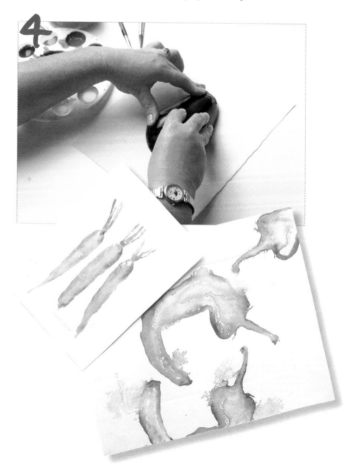

Lift vegetable carefully away to reveal print. Keep your brushes on hand to fill in any spaces or clean up paint edges while print is still wet (**Pic 5**).

If making more than one print, you will need to repaint the cut surface of the vegetable each time.

Allow print to dry, then pencil in any fine detail, such as seeds, stem detail or tiny leaves, and paint (**Pic 6**). Allow to dry thoroughly.

To make prints look more professional, you could emboss them. This involves depressing an area around the edges to give the impression that the paper has been press-printed. To do this, cut a piece of scrap cardboard to the size of the print paper. Cut a window from the cardboard, the same size as the inner rectangle ruled on the paper. The remaining cardboard frame becomes your template. Place paper print face-up over template, aligning edges. Use a burnisher to press around inner edges of template, creating a depressed edge, as shown in **Pic 7**.

Remember to sign your work.

Vegetables make a lasting impression in these delicate watercolor prints, which are very easy to do — simply paint the cut surface of a vegetable in appropriate colors and then press onto watercolor paper.

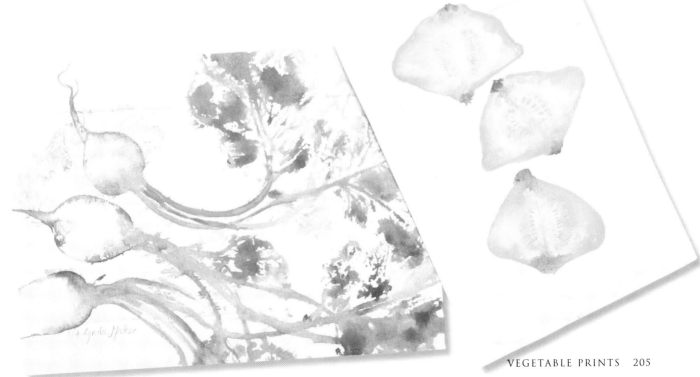

PAPER AND

DÉCOUPAGE

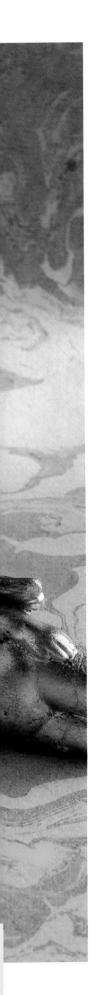

FINE FINISH

I t is hard to believe that this exquisite little box and brooch are not ancient family heirlooms, with their delicately hand-colored images of cherubs and garlands and age-darkened patina. But the cherubs started life as photocopies and, not so long ago, the box and brooch were still languishing, undecorated, on a craft shop shelf. With a little care and patience, you too can effect this magical transformation, and produce these charming découpaged "antiques".

MEASUREMENTS

Our box measures 6" x 4" x $3^{1}/8$", but the technique can be adapted to any size box. Brooch measures $2^{3}/8$" in diameter.

Box and brooch designed and made by Pamela Worsdall
Photography by Andrew Elton
Styling by Louise Owens

MATERIALS

- Photocopied pictures (see page 211)
- Unfinished pinewood box
- Wooden brooch front and brooch pin
- Ordinary writing tablet, or loose sheets
- Artists' colored pencils, such as Faber Castell Polychromos or Derwent: Light Flesh, Medium Flesh, Cream, Lemon Cadmium, Sky Blue, Ultramarine, Sap Green, Pompeiian Red, Van Dyke Brown, Burnt Ocher and Gold Ocher, or equivalent
- Gloss medium/varnish, such as Liquitex
- Brushes: 1" foam, 00 liner and $^{3}/_{4}$" Golden Nylon flat
- Découpage or curved-blade nail scissors
- 600 and 1200 ultra superfine wet-and-dry sandpapers and cork sanding block
- Artist-quality background paint, such as FolkArt or Blickrylic: Taffy, or equivalent
- Tack cloth, lint-free rag and disposable gloves
- Wallpaper paste
- PVA glue, archival quality
- Découpage roller (optional)
- Matte varnish, such as Liquitex or Jo Sonja's
- Crackle medium, such as Jo Sonja's or Delta
- Oil-based antiquing patina, such as Trichem or Modern Options
- Oil paint, such as Shiva: Burnt Umber
- Full gloss varnish, such as Grumbacher
- Turpentine or thinner, such as Bob Ross
- Dark brown contact suede
- Super glue (for brooch)

METHOD

Preparing illustrations

Photocopy black and white illustrations on opposite page, and enlarge or reduce to fit your box or brooch size. Place illustration on writing tablet or stack of loose sheets to cushion coloring-in. Using oil-based colored pencils with sharp points, color areas in, with short, light, single strokes (**Pic 1**). Shade by going over area again, or use a deeper colored pencil. Use darker colors for background and lighter for foreground. Oil-based varnish will yellow and tone down colors used, so make sure colors are strong.

Using foam brush, seal colored illustrations with two coats of gloss medium/varnish, front and back. When completely dry, use découpage scissors to cut out picture, taking care around delicate areas. Do not cut out all the background, as picture will become too fragile. The remaining areas can be concealed with background paint.

Preparing box or brooch

Sand box or brooch lightly and, using foam brush, paint with two or three coats of Taffy background paint. Sand lightly, remove dust with tack cloth then seal brooch and box (inside and out) with two coats of gloss medium/varnish.

Découpage

Arrange cut-out illustrations on box or brooch, and glue in place with a mixture of wallpaper paste and PVA glue (3:1). Brush some glue onto wooden surface, place picture on glue and cover with more glue. Gently press picture down with fingers or a roller to press out air bubbles and excess glue. Wipe excess away with a damp lint-free rag and allow to dry. Use 00 liner brush and background paint to hide any remaining background. Cut edges can be concealed with a black colored pencil or black acrylic paint and 00 liner (**Pic 2**).

Sealing and antiquing

Seal with gloss medium/varnish, then cover with four coats of matte varnish. Leave last coat to dry for one hour, then paint crackle medium over this, using short strokes and covering whole box or surface of brooch. As this dries it will crack the varnish. Leave to dry overnight.

To make cracking stand out, antique with antiquing patina and Burnt Umber oil paint as follows: With a soft cloth, rub patina over brooch or box, doing one side at a time. While still damp, rub in oil paint lightly, making it darker at edges and corners and around the illustrations (**Pic 3**).

Varnishing and sanding

Leave the box to dry for two or three days, then begin varnishing. Using the flat brush and full gloss varnish, apply 15 coats, remembering to vary the direction of each coat. Sand with 600 ultra superfine wet-and-dry sandpaper and cork sanding block, being careful at the edges (**Pic 4**). Keep the sanding area wet at all times. Dry off after sanding and use a tack cloth to remove dust; apply another five coats and sand again. The surface should start to appear uniformly dull.

Keep applying coats of varnish, now sanding after each coat, until no flaws remain and the surface is uniformly dull and even. Sand with 1200 ultra superfine wet-and-dry, then dry and clean.

For the final coat, for a gloss finish, thin the full gloss varnish with turpentine (80:20) and apply gently in a dust-free area. Leave to dry. The varnish will take a few months to cure completely, so treat with care.

The box can be lined with dark brown contact suede. Glue the brooch pin to the back of the brooch with super glue.

COUNTRY
SHADOW BOX

L ayers of cardboard and paper are the basis of this sturdy shadow box.

MEASUREMENTS

Finished box measures $20^1/_2''$ x $13^3/_4''$, including front face.

MATERIALS

- Large sheet medium tag board or heavy cardboard
- Pencil or stylus
- Metal ruler
- Craft blade or Xacto knife
- Masking tape
- Glue gun
- Gummed paper tape
- Clear sealer, such as Krylon or Jo Sonja's
- Brushes: foam and well-worn brush
- Wallpaper paste
- Newspaper, two colors if possible
- Florist's wire
- Two $^1/_3''$ brass rings, for hooks
- $1^1/_4$ yards hemispherical pearl beading
- One large wooden heart shape
- Eight small wooden heart shapes
- Gesso, such as Liquitex or Blickcrylic

Shadow box designed and made by Lynda Maker
Photography by Andre Martin
Styling by Louise Owens

- Artist-quality background paints, such as Jo Sonja's, Liquitex, Blickrylic, or Golden: Pale Beige and Heritage Blue, or equivalent
- Artist-quality flow formula acrylics, such as Jo Sonja's, Liquitex, Blickrylic, or Golden: Raw Sienna, Brilliant Alizarine, Titanium White and Burnt Umber, or equivalent
- Fine sandpaper
- Lint-free rag
- Water-based antiquing medium, such as Jo Sonja's or ChemTek
- Water-based satin varnish, such as Dick Blick, ModPodge, or Triple Thick

METHOD

The pattern for the front face is on page 216. Enlarge pattern 200 percent on a photocopier, then trace. Lay onto cardboard and re-trace using sharp pencil or stylus. Cut out, using the craft blade or Xacto knife.

Using the cutting diagram on page 215 as a guide, cut shelf and box pieces with a craft blade. Score seams as shown, by gently using the craft blade but not cutting all the way through (**Pic 1**).

Fold box along score lines and hold corners in place with masking tape. Stick seams together with glue gun.

Position horizontal shelves in place with masking tape, and glue in position (**Pic 2**). To ensure shelves fit snugly without bending to fit, it may be necessary to shave a fraction of an inch from length. Position and glue vertical shelves in the same manner. Remove masking tape.

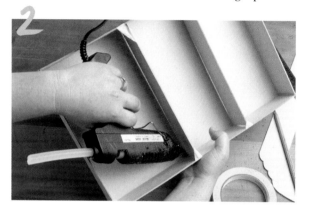

Fasten front face to the box with masking tape, glue seams and remove tape. Cover all seams with strips of dampened gummed tape. To prevent cardboard from warping, use the foam brush to apply a generous coat of clear sealer to whole box, inside and out (**Pic 3**).

Make wallpaper paste according to manufacturer's instructions. Tear or cut newspaper into strips no bigger than about 3" x 1", pass strips through the paper paste and glue to box, overlapping pieces as you work (**Pic 4**), eventually covering the entire box, both inside and out, with two layers.

Cut two short (5–6") lengths of florist's wire and twist together in the middle. Pass the ends through one small brass ring, then bend the ends of the wire out to form X-shaped prongs. Keeping the ring in the middle of the wire, place the wire on the back of the box, close to the side edge and approximately 3 inches down from the top (**Pic 5**).

Build up the papier mâché strips around the ring, covering all the wires under several layers. Repeat on the other side, with the remaining ring and wire, and allow to dry.

Position and glue the pearl beading around the edge of the front face. Glue the hearts in position, as photographed.

Using the well-worn brush, cover the entire box with a generous coat of gesso, brushing in the one direction to give a grainy look (**Pic 6**).

Paint the the inside and the back of the box in Pale Beige, allow to dry, then apply a mixture of Pale Beige and Heritage Blue. Paint the front face (front and back) with a mixture of Pale Beige and Heritage Blue, then apply a second coat of Pale Beige.

For the red hearts, mix a little Raw Sienna into Brilliant Alizarine, to "dirty" it a little. For the antique pink hearts, add Titanium White to the Alizarine–Sienna mix. Finally, add a few simple flourishes in Raw Sienna.

When completely dry, gently sand to bring base colors through (**Pic 7**). Do not sand over the beading, as you could risk revealing the pearl. Instead, with Heritage Blue paint on the fingertip, touch each bead with a little blue to make it appear to be showing through. When you have achieved the desired look, brush away any dust.

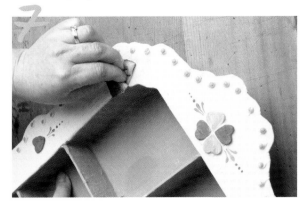

Using lint-free rag, dab antiquing medium all over the box. This will prevent it from absorbing too much color. With your medium-dampened rag, pick up a little Raw Umber paint and rub this onto all surfaces (**Pic 8**), then wipe off excess. Allow to dry.

Finally, apply a light coat of water-based satin varnish to protect the paintwork (**Pic 9**).

Use the cutting guide at right to outline the shelf and box pieces on your cardboard. Cut out carefully, using a craft blade or Xacto knife. Score the lines where indicated, using the craft blade and making sure you do not cut right through.

Tips for success

- When cutting through thick board, it is best to use a metal ruler. This helps to stop the craft blade running over the ruler.

- Never try to cut through the board in one pass. Two or three gentle cuts will easily slice the board and not your finger!

- Wallpaper paste, found in most hardware stores, is available in small packets.

- It is a good idea to use a different-colored newspaper (inserts, for example) for the second layer. This helps you to see exactly where you have been.

- An expensive brush is not necessary to paint on the gesso or background colors. A well-worn brush helps you to achieve the grainy look of this piece.

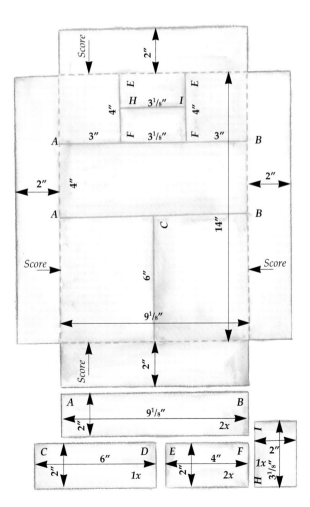

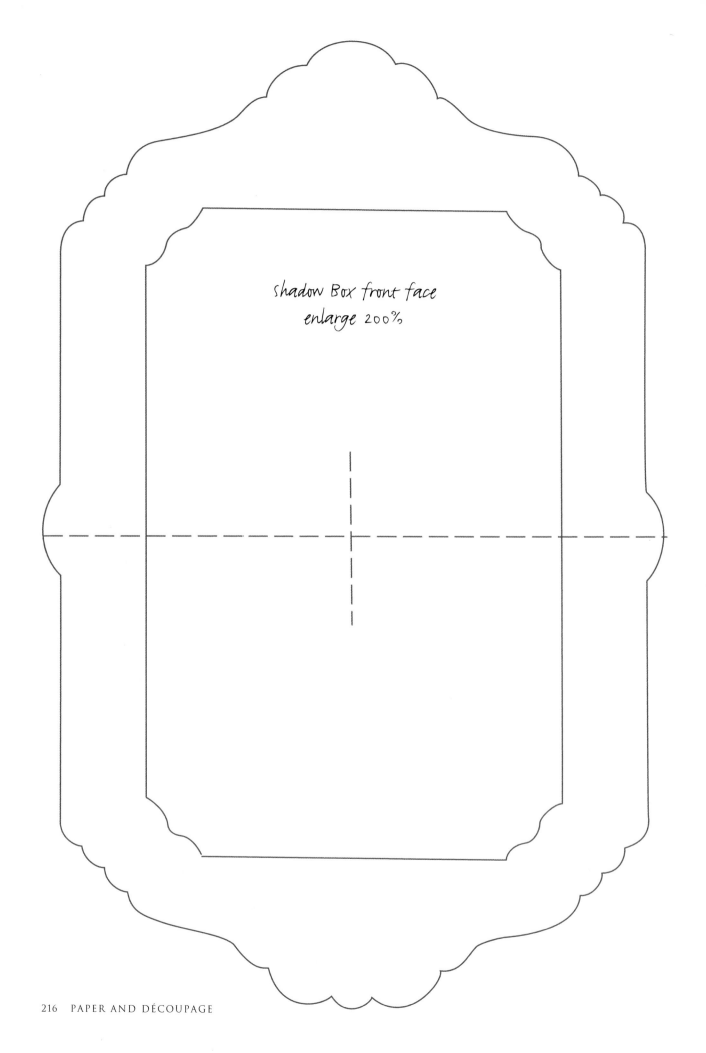

shadow Box front face
enlarge 200%

PRESSED FLOWER GIFTWRAP

This pretty giftwrap is easy and inexpensive to make from simple waxed paper and whatever flowers you have available in the garden. Small flowers, individual petals, leaves and bits of fern — all can be pressed and used to create your own individual wrappings.

Pressing Flowers

Use only dry, undamaged flowers or leaves for pressing. Simply place specimens between the pages of an out-of-date phone book and place another phone book on top. Leave alone for six weeks. Or you could use a Microfleur flower press, available from Microfleur USA, P.O. Box 280, Minden, NV89423, ph (888) 883 5387.

Giftwrap designed and made by Anabelle Lister
Photography by Catherine Muscat

MATERIALS

- Pressed flowers and leaves (see Box at left)
- Waxed paper
- Sheet of unbleached calico (or an old cotton sheet)
- Ironing board and iron

METHOD

Turn the iron to very hot, no steam.

Lay the calico over the ironing board with the overhang on your side of the board. Now unroll some waxed paper (waxed side up) over the full length of the ironing board.

Place the pressed material in the desired pattern on top of the waxed paper. When satisfied with the layout, gently unroll more waxed paper over the top of your work (waxed sides together), and cut to the same size.

Take care with this next step. Carefully fold the overhanging calico sheet back over the "flower sandwich", making sure the layers of waxed paper underneath are aligned properly.

Iron layers carefully. Allow work to cool slightly, then gently peel the cloth back to reveal a sheet of pretty homemade giftwrap.

MAPPED OUT

N*ow is the time to update your road map or atlas collection, especially when you see what you can make! Transform a wastepaper basket and desk set from ho-hum to handsome by covering them with craftily aged maps.*

MATERIALS

- Metal wastepaper basket
- Empty smooth-sided tin can, opened at one end
- White vinegar
- Very fine, artist-grade steel wool (No. 0000)
- Tack cloth and lint-free clean rags
- Metal primer
- Brushes: 2" foam, 1" varnish brush, No. 3 round and No. 4 fitch
- All-purpose sealer, such as BullsEye 1-2-3, Royal Gard, or Krylon
- Papier mâché "book box" or slipcase
- Artist-quality flow formula acrylic: Black
- Plastic business card holder (from stationery shops)
- Road maps or atlas pages
- Craft blade or Xacto knife
- Wallpaper paste
- PVA glue, archival quality
- Rollers: 4" rubber and 2" foam

Project created by Pam Worsdall
Photography by Andrew Elton
Styling by Louise Owens

- Crackle medium, such as Delta or Jo Sonja's
- Quick-drying, water-based satin varnish, such as Liquitex, Dick Blick, ModPodge, or Triple Thick
- Oil-based antiquing patina, such as Modern Options
- Oil paint, such as Shiva, Winsor & Newton, or Rembrandt: Burnt Umber
- Disposable gloves
- 1200 ultra superfine wet-and-dry sandpaper
- Antique pine wax polish, such as Black Bison or Dorland's, and polishing cloth
- Liquid leaf, such as Gold Brush'nLeaf, or gilding kits
- Black self-adhesive velour
- Artist's acrylic gouache, such as Jo Sonja's, Winsor & Newton, or Dick Blick: Rich Gold, or equivalent
- Gold protective corners and latch

METHOD

Clean exterior of metal items with a solution of half vinegar and water. Dry item well, then sand shiny surface with 0000 steel wool to roughen. Remove any dust with a tack cloth, and apply metal primer with 2" foam brush. Allow to dry, then seal with all-purpose sealer.

Paint sides of papier mâché book box with Black. Allow to dry, then seal with all-purpose sealer.

Seal plastic card holder and both sides of map sheets with all-purpose sealer.

Apply a mix of wallpaper paste and PVA glue (3:1) to each item, and lay a map over the glue, using rubber roller to smooth out any glue or air bubbles. Clean off excess glue with a dampened cloth. Continue gluing maps, overlapping edges of pages and trimming to fit edges of item being covered. When dry, remove any excess glue using a 50/50 vinegar and water mix. When completely dry, seal with all-purpose sealer and allow to dry again.

Mix crackle medium with satin varnish in a ratio of 1:1 and paint this over the sealed maps, using the 2″ foam brush. Allow to dry for about an hour, then use the 2″ foam roller to apply a coat of satin varnish. This will crack as it dries, forming a cobweb-like pattern. A hairdryer may be used to speed up the drying time. (It may be advisable to practice this technique first on a piece of board.)

It is necessary to antique the items in order to make the crackle appear. Moisten lint-free rag with antiquing patina and, wearing disposable gloves, rub this over the cracked surface. Pick up some Burnt Umber oil paint with patina-dampened rag and rub this into the cracks. If antiquing is too dark, it can be lightened by using more antiquing patina to remove some of the oil paint. Allow to dry for 24–48 hours.

Using 1″ varnish brush, apply 10 coats of satin varnish in alternating vertical and horizontal directions. When final coat is dry, lightly sand with wet 1200 wet-and-dry sandpaper. Apply another 5–10 coats of varnish, sanding lightly between the last few. Finish by rubbing antique pine wax polish into surface with 0000 steel wool and buffing when it is dry. Remove any dust with a tack cloth.

Paint edges of wastepaper basket, card holder and pencil holder with liquid leaf, using a No. 3 round brush. Line pencil holder and book box with black self-adhesive velour.

Using fitch brush, dry brush some Rich Gold along sides of book box and paint some gold stripes on the "spine". Paint edges of box gold and protect all gold work with three coats of satin varnish.

Glue on gold corners and latch, as photographed.

QUILLED EUCALYPTUS LEAVES AND BLOSSOMS

*A*s they worked in quiet isolation, rolling intricate filigree shapes from thin paper strips, the cloistered nuns of the 15th century could never have imagined how far their simple art of quilling would one day travel. But these beautiful eucalyptus leaves and blossoms, now a favorite symbol of an unimaginable antipodean land, are the direct descendants of that far-off craft. Tough little eucalyptus seeds, known as gumnuts, sinuous grey-green leaves and colorful ragged blossom are all captured with startling realism in the coils and twists of a few narrow paper strips.

MEASUREMENTS

Quilled designs measure approximately $3^3/4''$ across x $4^1/2''$ high. Backing card measures $4^3/4''$ x $6^3/4''$.

Quilled flowers designed and made by Ester Murray and Marilyn Renshaw of Craft Lover's Crafty Cards
Photography by Ian Hofstetter
Styling by Lisa Hilton

LEMON GUM LEAF OUTLINES

MATERIALS

- Quilling papers in the following widths and colors: $^1/_{16}''$ yellow, $^1/_8''$ jade green, $^1/_8''$ tan, $^3/_8''$ jade green, $^3/_8''$ lemon, $^3/_8''$ red, $^3/_4''$ jade green (see **Note**, below)
- Quilling tool (see **Note**, below)
- Fine-pointed, sharp scissors
- PVA glue, archival quality
- Toothpick or skewer
- Tracing paper
- Cream or white background paper or card
- Ruler
- Craft blade
- Tweezers

Note: *Quilling papers and tools are available from craft or art supply stores.*

METHOD

Lemon Scented Gum Following **General Quilling Instructions** on page 223, make nine Open Gumnuts from 8-inch lengths of $^1/_8$-inch tan paper.

Make three Single Blossoms, using 4-inch lengths of $^3/_8$-inch lemon paper, and insert into three of the Open Gumnuts.

Cut a $1^1/_8$-inch strip of $^3/_8$-inch jade green paper. Roll up lengthwise to form a tube-shaped stem. Secure long edge with a little glue. Bend a little in the middle for a more realistic look.

Trace Lemon Gum Leaf outlines, printed on this page, onto tracing paper.

From $^3/_4$-inch jade green paper, cut two large and five small leaves, using a template or transferring the outline directly onto paper.

Lightly score down the center of each leaf using point of quilling tool. Score small veins crosswise as well, if desired. Gently curve edges of leaves. From a scrap of green, cut a $^1/_{16}$-inch strip, $^5/_8$-inch long, to use as an extra stalk between the gumnuts.

Referring to the photograph above, arrange the leaves, blossoms and gumnuts on the background paper. When you are pleased with the arrangement, secure in place with a little glue, using tweezers to place components where necessary. Use glue very sparingly; it should not be visible. Do not glue entire under-surface of leaves to background; for a more realistic effect, place a little glue at center back and allow the edges to curl up from the background.

Allow to dry and frame as desired.

Red Flowering Gum
Following **General Quilling Instructions** on opposite page, make three Closed Gumnuts from $^1/_8$-inch jade green paper, each consisting of one 4-inch length and one 8-inch length.

Make four Double Blossoms, using 8-inch lengths of doubled red and yellow paper. For flower bases, make four Open Gumnuts, using 8-inch lengths of $^1/_8$-inch jade green. Make one smaller Double Blossom, using a 4-inch length of doubled red and yellow paper for flower, and a 4-inch length of jade green for base nut. Insert the base of this smaller blossom into an open gumnut, made from an 8-inch length of $^1/_8$-inch jade green paper.

For leaf stems, cut a $3^1/_8$-inch strip of $^1/_8$-inch jade green paper. Cut this strip in half lengthwise, tapering both ends. Fold one of these narrower strips crosswise so that one stem is 2 inches long, and the other $1^1/_8$ inches long. Reserve remaining piece for third stem.

Trace Red Gum Leaf outlines, printed on this page, onto tracing paper. From $^3/_4$-inch jade green paper, cut one of each leaf shape, using a template or transferring the outline directly onto paper. Lightly score down the center of each leaf using point of quilling tool.

Referring to the photograph below, arrange the leaves, blossoms, stems and gumnuts on the background paper. When satisfied with the arrangement, glue into place, using tweezers to position pieces where necessary and remembering to use glue sparingly so that it is not visible.

Glue leaf stems in place on edge, turning them flat only where they join the leaves. For a more realistic effect, do not glue the entire undersurface of the leaves to the background paper; place a little glue at the center back and allow the edges to curl up from the background.

Allow to dry and frame as desired.

General Quilling Instructions

TIGHT ROLL

This is the basis for all the quilled shapes in this project. Cut desired width of quilling paper to specified length. If using a needle tool, place end against needle and, using your thumb and forefinger, commence rolling the paper around the needle (do not turn tool with other hand). If using a slotted tool, place the end of the paper in the slot and turn the tool around. When using either tool, try to keep the edges even as you roll, and keep a firm tension on the coil. When the entire length has been rolled, secure end with a small amount of glue applied with a toothpick. Remove from tool.

OPEN GUMNUT (PIC 1)

a From required length of paper, make one Tight Roll.

b Using rounded end of tool or similar blunt instrument, gently push center out to give a rounded shape.

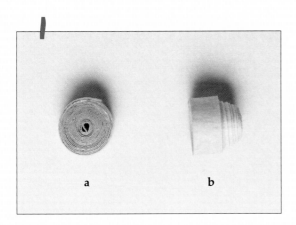

CLOSED GUMNUT (PIC 2)

a Make two Tight Rolls, making one from a piece of paper twice the length of the other.

b Gently push out the center of the larger roll to make an Open Gumnut. Push out the center of the smaller roll using a finer tool, such as a toothpick, to give a pointed end.

c Glue the smaller, pointed nut into the larger one to complete the gumnut.

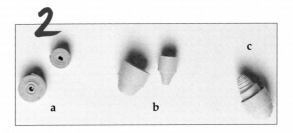

SINGLE BLOSSOM (PIC 3)

a Using sharp, fine scissors, snip evenly along required length of paper, snipping almost across full width of strip (but not quite — leave $1/16$ inch or so for inserting in tool), making each snip approximately $1/16$-inch wide, to form a fringe.

b Make a Tight Roll from fringed strip.

c Glue fringed roll into an Open Gumnut.

d Open out fringe using your fingernails or toothpick.

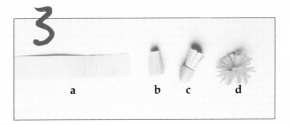

DOUBLE BLOSSOM (PIC 4)

a Glue a $1/16$-inch strip of yellow paper to the edge of a $3/8$-inch strip of red paper and, when dry, fringe along length, cutting through yellow strip.

b Make an Open Gumnut.

c Roll the fringed red strip around the outside edge of the Open Gumnut and, when dry, open out the fringe using your fingernails or a toothpick.

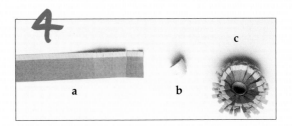

A BRIGHTER
SHADE OF PAIL ...

These lidded pails are a long way from the cowboy's campfire and will not be "pale" for long. As unusual gifts, they will be hard to beat, especially when filled with a batch of freshly baked cookies. Each lidded pail can feature a different theme, from cartoon characters to famous food labels, and any image, or series of images, is suitable.

MEASUREMENTS

Our lidded camp pails measure $4^3/4$", $6^5/8$" and 8" high, excluding their lids, but the technique can be adapted to any size lidded pail.

MATERIALS

- Three lidded pails
- White vinegar
- Rustproof undercoat or metal primer, such as Krylon
- Assorted images
- Gloss medium/varnish, such as Liquitex
- Brushes: 1" foam, 1" coarse, 1" varnish and No. 6 flat
- Découpage scissors
- Impasto medium, such as Artisan
- Gesso, such as Liquitex

Lidded pails designed and découpaged by Pamela Worsdall
Photography by Andrew Elton
Styling by Lisa Hilton

- Artist-quality background paints: Heritage Blue, White, Lichen Grey, Leaf Green and Pale Beige
- Sandpapers: P180 fine, and 600 and 1200 ultra superfine wet-and-dry
- Kleister medium, such as Jo Sonja's
- Plastic clingwrap
- Double-coated removable tape
- Wallpaper paste
- PVA glue, archival quality
- 4" rubber roller
- Lint-free towelette
- Oil-based artist's pencils for touch-up (optional)
- Water-based satin varnish, such as ModPodge, Triple Thick, or Dick Blick
- Japan gold size, such as Winsor & Newton
- Gum arabic, such as Winsor & Newton
- Oil paint, such as Winsor & Newton: Burnt Umber (green and beige pails) and Paynes Grey (blue pail)
- Oil-based satin varnish, such as Damer by Shiva
- Wax gilding paste, such as Treasure Gold

METHOD

Découpage Wash lidded pails in warm water and detergent, and rinse with equal parts vinegar and water to remove any grease and dirt. When completely dry, coat cans with rustproof compound on the outside.

Select required pictures. Prepare découpage images by coating back and front with gloss medium/varnish, using the 1" foam brush. When completely dry, cut out pictures carefully with découpage scissors.

Blue Pail: Mix some impasto medium and gesso together and apply this in a random pattern over the pail with the coarse brush to give a textured base for the paint. When dry, apply a coat of Heritage Blue mixed with White, in a ratio of 1:1, using the foam brush. Next, load some Heritage Blue on the coarse brush and dry-brush this over the lighter blue mix.

Green Pail: Prepare with impasto/gesso, as for Blue Pail. With the foam brush, give the pail a coat of Lichen Grey. After drying, paint over with Leaf Green. Sand this back with P180 to let the paler color show through.

Beige Pail: Paint with two coats of Pale Beige. Mix Lichen Grey with kleister medium, in a ratio of 1:1, and paint onto the pail. Dab with crumpled clingwrap to remove some paint and leave a mottled effect.

When all paint is dry, seal each pail with gloss medium/varnish.

Position cut-outs on pails with removable tape until a pleasing arrangement is achieved. Glue into place with a mix of wallpaper paste and PVA glue (3:1), smoothing out air bubbles or excess glue with rubber roller and wiping over with damp cloth. Remove excess dried glue by wiping over with equal parts of vinegar and water.

Touch up any obvious cut edges with oil-based artist's pencils or matching paint and a fine liner brush. Seal everything with gloss medium/varnish. When dry, varnish pails with six coats of water-based satin varnish.

Craqueleur Using a No. 6 flat brush, paint each pail with one coat of Japan gold size, making sure it is completely covered with an even coat. Allow to dry until just tacky (about two hours, depending on weather conditions — test lightly with a knuckle).

When gold size is dry, apply liquid gum arabic. This coat should be neither too thin (cracks will be too fine and shallow) nor too thick (cracks will be very wide apart with a long drying time). Let this layer dry for 30 minutes — then the process can be speeded up by gently using a hairdryer over the surface. Leave the cracks to develop fully overnight.

To emphasize cracks, antique them using oil paint, in the following manner: Using a soft cloth, rub Burnt Umber oil paint into cracks on the green and beige pails, and Paynes Grey into cracks on the blue pail. Wipe off any surplus paint almost immediately with a clean cloth.

Finishing Leave pails at least one week for oil paint to dry, then varnish with oil-based varnish. Apply at least 10 coats of varnish, then sand lightly with wet 600 wet-and-dry sandpaper. After another two coats of varnish, sand with 1200 wet-and-dry sandpaper, then apply a finishing coat of varnish.

Fittings Handles, rims and so on can all be rubbed with wax gilding paste by finger, or with a soft cloth, to give a gilded appearance. Leave to dry, then buff with a clean cloth.

Lavinia, Savinia and Vavinia
Duckylene, Luckylene and Zuckylene,
Tiglath-Pileser and Tilgath-Pilneser,
Abinadab, Ahinadab and Aminadab,
Abimelech, Ahimelech and Elimelech,
Felix, Kelix and Selix,
Alpheus, Dalpheus and Ralpheus,
Balak, Halak and Lamech,
Are all good names for dolls.
Randal, Sandal and Vandal,
Arabella, Carrabella and Clarabella,
Harriet, Marriet and Varriet,
Abilene, Mabilene and Rabilene,
Erwin, Kirwin and Mirwin,
Agar, Dagar and Zagar,
Alice, Dalice and Zalice,
Bab, Tab and Zab,
Edwin, Fredwin,
Clara, Lara, Sara and
Dariel and Zariel,
Gibeon, Tibeon and Zibeon,
Jessie, Kessie and Sessie,
Dias, Pius, Thias and Zius,
Doll, Moll, Poll and Noll,
EVE
TOBY
EVE
UNA

LITTLE WOMEN

With their demure expressions and old-fashioned clothes, it is hard to believe that these adorable maidens started life as humble papier mâché. They are durable enough for playthings, but would also add a lovely country accent to a kitchen cabinet shelf or bookcase.

MEASUREMENTS
Finished doll is approximately 9" tall.

MATERIALS

- Paper Clay: Instant Papier Mâché Mix
- Sharp-ended wooden craft sticks
- Wallpaper paste
- Newspaper, in two colors if possible
- Liquid polymer medium, matte or gloss
- Fine-grade sandpaper
- Craft blade or Xacto knife
- Gesso, such as Liquitex or Blickrylic
- Water-based clear sealer, such as Jo Sonja's, Bulls Eye 1-2-3, or Krylon

- Artist-quality flow formula acrylics: Ash Pink, Burnt Sienna, Mars Black, Titanium White, Burnt Umber and (for black doll only) Raw Umber, or equivalent
- Brushes: flat, for general painting and varnishing, and 10/0 liner, for face
- Water-based antiquing medium, such as Jo Sonja's
- Water-based satin varnish, such as Liquitex, Palmers, Dick Blick, or ModPodge
- Fine skewer or large needle
- Small amount calico, for Body
- Polyester fiberfill
- 8" x 16" cheesecloth or thin fabric, for Bloomers
- 12" x 20" fabric print, for Dress
- 16" square contrast fabric print, for Pinafore
- Blunt-ended darning or tapestry needle
- Scrap of crochet cotton or similar, for drawstring
- Heavy elastic thread, for gathering
- $^3/_4$ yard x $^1/_{16}$"-wide ribbon, for Pinafore and hair ties
- Doll hair (available in craft supply stores)
- Craft glue
- Purchased straw hat (optional)

PATTERN PIECES
All pattern pieces for doll's body and clothes are printed on page 231. Trace Body, Bloomers, Dress and Pinafore.

Dolls designed and made by Georgina Bitcon

CUTTING

Note: *Remember to **add** seam allowance to all pieces before cutting, as well as hem allowance on lower edge of Bloomers and Dress, and casing allowance on upper edge of Bloomers.*

From calico, cut two Bodies.

From cheesecloth, cut two Bloomers on the fold.

From fabric print, cut two Dresses.

From contrast print, cut four Pinafores.

METHOD

Doll Mix up a small amount of Paper Clay according to directions on packet. Break off the point of five craft sticks.

As though you were making ground meat kebabs, mold each of the doll's limbs around a craft stick (**Pic 1**). The finished limbs should be 3½" to 4" long, but if they're too long, trim them when dry. Carefully shape rudimentary hands on the arms.

To make the feet, stand a leg upright, then add another small amount of clay to the bottom, and mold into shape (**Pic 2**). Make each pair of arms and legs roughly the same size.

To shape the head, take a piece of clay, about the size of a pingpong ball, and roll and squeeze into a ball. Insert a craft stick into the ball, then, with more clay, mold a neck around the stick, making sure it becomes bonded to the head. Add a tiny amount of clay to the front of the head and smooth into a nose (**Pic 3**), flattening the face slightly on either side of the nose.

Place molded pieces on a tray and allow to dry for a couple of days, turning them occasionally and re-shaping if necessary so that they do not become flattened on one side as they dry. When they are partially dry, stand them upside down in a glass. (The drying process can be shortened in a very slow oven, if necessary, but remember to keep turning.)

When pieces are completely dry, they need to have a couple of layers of traditional papier mâché added, for strength. Do not be tempted to skip this step — the brittle limbs break very easily. Mix up wallpaper paste according to manufacturer's instructions. Tear newspaper into small pieces, dip into paste and apply to head and limbs (**Pic 4**), covering each with two layers. (It is easier to keep track of the layers if you use different-colored newspaper each time.) Allow to dry thoroughly.

Apply polymer medium to head and limbs, as desired, for a smooth surface (**Pic 5**). You may want to skip this step for a more rustic look, but it is easier to paint facial features on a smooth surface. We left our arms and legs fairly rough, but created a smooth head. When filler is dry, it can be sanded back until smooth. Repeat process until you are satisfied.

At this stage, you can carefully work craft sticks free and cut limbs to an exact length, if necessary, using a craft blade. Replace sticks to continue.

Paint head and limbs with gesso and allow to dry. Sand lightly, then seal each piece with clear sealer, including around cut end. Allow to dry.

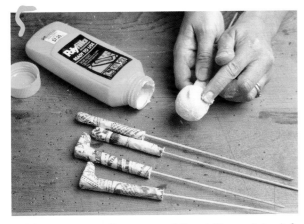

Mix a very small amount of Burnt Sienna into Ash Pink to create a brownish skin tone, and paint head and arms (**Pic 6**). (For a black-skinned doll, paint head and arms in Raw Umber.) For perfect coverage, use two coats, allowing to dry between coats.

For stockings, mix a grey shade from Mars Black and Titanium White and paint legs. (You can also paint legs in stripes, if desired.) When dry, paint foot and lower leg with Burnt Sienna, to simulate boots. When dry, paint sole, outline boot and add lace details in Mars Black or Burnt Umber, using liner brush (**Pic 7**).

Using a pencil, lightly mark the position of each eye with an elongated cross. (The eyes are a little above the halfway point on the face.) Now mark the position of the mouth, using two upside-down Cs for the upper lip and one C for the lower lip (**Pic 8**).

Using Titanium White and the liner brush, paint in a white oval over each pencil cross for the whites of the eyes (**Pic 9**).

Add Titanium White to a little Burnt Sienna plus a dot of Burnt Umber, and carefully fill in the lips. Add a touch of Titanium White to Burnt Umber to make it a little lighter, and paint a circle in the center of each white eye (**Pic 10**).

Water down this mixture just slightly to make it more fluid, and paint eyelids and eyebrows (**Pic 11**).

Add smaller pupil circles to the eyes, using Burnt Umber or Mars Black, then add the tiniest dot of Titanium White to both eyes for highlights. Finally, add a little extra Burnt Sienna to your original skin shade and paint two round cheeks (**Pic 12**).

Allow face and limbs to dry thoroughly, then paint each with clear sealer and allow to dry again.

Mix Burnt Umber with antiquing medium and apply with a brush or damp rag, then rub off, leaving just a trace of color, for an "antique" finish (**Pic 13**).

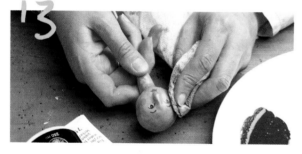

When pieces are thoroughly dry, seal with a coat of satin varnish and allow to dry again. Carefully withdraw craft sticks.

Using a fine skewer or large needle, push holes in upper edges of arms and legs, and in neck, pushing from side to side for one set of holes (**Pic 14**), then making a second set at right angles to the first.

Do not work too close to the edge, or the clay may crumble.

With right sides together, stitch Body pieces together, leaving open, as indicated, at armholes, neck edge and lower edge. Clip to stitching at underarms, then turn right side out. Turn under seam allowance at armholes and, with a double thread, run a gathering thread around edge. Insert arm into armhole, pull up gathers around arm and push needle across holes in upper arm, like sewing on a button, to secure. Tie off firmly. Repeat this process for remaining arm and legs.

Fill Body with polyester fiberfill, but not too firmly or limbs will not swing freely. Run a gathering thread around neck edge, as before, pull up gathers and secure head firmly in place with stitches from hole to hole.

Clothes Stitch narrow hems on lower edge of each Bloomer piece, and stitch a narrow casing along upper edge of each. Stitch Bloomers together at center front and center back, then around inside leg seam, using narrow French seams or zigzagging raw edges, as cheesecloth is inclined to fray. Turn Bloomers right side out. Thread darning needle with crochet cotton and, starting on one side of center front seam, work needle through casing, making a small jump over center back seam and re-emerging on other side of center front seam. Place Bloomers on the doll, pull up drawstring to fit waist and tie in a bow. Cut off excess thread and knot ends.

With right sides together, stitch Dress pieces together, leaving opening at neck edge as indicated. Snip to stitching at underarm. Turn under seam allowance at neck and sleeve edges and finger press. Thread a needle with heavy elastic thread and, securing end firmly, work a line of small running stitches around neck and sleeve edges. Pull up elastic to fit neck and arms, and secure ends. Sew a narrow hem on lower edge of Dress. Turn Dress right side out and place on doll.

With right sides together, stitch Pinafores together in pairs, sandwiching 4-inch ribbon ties in each side seam, as indicated, and leaving shoulders open, as well as an opening for turning in lower edge. Clip curves around neck edge and turn Pinafores right side out. Slipstitch each opening closed, and press. With right sides together, stitch Pinafores together at shoulders, keeping inside shoulder seams free. Turn in seam allowance on inside shoulder seams and slipstitch folded edges together. Place Pinafore on doll and tie at sides.

Finishing Glue hair to doll's head and arrange as desired, finishing braids with ribbon ties.

Pantaloons = Bloomers

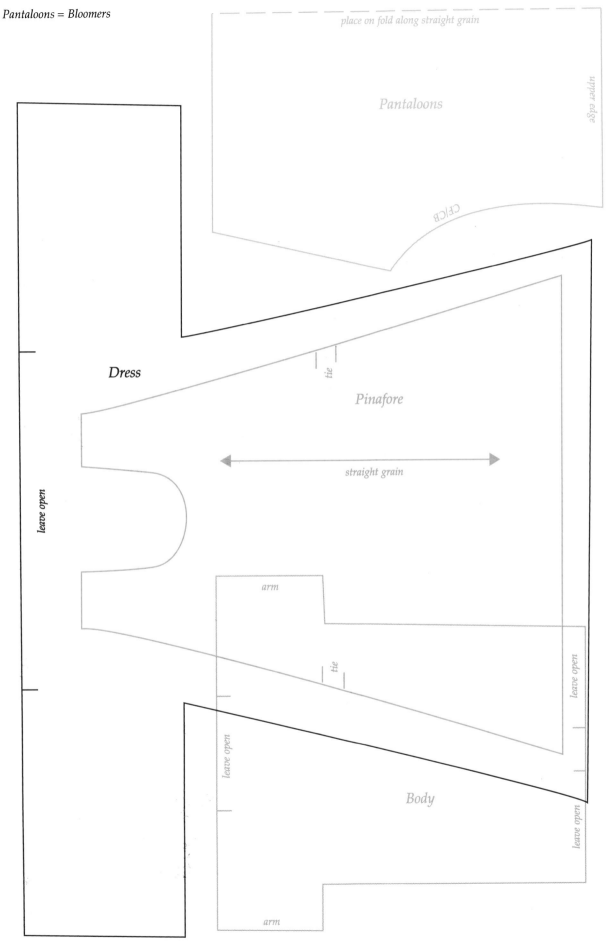

place on fold along straight grain

Pantaloons

upper edge

CF/CB

Dress

tie

Pinafore

straight grain

leave open

arm

tie

leave open

leave open

Body

leave open

arm

GENERAL CRAFT

MAN OF STRAW

P*erhaps a less common sight than he used to be, the scarecrow is nonetheless one of the most enduring and well-loved symbols of country life. Our splendid little fellow would add an instant rustic touch to a kitchen shelf, or a quaint highlight to a quilt display.*

MEASUREMENTS
Finished scarecrow is approximately 12^1/$_4$″ tall.

MATERIALS
- 10″ square calico, for Body
- 8″ square of two contrasting print fabrics, for Pants and Shirt
- Small amount brown paper
- Matching sewing thread
- Red and black embroidery floss
- Red colored pencil
- Polyester fiberfill
- Raffia

Project designed and stitched by Janene Nicholls
Photography by Catherine Muscat

- Large-eyed or straw/milliner's needle, for sewing with raffia
- One 10^3/$_4$″ length of ^{1}/$_2$″ dowel
- Two 5^1/$_2$″ lengths of ^{3}/$_8$″ dowel
- Small amount dried moss, for hair
- Craft glue

PATTERN PIECES
All pattern pieces are printed on page 237. Trace Body, Shirt Front/Back, Pants and Hat.

CUTTING
Note: ^{1}/$_4$ *inch seam allowance is **included** on all pieces, except Hat, which is cut without allowance.*
From calico, cut two Bodies.
   From one print, cut one Shirt Front (on the fold) and two Shirt Backs (along center back opening, as shown on pattern piece).
   From contrast print, cut two Pants.
   From brown paper, cut one Hat.

SEWING
With right sides together, stitch scarecrow Bodies together, leaving bottom edge open. Trim seams, clip curves and turn right side out.
   Using black embroidery floss, work backstitch eyes and satin stitch nose, as shown on the pattern piece. The mouth is embroidered in red running stitch. A red pencil can be used lightly for cheeks.

Fill Body quite firmly with polyester fiberfill and slipstitch opening closed.

With right sides together, stitch Shirt Front to Shirt Backs across shoulder seam, leaving opening for neck as indicated on the pattern. Press under seam allowance on front and back neck opening. With right sides together, stitch side and sleeve seams in one operation. Clip underarm corners, turn Shirt right side out and press.

Place Shirt on Body and baste back opening to neck. With a couple of strands of raffia threaded in large-eyed needle, and beginning at center front neck edge, run a gathering stitch around neck edge of Shirt, draw up to fit neck and tie in bow at center front.

Run a raffia gathering thread around raw edges of sleeves, but leave ungathered for the moment.

With right sides together, stitch side seams of Pants. Stitch along given stitching line for inner leg seam, then carefully cut along slash line, cutting diagonally in towards stitching at top of slash. Turn Pants right side out and press.

Starting at center front of Pants, run a raffia gathering thread around the waist, approximately $5/8$ inch below raw edge. Run similar gathering threads around lower edges of Pants, approximately 1 inch from raw edge.

Place Pants onto Body and pull up raffia drawstring to fit waist firmly, adding a little stuffing to give shape to Pants before tying ends in a bow at center front.

Insert long dowel through sleeves, and position it evenly across back of scarecrow. Before tying off raffia drawstrings at sleeve edges, insert small bunches of raffia into sleeves, leaving some showing (to give impression that scarecrow is stuffed with straw). Pull up drawstrings around dowel and tie off securely.

Insert shorter dowel pieces into trouser legs and add a little stuffing as well as raffia (in the same manner as arms) before tying off.

Glue dried moss to head for hair.

Run a raffia gathering thread around Hat circle, about $3/4$ inch from edge. Pull up gathers carefully to fit head, then tie raffia in bow at the front. Glue Hat to scarecrow's head over his hair.

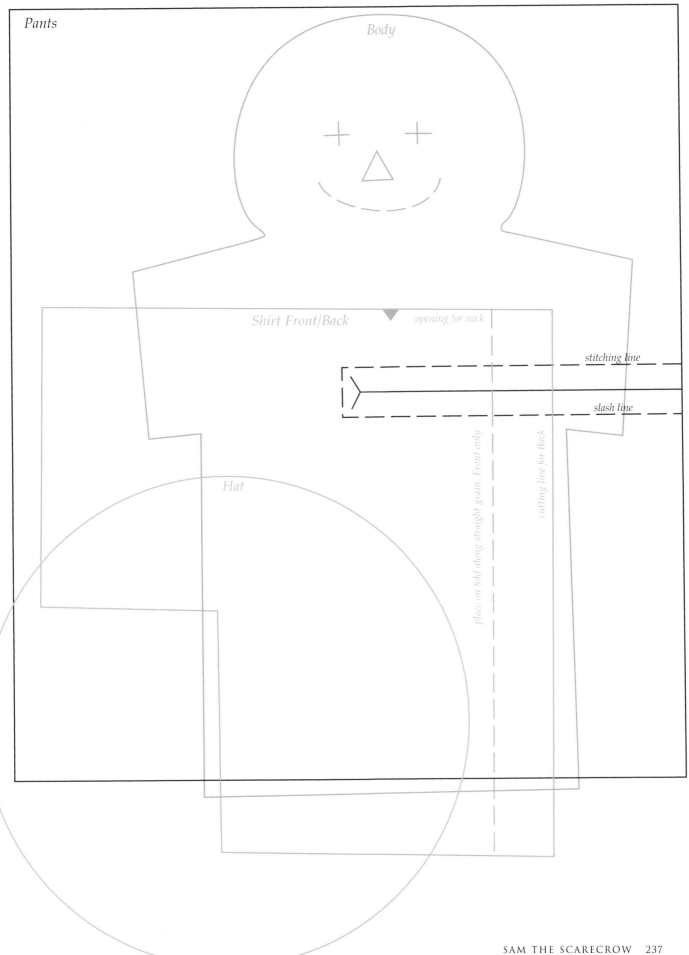

Pants

Body

Shirt Front/Back

opening for neck

stitching line

slash line

place on fold along straight grain. Front only

cutting line for Back

Hat

AUTUMN PRESSINGS

Autumn leaves — each a lasting reminder of a season that is all too brief — make unusual and highly decorative découpage materials for a variety of inexpensive or recycled containers.

MATERIALS

- Items to découpage, such as recycled cans or papier mâché boxes
- Colorful autumn leaves
- Microfleur microwave flower press (see **Note**, below)
- White vinegar
- Anti-rust spray
- Artist-quality background paints, such as Jo Sonja's: Vellum and/or Olive Green, or equivalent
- Brushes: $^3/_4$" flat, varnish brush and 1" foam
- All-purpose sealer, such as Krylon or Royal Gard
- Tacky craft glue
- Disposable lint-free towelettes
- Oil-based satin varnish, such as Damar by Shiva
- White gesso, such as Liquitex or Blickrylic
- Sandpaper
- Lead pencil
- Craft blade or scissors
- Old toothbrush

Note: *Leaves can be pressed in the traditional manner, although we recommend using a Microfleur, as it preserves the color beautifully and is very quick — see Box on page 217 for information on pressing flowers and leaves and details of the Microfleur.*

Photography by Louise Lister

METHOD

Press assorted autumn leaves in the Microfleur according to manufacturer's instructions, or between the pages of an outdated phone book, and set aside.

Tin Canister Wash canister and lid with detergent and warm water, then rinse. Wipe over with vinegar and water (1:1) and dry. Spray on two coats of anti-rust paint and allow to dry.

Paint with two coats of Vellum and one rough coat of Olive Green, using the $^3/_4$" flat brush and allowing to dry between coats. Apply one coat of all-purpose sealer.

Experiment with placement of leaves, covering most of the canister and ensuring that the most interesting leaves stand out. Paint back of each leaf with a thick layer of glue and press onto canister, smoothing out excess with a damp towelette. Hold leaf in place while the glue sets. Continue around canister, overlapping leaves. The lid has a zigzag line of small leaves around the side and a circular pattern of leaves on the top.

Leave to dry overnight, then check if any edges need extra glue. Dry and seal with all-purpose sealer.

When dry, varnish with 10 coats of satin varnish, using the varnish brush and allowing to dry between coats.

Oval Papier Mâché Box Apply two coats of white gesso to all surfaces, inside and out, using the foam brush and allowing to dry between coats. Sand lightly after the second coat, then apply two coats of Vellum. Allow to dry, and seal with one coat of all-purpose sealer.

When dry, place the lid on the base and lightly mark the overlap with pencil. Do not glue leaves above this line or the lid will not close.

We used large leaves for this box. Position a leaf on the box base, mark on it with pencil the length required, then trim carefully with a craft blade or scissors. Apply the tacky glue to the back of the leaf, allow to set slightly, then smooth leaf onto the box, removing excess glue with a damp towelette. Overlap leaves — one up, one down — around the base.

For lid, place leaves pointing towards the center, starting at the top, then the sides and finally the bottom. The side of the lid has small cut sections of the leaves overlapping. When dry, check if any extra glue is required, then seal and varnish, as for Tin Canister.

Octagonal Papier Mâché Box
Apply gesso as for the Oval Box, then paint with two coats of Vellum, inside and out. Make up a watery mix of Olive Green and use the toothbrush to spatter this over the Vellum, inside and out.

The base has vertical overlapping leaves glued in place after being trimmed to fit (be careful not to carry them under the lid). The lid has a formal arrangement of four leaves placed diagonally in a diamond pattern around the edge, then a cross shape in the middle with a small leaf in the center.

When dry, check that all is glued down, then seal and varnish, as for the Tin Canister, opposite.

TAKE A LEAF

One of the best ways to focus attention on the beauty of autumn leaves is to feature a single lovely specimen in a frame. Plain wooden frames, rustic mats and textured mounts, such as those shown here, all complement the leaf's natural beauty and do not interfere with its sculptural simplicity. Sometimes you can be lucky enough to find "skeletonized" leaves, their fragile network of veins all that remains after the ravages of weather and insects. But if such leaves are difficult to find, we show you how to help Nature along a little and skeletonize your own specimens for framing.

Small Frame

MEASUREMENTS

Our frame measures 9" x 10", but any size frame can be used.

MATERIALS

- Unfinished wooden frame
- Artist's acrylic gouache, such as Jo Sonja's, Winsor & Newton, Dick Blick, or The French School: Brown Earth and Raw Sienna, or equivalent

Leaf pictures designed and made by Pamela Worsdall
Photography by Louise Lister

- Clear glazing medium, such as Jo Sonja's
- Clean rags
- 150 fine sandpaper
- Old toothbrush
- Furniture wax
- Assorted leaves
- Microfleur flower press (see Box on page 217)
- Burlap fabric
- Spray adhesive
- Tacky craft glue

METHOD

Prepare a stain for the frame by mixing Brown Earth and Raw Sienna (2:1), then mixing one part of this paint mix with three parts clear glazing medium. With a damp rag, rub a thin coat of stain over frame, removing any excess as you go. When dry, sand lightly. If desired, thin some Brown Earth with water and use toothbrush to give the frame a light spatter. Finish with a coat of wax rubbed in with a clean, soft cloth. Buff when set.

Choose an interesting leaf and press in the Microfleur. Cut a piece of burlap to fit the frame glass and fringe the sides. Spray the back with adhesive and smooth onto the backboard of the frame. Brush some tacky glue onto the back of the pressed leaf and press firmly onto the burlap, holding until set.

Narrow Frame

We used a 10¹/₄" x 13³/₄" frame.

MATERIALS

- Pine frame
- Artist-quality background paints, such as Jo Sonja's or Liquitex: Vellum and Olive Green, or equivalent
- 150 fine sandpaper
- Old toothbrush
- Furniture wax
- Soft cloth
- Assorted leaves
- Microfleur flower press (see Box on page 217)
- Cream-colored Canson paper
- Tacky craft glue
- Corrugated cardboard
- Lead pencil
- Craft blade
- Ruler
- Artist's acrylic gouache, such as Jo Sonja's or Dick Blick: Brown Earth and Raw Sienna, or equivalent

METHOD

Paint frame with one coat of Vellum. When dry, rub with sandpaper in direction of grain to reveal unfinished wood in parts. Thin some Olive Green with water and use toothbrush to spatter the frame lightly. Finish frame by rubbing in one coat of furniture wax with a soft cloth, allow to set, then buff clean with a cloth.

Choose an interesting eucalyptus leaf and press in the Microfleur.

Cut a piece of Canson paper to size and glue this onto the backing board with a thin layer of tacky glue. Cut a piece of corrugated cardboard to the same size. Decide where the leaf will be placed and, on the flat back of the cardboard, draw a rectangle to frame the leaf. Use a craft blade and ruler to cut this out. Again working from the back, pencil leaf shapes around the rectangle, and cut them out. (If the cardboard is too grey in color, it can be painted with a wash of Brown Earth and Raw Sienna (1:3) to make it warmer, or any other color you prefer.) Place the corrugated mat on the Canson paper and position the leaf. Glue the leaf in place with the tacky glue, then the cardboard mat around it. Tape the frame and mount together.

Skeletonized Leaves

MATERIALS

- Unfinished wooden frame — we used size 13³/₄" x 16"
- Artist-quality background paints, such as Jo Sonja's: Vellum and Forest Green, or equivalent
- Clear glazing medium, such as ModPodge
- Clean rag
- 150 fine sandpaper
- Furniture wax
- Washing soda crystals (sodium carbonate)
- Leaves with good veins (see **Note**, below)
- Tongs and blunt knife
- Newspaper
- Paper towel
- Black spray craft paint
- Cream-colored Canson paper
- PVA glue, archival quality
- Burlap fabric
- No. 6 flat fitch brush

Note: *Ivy works well, but experiment with other leaves. Very new or very old leaves do not seem to work as well.*

METHOD

Mix Vellum and Forest Green (1:1), then mix paint with clear glazing medium (1:6). Using a damp rag, rub this stain over the frame, wiping off excess. Allow to dry, then sand to reveal the grain, and finish with one coat of wax applied with a soft cloth.

Mix three tablespoons of washing soda with 4¹/₂ cups of water and heat to boiling in a (non-aluminum) saucepan. Add leaves (no stems) and simmer for 30 minutes, gently stirring now and then to keep leaves submerged. Working on one leaf at a time, remove leaves from saucepan with tongs, dip in clean water and place on newspaper. Holding leaf down with top side up and using a blunt knife, gently scrape away outer surface of leaf, working from main veins out towards edge. Dip leaf in washing soda solution again for 10 seconds, then place on newspaper, lower side up, and remove this layer as before. Place flat on paper towel to dry. The skeletons can be sprayed with black paint to make them stand out in the frame.

Cut a piece of Canson paper to fit the backing board and glue down. Cut four strips of burlap wide enough to form a ⁵/₈-inch mat in from the frame to outline the leaves, and glue strips onto the paper. Using the flat fitch brush, very gently apply some PVA glue to the skeleton's main vein and edges. Position onto the paper and gently press flat with a piece of paper towel, removing it quickly before the glue starts to set. Glue other skeletons in place in same manner and attach mount to frame with tape.

THE EGG
AND DYE

P ut a little tradition back into Easter with a clutch of engraved eggs, which have long been part of European Easter celebrations. Although motifs differ from country to country, the essential technique of scratching onto a dyed egg is the same throughout Europe. It is not a difficult process, and a collection can be built up over many years, personalized with recipients' names or perhaps engraved with the date and place of your celebrations. But if engraving seems too much trouble, the simple dyed eggs themselves are very sculptural.

MATERIALS

- Hen eggs (we used 2oz size)
- Dylon Multi-Purpose Dyes in chosen colors (available from art materials suppliers; one tin of dye will be enough for several eggs)
- White vinegar and cooking salt
- Glass or ceramic containers
- Newspaper
- Fine skewer or darning needle
- Craft blade or Xacto knife
- Olive oil

Eggs decorated by Georgina Bitcon
Photography by Andre Martin
Styling by Vicki Liley

METHOD

Eggs must be dyed before they are blown, as it is very difficult to weight an empty egg.

Mix half a container of Dylon dye with 2 cups of hot water, three tablespoons of white vinegar and $1^1/_2$ tablespoons of salt. Stir until salt is dissolved and allow to cool completely. Do not be tempted to put eggs into dye until it is completely cool or the contents might cook a little and you will not be able to blow the egg.

Place two or three eggs into dye and weight with an old saucer, if necessary, so that they are completely submerged. Allow to remain in dye for an hour or so, or until they are as deeply colored as you desire. Remove from dye and rinse under gently running water, then place on several thicknesses of newspaper to dry.

Using a fine skewer or darning needle, carefully make a hole in both ends of an egg, poking skewer into egg to break yolk. Holding one end over a bowl, blow hard so that contents of the egg are expelled into the bowl, until egg is empty. Discard contents. Allow egg to dry again.

We have reproduced some rustic designs at left, but these are for use as a guide only, as it is virtually impossible to trace onto the curved surface of an egg. If you are nervous, you can use a lead pencil or light colored pencil to sketch a basic outline onto an egg, but remember that the designs are more appealing if they are naïve. If you feel you really cannot draw a simple chicken or rabbit, it is easy to divide your egg into segments, either vertically or horizontally, and fill in the stripes with different patterns. The result is still very effective.

Using the point of a sharp craft blade or Xacto knife, scratch a pattern onto the surface of the egg, using short scratching strokes to remove the dye and expose the natural color beneath. Do not grip the egg too firmly — remember it is fairly fragile — and do not design too complicated a pattern, as too much engraving will weaken the shell.

When design is complete, moisten your fingers with a tiny amount of olive oil and rub over the surface of the egg to give a soft glow. If you use too much oil, wipe off the excess with a tissue.

FABULOUS FAKES

*P*reserve the sculptural beauty of a simple vegetable by casting it in plaster. These bell peppers were all cast in the same mold, then painted different colors and given a touch of the exotic with gold stems. Bell peppers are ideal for casting, but so too are eggplants and small squash — in fact, any shape that is not too intricate will make a perfect mold, and can be used again and again.

MATERIALS

- Bell pepper, or vegetable of choice
- Straight-sided container (see **Note**)
- Petroleum jelly
- Wet clay
- One 8" length of $^5/_{16}$" dowel
- Dow Corning Silastic 3481 Base & Curing Agent kit, 2lb pack, or Por-a-Mold kit (available through art suppliers)
- Small amount Plasticine
- Plaster of Paris
- Sandpaper

- Craft blade or Xacto knife
- Clear sealer, such as Jo Sonja's or Krylon
- Artist-quality flow formula acrylics, such as Jo Sonja's: Napthol Crimson, Burgundy, Venetian Red, Chromium Green Oxide, Antique Green, Pthalo Blue, Dioxazine Purple and Paynes Grey, or equivalent
- 1" flat brush
- Water-based antiquing medium, such as Jo Sonja's
- Disposable lint-free towelettes
- Gold gilding wax, such as RubnBuff, or a gilding kit
- Water-based satin varnish, such as Liquitex or Jo Sonja's

Note: *Choose a container that allows approximately $^3/_4$" around all sides of the object you wish to mold, but not much more. This will ensure a solid mold, but will not unnecessarily waste the silastic medium. When choosing the container, also consider the way in which you want to orientate the object in a two-part mold — any parts that curve back on themselves should be molded sideways so that the mold can be pulled apart easily.*

Bell peppers made by Caroline Halliday
Photography by Joe Filshie
Styling by Georgina Dolling

METHOD

Grease base and sides of container with a substantial amount of petroleum jelly. Place the bell pepper, or object to be molded, in the bottom of the container, and pack wet clay to approximately halfway up its sides, smoothing the surface of the clay as flat as possible. Push 2-inch lengths of dowel into the clay around the bell pepper, about $^3/_4$ inch deep. These will form positional pegs, and ensure that the halves join accurately in the casting process (**Pic 1**).

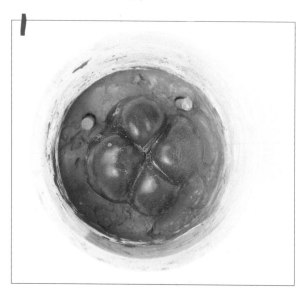

Mix the kit ingredients together in accordance with the manufacturer's instructions. Mix only enough to cover the bell pepper completely to a thickness of approximately $^1/_2$ inch above the piece. Pour the mix over the bell pepper (**Pic 2**) and allow to set for 24 hours.

When set, invert container and tip contents out. Wash clay from bell pepper and mold, and return both to container, with mold at the bottom and bell pepper

and positional pegs in place in the mold. Make two small sausages of Plasticine and place on top of the bell pepper, as shown in **Pic 3**.

The Plasticine sausages will form channels — one will be used for pouring the plaster, the other for an airhole. We used the bell pepper stem as one channel; the other should be on the next highest point of the bell pepper (if there is not a clear high point, several pouring holes can be made to ensure every "bump" will be filled). Smear petroleum jelly over mold, bell pepper, Plasticine and dowel. Mix remainder of kit material together as before, and pour over bell pepper to form second part of mold. Allow to set 24 hours.

When set, tip contents out of container, pull mold apart (**Pic 4**) and remove bell pepper and Plasticine.

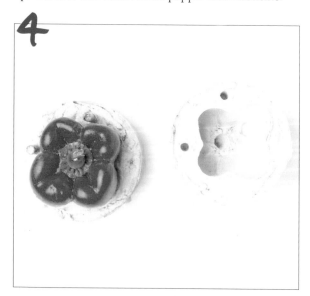

Rejoin the halves of the mold and secure with several elastic bands. To a container containing approximately $1^1/_4$ cups of water, add plaster of Paris until the mixture has the consistency of thick cream. Pour plaster into mold through one channel (**Pic 5**), ensuring it fills the mold completely by tapping to remove excess air bubbles and tipping mold at an angle away from pouring hole to fill all areas. Fill mold until plaster shows at both holes.

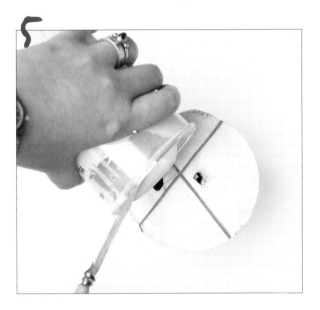

Allow plaster to set completely, approximately six hours, and pull base of mold away from the bell pepper.

Carefully remove cast from remainder of mold. With a craft blade or Xacto knife, cut away any rough joints and the plaster "plugs" that the pouring hole and airhole have left (**Pic 6**).

If there are any unwanted air bubbles or irregularities, mix a little plaster to the consistency of putty and use your finger to smear it into the holes (**Pic 7**). Allow plaster to cure for approximately 24 hours. This curing time will vary with the weather, but plaster should be completely dry before sealing and

painting, otherwise the paint will peel. When dry, sand surface lightly until smooth.

Seal surface with clear sealer. When dry, paint as follows:

For the red bell pepper, paint with two coats of Napthol Crimson, allowing to dry between coats. Paint stem in Burgundy. Leave to dry for 24 hours. Mix Venetian Red and antiquing medium together in equal amounts to form a glaze. Apply a generous coat to the surface of the bell pepper, but not the stem. Drag a clean, damp towelette lightly down the surface to reveal lighter color underneath. If you wipe too much glaze off, reapply paint and drag again. Allow to dry.

For the green bell pepper, mix Chromium Green Oxide with Antique Green in equal amounts and paint sealed plaster with two coats, allowing to dry between coats. Paint stem with Burgundy. Leave to dry for 24 hours. Add a touch of Pthalo Blue to basecoat color, then mix this with an equal amount of antiquing medium. Apply and drag this glaze with a damp towelette, as for red bell pepper. If desired, apply a second glaze of Chromium Green Oxide mixed with an equal amount of antiquing medium when the first glaze has dried.

For the purple bell pepper, paint bell pepper and stem in two coats of Burgundy. Allow to dry for 24 hours. Mix together Dioxazine Purple and Paynes Grey (1:2). To this mix, add an equal amount of antiquing medium, and apply and drag the glaze, as for red bell pepper.

Apply a small amount of gold gilding wax to bell pepper stems, allowing Burgundy to show underneath, or, using a gilding kit, paint stem with gold size, apply gold leaf and finish with gold leaf sealer.

When you are happy with the look, apply several coats of satin varnish over the entire surface.

BREAD OF LOVE

O nce you get started on these bread dough teddy bears, we guarantee your "family" will just grow and grow! Hot sellers at craft fairs, these dear little fellows are also great favorites with children, who, incidentally, will love helping you to make them. They are easy to model from the most inexpensive of materials: flour, salt and water. Whether you choose the portrait bears or the lively cubs around the honey pot, the basic technique is the same, and the decorative details are limited only by your imagination. And once you have mastered these basic bears, you will find it easy to try different sizes, shapes and clothing; simply experiment with baking times according to the size and thickness of each model.

Bread dough teddies created by Theresia Cookson
Photography by Joe Filshie
Styling by Georgina Dolling

Bread Dough

BASIC MATERIALS
(for one batch of dough)

- 2 cups all-purpose flour
- $1/2$ cup salt
- Food coloring or acrylic paints in desired colors (see **Note**, below)
- 1 teaspoon glycerine or vegetable oil (optional)
- 1 cup warm water

Note: *Dough can be colored with food coloring or acrylic paint before baking, or painted after baking. We colored our dough with acrylic paint, using brown, blue, dark green, white and yellow.*

BASIC INSTRUCTIONS

For each batch of dough, first mix the dry ingredients well. If making colored dough, add approximately one teaspoon of food coloring or acrylic paint to the warm water to give a stronger color than that required in the finished piece (colors will fade during baking). For a true white dough, white paint can be added; if left plain, the dough will bake to a pale cookie color. For a smoother, more elastic dough, add glycerine or vegetable oil to the water, then slowly add water mix to dry ingredients, stirring until well combined.

Knead mixture well for at least 10 minutes until it is smooth and elastic. Wrap in a plastic bag or plastic clingwrap, and leave to rest for 20 minutes before modeling.

Portrait Bears

MEASUREMENTS

Each portrait bear is approximately $6^3/4''$ tall.

MATERIALS

- Basic Materials, as on page 249
- Thin cardboard, for templates
- Rolling pin
- Aluminum foil
- Assorted modeling tools: knife, skewer, pastry wheel, aspic cutters, garlic press, as desired
- Peppercorns
- Artist-quality acrylic paint: Black and White
- Fine paintbrush
- Oil-based gloss varnish, such as Damar by Shiva, or Cassein (do not use water-based varnish)
- $8'' \times 9^1/2''$ pine frame
- Small wood cut-outs, to decorate frame (optional)
- Craft glue

PATTERN OUTLINES

Pattern outlines for portrait bears' clothing are printed on page 253. Trace Underskirt, Dress, Apron, Collar and Trousers. Transfer to thin cardboard and cut out, to use as templates.

METHOD

Modeling Make one batch of brown dough for the body, and as many half-batches of colored dough as needed to make the clothes — we used blue, green, yellow and white. If preferred, you can leave all dough natural and paint it after baking. In our finished portraits, we used colored dough, but added extra painted detail to the clothes after baking.

Model bear's body first by rolling a golfball-sized piece of dough (**Pic 1**). Now roll and flatten it to form a cylinder approximately 3 inches long and $1/2$ inch thick (**Pic 2**). Place dough on a piece of aluminum foil now, as it will be easier to place directly into oven later.

Using a knife, create legs by cutting halfway up the cylinder, and pulling the ends apart a little. Using the blunt end of a pencil or modeling tool, make holes in the bottom of the legs in which to insert feet (**Pic 3**).

To make feet, roll marble-sized balls of dough into cone shapes, and insert narrower end of each cone into holes in legs (**Pic 4**). To make parts stick together, dip your finger in water and dampen section to be joined. Mark "toes" on feet using modeling tool or blunt knife.

From colored dough (we used green), roll out a piece $1/8$-inch thick, and use Underskirt template to cut to shape (**Pic 5**). Curve Underskirt slightly upwards and, if desired, mark "stitches" along hem line using a pastry wheel (**Pic 6**). Dampen top edge of Underskirt to attach to body. Center across legs, leaving feet showing, and gather by pinching where required (**Pic 7**).

Repeat these steps for Dress, rounding off lower corners before positioning. Leave $3/4$ inch of Underskirt showing and form pleat in dough at center front (**Pic 8**).

Roll and cut Apron from a different-colored dough (we used yellow) and position over Dress, using a skewer or other sharp point to pinprick edge to form decorative stitches (**Pic 9**). If desired, embellish Apron with tiny heart shapes and/or buttons, cut from contrast dough using aspic cutters.

To make sleeves, roll out a cylinder about 6 inches long and $5/8$-inch thick in desired color and attach across top of body, folding each "arm" into position as desired. Mold small pieces of dough into oval shapes for paws, attach to ends of sleeves, as for feet, and mark paws.

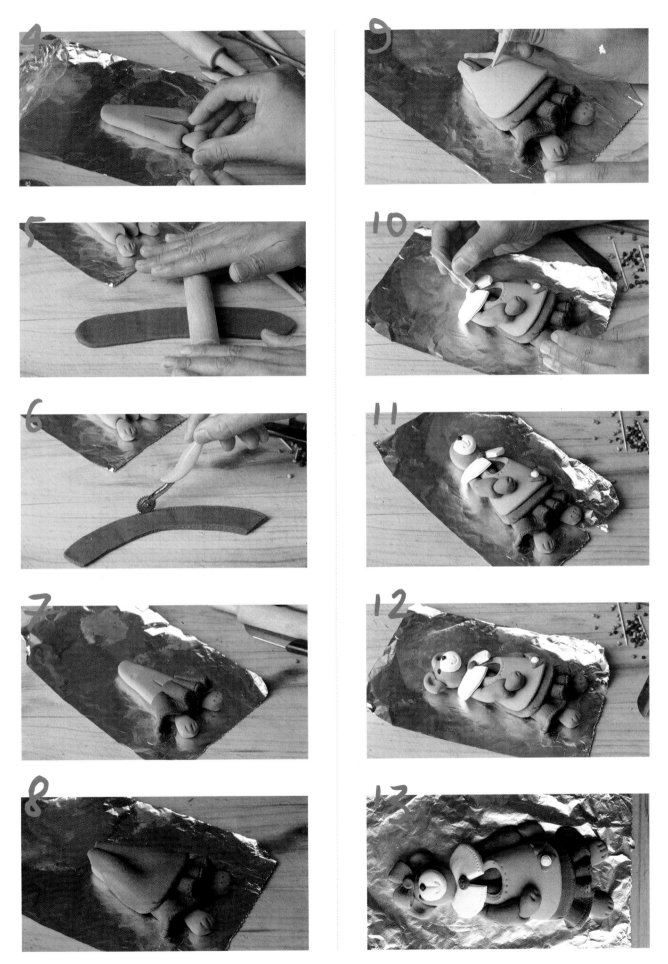

Roll out a piece of white dough and, using template, cut a Collar. Use a pastry cutter to decorate lower edges, if desired. Moisten back of Collar and attach to top of body. Make a button for Collar by cutting a $^3/_8$-inch circle of contrast dough, then marking a smaller circle in center with a tiny tube or drinking straw (**Pic 10**). Use a skewer or pin to mark center of button with four tiny dots.

To make the head, mold a walnut-sized piece of brown dough into a slightly flattened oval. Attach to neck above Collar, moistening with water for good adhesion.

To make muzzle, roll a white ball of dough that is about half the size of the head, cut in half and attach cut side to front of face. Push a peppercorn into muzzle for the nose and, using a blunt knife or modeling tool, mark the mouth as shown in **Pic 11**. Push peppercorn eyes into head just above muzzle or, if preferred, paint on eyes after baking.

For ears, roll a small ball of brown dough and cut in half. Flatten each half slightly and position on each side of head. Using your finger or a blunt modeling tool, indent the center front of each ear (**Pic 12**).

For the hair bow, roll out a rectangle, $2^1/_2$" x $^3/_4$", of blue dough. Fold ends behind to the center, forming a loop, then pinch loop in the center, forming a bow shape. Attach to bear's head between ears. Roll a tiny circle and flatten, to form center of bow, and attach (**Pic 13**).

Boy bear variation: The boy portrait bear is modeled in a similar manner to the girl, except for the following variations:

Roll and cut the boy's legs as for the girl bear, but use the same-colored dough as you will use for the boy's shirt. After cutting the legs, use the Trousers template to make his pants. Attach over legs, adding a small extra cushion of dough beneath the upper section to form his belly, if desired. Add rectangular cuffs to lower edges of Trousers, decorating edges with a pastry cutter. Add small contrast dough "patches" to Trousers, if desired. Apply sleeves and paws, as for girl bear, but, before adding Collar, cut two narrow strips for suspenders and run these from shoulders to top edge of Trousers. Add tiny buttons. Create head as for girl bear, but, before adding ears, cut another Collar shape (without the center split) and attach this to the head, curved edge to the front, forming a simple hat. Attach the ears to the top of the hat.

Extras: If desired, use aspic cutters and a garlic press to make a bouquet of flowers for girl teddy's paw. Use the garlic press to extrude a mass of thin green stalks for your flowers. The teddies can also hold books, their own toy teddies, or anything else you wish to model.

Baking Carefully transfer your completed bear (still on its aluminum foil) to a baking tray. Bake at approximately 250°F until completely hard and dry, between 12 and 15 hours, depending on the size and thickness of the piece. Remove from the oven. Allow to cool, then if any sections are loose, re-glue them into position.

Painting and varnishing Using a fine paintbrush, outline muzzle details in black, and add a white dot to center of each peppercorn eye. Paint clothing, as desired, using the photographs on this page as a guide.

When dry, seal with at least two coats of gloss varnish and allow to dry. It is vital to finish all pieces with at least two coats of varnish to protect them from moisture and humidity. If possible, keep pieces in a dry and sunny spot. If your dough object does go soft even after varnishing, put it outside in the sun or in a sunny dry room until it hardens again, when it can be re-varnished.

Finishing Attach figure and decorative wooden cut-outs to pine frame using craft glue.

Sitting Bears

MEASUREMENTS
Finished bears range from $2^1/_2$" to 4" high.

MATERIALS

- Basic Materials, as on page 249
- Aluminum foil
- Rolling pin
- Assorted modeling tools: knife, skewer, pastry wheel, aspic cutters, garlic press, as desired
- Peppercorns
- Fine paintbrush
- Artist-quality acrylic paint: Black
- Oil-based gloss varnish, such as Damar by Shiva (do not use water-based varnish)

METHOD
Knead one batch of brown dough and a half-batch of two or more other colors (we used white, blue, yellow and green).

For the body, take a walnut-sized ball (2 inches diameter) of brown dough and gently elongate it into more of a cone shape, about 2 inches high and $1\frac{1}{8}$ inches across base. (This will give a finished bear about $2\frac{3}{4}$ inches high. For larger bears, use proportionately more dough for each segment and allow extra baking time.) Place body on a piece of aluminum foil.

From brown dough, shape two legs in the form of tapered "sausages", each about 2 inches long, $\frac{3}{4}$ inch in diameter at thickest end and tapering away to almost nothing at the opposite end. Make a circular indentation on each thickest (foot) end. Moisten lower edge of body and curve legs around sides of body to attach, leaving space between them for honey jar.

Roll out a piece of colored dough $\frac{1}{8}$ inch thick and cut a rectangle, approximately 1 inch wide and long enough to wrap around the bear's body. Moisten one side of the rectangle and wrap around bear's body, pinching in excess dough at neck edge and butting edges at center back for a smock front, or bringing edges to the center front and folding upper corners back slightly to give the appearance of a jacket collar.

Using dough in the same color as the shirt/jacket, roll two $1\frac{1}{2}$-inch balls and shape into tapered "sausages" for sleeves, just slightly shorter than legs. Attach arms to side of body. Roll two small balls of dough for paws, pinching one side of each to form a cone. Indent ends of sleeves, moisten indentations and insert paws. Mark claws on paws with a skewer. Decorate jacket/shirt front with buttons and hearts or flowers, as desired. A kerchief can be made by following the instructions for the girl bear's bow, on opposite page. Position bow on bear's neck, then add extra tails, as well as a narrow strip around neck itself.

For the head, roll a $1\frac{1}{8}$-inch brown ball. Flatten one side of a $\frac{3}{4}$-inch white ball of dough and apply to front of face for muzzle. Push head onto body, using a little water to moisten contact point. Press peppercorns into face and muzzle for eyes and nose, and mark mouth with a modeling tool or blunt knife.

If making a bear without a hat, mold ears as for Portrait Bears, on opposite page, and adhere to each side of head.

To make a hat, the simplest method is to cut a semi-circle (the size will depend on the size of your bear's head) and arrange around top of head into a brim shape. If you want a complete hat (so that bear can be viewed from the back), cut a donut shape for the brim and place onto bear's head. Next, cut a circle that will cover exposed area of crown and smooth over the bear's head to meet the brim. On both styles of hat, fold brim back a little at front and decorate as desired.

Roll a small brown ball of dough for honey jar, and slightly flatten base. If leaving jar open, push your little finger or the end of a pencil into the center of the ball, and mold into a pot shape. If you would prefer a lid, flatten a small disc of dough and place onto jar. Place a pea-sized ball of dough on lid for knob. Position the jar between the bear's legs.

Lift bear (on aluminum foil) onto baking tray and bake at 250°F for approximately 10 hours or until completely dry. Paint details as required and seal with two coats of gloss varnish.

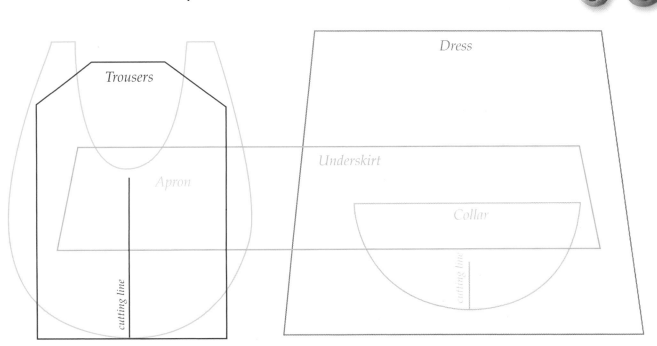

Trousers

Dress

Apron

Underskirt

Collar

cutting line

cutting line

NATURE WINDOWS

These elegant, minimalist frames are easy to make using sheets of glass, or plexiglass, and copper foil. The simple beauty of delicate ferns, grasses or even a single perfect leaf is highlighted by the transparent background and thin frame. Your favorite print can also be treated in this manner, but a mount should be used to prevent the print sticking to the glass. Pictures can be hung on walls or in windows, or simply stood against a support.

MEASUREMENTS

Frames can be made to any size, but remember that the larger they are, the heavier they will be and the more difficult to hang.

MATERIALS

- Two sheets $^1/_{16}$″ glass, cut to required size
- Clean cotton gloves
- Flowers, grasses or ferns
- $^3/_8$″-wide self-adhesive copper foil tape
- Black patina
- Fine copper wire, for hanging (optional)
- Soldering iron, solder and flux (optional)
- Paintbrush, for patina

Note: *Foil tape, copper wire and black patina can be purchased from stained glass suppliers.*

Frames created by Caroline Gunter

METHOD

Flowers, grasses and ferns should be thoroughly dried and then pressed (see Box on page 217).

Wearing clean cotton gloves to avoid leaving fingerprints, thoroughly clean both sheets of glass (**Pic 1**). For a very shiny, lint-free surface, rub glass with crumpled dry newspaper.

Lay pressed plants onto one glass surface and arrange the design. Carefully top with remaining glass sheet. Cut two strips of copper foil tape the length of glass sides plus an extra $^3/_4$ inch. Remove backing from foil and tape two parallel sides together, wrapping foil around edges from front to back and allowing $^3/_8$ inch to extend at either end (**Pic 2**). Make sure tape edges are even along frame front.

Snip tape ends in along corner folds to glass, then fold pieces neatly over one another. Tape remaining two sides with foil in the same manner, folding and trimming ends neatly. Smooth foil against glass with your fingernail (**Pic 3**).

Paint foil with black patina to remove the shiny new look of the copper foil.

If you wish, solder fine wire loops firmly to the corners for hanging.

SEW PRACTICAL

For sewing friends, this is an exquisite gift that will be much treasured for its usefulness. The dainty chatelaine features a scissors scabbard and matching needle holder. Each piece is covered in a fine sprigged fabric and finished with delicate Palestrina knot stitch worked in variegated hand-dyed thread.

MEASUREMENTS

Scissors scabbard measures $5^1/2$" x $2^3/4$" and holds embroidery scissors up to $3^1/2$" in length; needle holder measures $3^1/4$" x $2^1/4$".

MATERIALS

- 8" x 10" piece firm cardboard, such as mat board
- 8" x 16" piece thin batting
- $1/4$ yard x 36" fabric
- 4" x $3^1/4$" piece flannel lining fabric
- Craft blade or Xacto knife
- Two skeins Watercolor thread (see **Note**)
- Glue stick
- Sewing thread to match fabric
- Size 8 straw, or milliner's, needle
- Size 5 or 6 crewel needle
- Small plastic snap

Chatelaine designed and stitched by Alison Snepp
Photography by Catherine Muscat

- Pins
- Pinking shears

Note: *If Watercolor is not available, substitute a variegated perle thread. Watercolor Thread is made by The Caron Collection, 67 Poland Street, Bridgeport, CT 06605, ph (203) 333 0325.*

TEMPLATE OUTLINES

Template outlines are printed on page 259. Trace Scabbard A and Scabbard B.

CUTTING

From cardboard or mat board, cut one Scabbard A and one Scabbard B. Cut also two rectangles, each 2" x 3", for needle holder.

From batting, cut two Scabbard As and two Scabbard Bs. Cut also two rectangles, 3" x $4^3/8$", for needle holder.

From fabric, cut two Scabbard As and two Scabbard Bs, adding $5/8$-inch seam allowance on all sides. Cut also two rectangles, $5^1/2$" x $4^1/4$", for needle holder.

METHOD

Twisted cord Cut three $4^1/3$-yard lengths of Watercolor thread and separate strands. Turn one strand of each length around so that it faces in the opposite direction to the other two — this will distribute the colors attractively through the cord. Place all the lengths of thread together and tie them in a knot at one end. Close the knot in a tightly fitting drawer, stand at the other end of the length of thread and wind the threads together until they are firmly twisted. Without letting go of the twisted threads, tie the end you have twisted to the knot in the drawer and let the cord twist back on itself, distributing the twists evenly to make the cord. Tie a knot at the folded end of the cord also. (This will be used to form the shape of a tassel.)

Scissors scabbard Glue one piece of the batting to each side of cardboard pieces.

Press fabric pieces. Thread the straw, or milliner's, needle with a doubled length of sewing thread, knot one end and hand-stitch a row of gathering stitches $1/4$ inch in from the edge of the Scabbard A fabric pieces.

Place the padded cardboard Scabbard A piece in the middle of the wrong side of one fabric Scabbard A and pull up gathering stitches until the fabric fits snugly around the cardboard. Do not cut the gathering thread, but use it to lace the fabric into the seam allowances from side to side across the wrong side of Scabbard A. Distribute the gathers evenly as you lace until the fabric is smooth. When this lacing thread runs out, start another doubled length of thread and continue lacing.

Place the second fabric Scabbard A (the lining) over the back of the laced section with right sides facing

Once worn by women around their waist, with keys and various household items attached, a chatelaine is now usually found in the sewing basket, where it prevents scissors and other small items from going astray. This chatelaine, consisting of a needle holder and scissors scabbard, is functional in the prettiest possible way.

outwards. Carefully turn in the seam allowance of the lining to fit, and pin in position. Hand-stitch the lining to the main piece around the edges. If you bend the straw, or milliner's, needle a little, you will find it easier to sew along the rigid edge of the cardboard.

Sew fabric Scabbard Bs to the padded cardboard Scabbard B in the same manner.

Cut off a 20-inch length of Watercolor thread, and a 12-inch length as well. Separate the three strands of each length. Place the three longer lengths of thread together again and make a simple tassel by winding the threads around three fingers of your hand. Tie the top of the tassel with one of the shorter lengths, then bind the neck of the tassel with another shorter length. Cut lower loops of tassel to form fringe.

Using the tying threads at the top of the tassel, sew it to the bottom of Scabbard A, just inside the edge so that the stitches will not be seen when the two sections of the scabbard are sewn together.

Pin the two fabric-covered sections together, matching the curve at bottom of scabbard. Sew them together around side and lower edges, using a doubled length of sewing thread in the bent straw, or milliner's, needle.

Thread the crewel needle with a single thickness of Watercolor thread and stitch the twisted cord to the top curve on the scabbard, about $2^1/2$ inches from one end of the cord, then work Palestrina knot stitch (see **Embroidery Stitch Guide** on page 58) over the top of the cord as you work around the finished scabbard.

Needle holder Glue needle holder cardboard pieces to one piece of batting so that there is a $3/8$-inch gap between the two pieces at the center. Glue remaining piece of batting to other side of cardboard pieces. The gap between the pieces of cardboard will allow the needle holder to fold in half easily.

Lace one piece of fabric around padded cardboard section, with right side out, taking care to maintain gap between the two pieces of cardboard. Place second piece of fabric (lining) over wrong side of cardboard, with right side of fabric facing outwards. Turn in the edges of the lining to fit and pin in position. Hand-stitch around outside of needle holder using the straw, or milliner's, needle — this is easier if the needle is slightly bent.

Sew one piece of the snap onto the middle of each inside long edge of the needle holder, close to edge.

Fold the flannel in half (to form a 2" x $1^1/2$" rectangle) and pink around the outside, trimming so that the flannel will sit easily inside the snap when the needle holder is closed. Sew the fold of the flannel invisibly to the inside fold of the needle holder using sewing thread.

Use a single strand of Watercolor thread to embroider a row of Palestrina knot stitch around the outside edge of needle holder. Sew the other end of the twisted cord to the middle of the outside spine of the needle holder, using sewing thread and positioning stitching about $2^{1}/_{2}$ inches from end of cord.

Work a row of Palestrina knot stitch along the outside spine, working over the twisted cord when you come to it.

Cord tassels Cut two 20-inch lengths of Watercolor thread and two 8-inch lengths. Separate the strands. Working with three 20-inch strands at one time, wind the threads around three fingers of your hand. Cut the loops along one side only. Arrange the thread around a knot at one end of the cord (**Diagram 1**). Tie them onto the cord just above the knot, using three 8-inch strands (**Diagram 2**). Allow the top threads to fall down over the tie just made and become part of the tassel fringe (**Diagram 3**). Bind the neck of the tassel just below the knot with another three 8-inch strands (**Diagram 4**). Tie the binding off, thread the tied-off ends, one at a time, behind the binding, unthread needle and allow thread to become part of the tassel fringe.

Make another tassel at the other end of cord in the same manner, using remaining cut threads. Trim tassel fringes evenly and to the same length as each other.

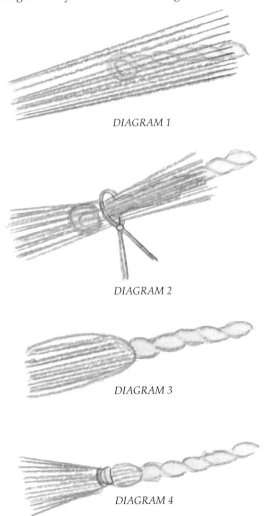

DIAGRAM 1

DIAGRAM 2

DIAGRAM 3

DIAGRAM 4

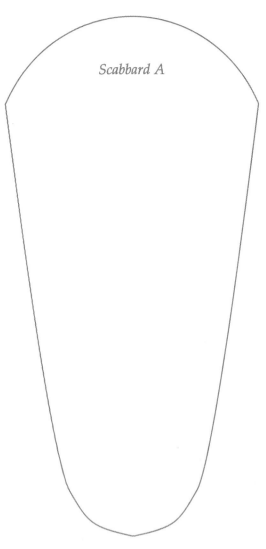

Scabbard A

Scabbard B

A TOUCH OF SPICE

These are pomanders with a difference! Simple Oasis spheres have been completely covered with scented seeds and leaves, and the resulting eye-catching and sweetly fragrant balls would make an unusual and striking centerpiece. We used star anise, coffee beans and bay leaves but, once you have mastered the basic technique, you can experiment with lots of different seeds, scented or not.

MEASUREMENTS

Our balls are about the size of an orange, but the method can be applied to any size ball.

MATERIALS

- Oasis spheres, or styrofoam balls, of desired size (from florists' supplies)
- Coffee beans
- Star anise, broken into segments
- Bay leaves
- Glue gun

Pomanders designed and made by Sonja Falkiner
Photography by Andre Martin
Styling by Lisa Hilton

METHOD

Star Anise Pomander Using star anise, this pomander is worked in a spiral from center to top and, again, from center to bottom. Starting at center of ball, run a 2-inch thread of glue along circumference. Attach star anise, with pointed section of each subsequent piece slightly overlapping the one in front (**Pic 1**). Continue in 2-inch sections around the circumference.

When the beginning point is reached, start working the spiral by overlapping the first row, making sure that the pointed section of the anise pieces faces in the same direction throughout (**Pic 2**).

Continue working the spiral until the top is reached and filled (**Pic 3**).

To start the second half, start about 2 inches in front of the beginning point and work back to it (**Pic 4**).

Work the second half of the ball in the same way as the first, ensuring that all points of anise face the same direction as those on the first half (**Pic 5**).

Coffee Bean Pomander A variation of the Star Anise Pomander can be made using coffee beans. Follow the same procedure as above, ensuring that the inside of the bean, which is more texturally interesting, faces out and one end of the bean points away from the ball.

Bay Leaf Pomander This pomander is worked from the top to the bottom in overlapping layers of leaves, gently shaped and glued in place. Not all the leaf surface is glued, so that the finished pomander looks a little like an artichoke. It is recommended that you use all the leaves — even those that are somewhat tattered and broken, as they can add their own special charm to the pomander.

To begin, mark the top and bottom of the ball with your thumb. Place a spot of glue in center top and attach leaves by their tips so that they overlap slightly. For this step, choose leaves with perfect tips (**Pic 1**).

Allow to set while glue dries (**Pic 2**).

Place spots of glue at points where leaves begin to overlap (**Pic 3**).

Cover each spot with a new leaf, pressing the tip firmly in the glue to spread it and gently bending and shaping all leaves against the ball (**Pic 4**).

Keep working over the whole ball, positioning and overlapping leaves to cover sides of leaves in previous layer (**Pic 5**).

From this point — where one more layer will complete the ball — the goal is to have all the leaves finishing at the center point. Place a blob of glue at the center point. Continue gluing and pressing all the leaves into this center point (**Pic 6**).

INDEX